D0397360

SALINAS PUBLIC
SALINAS
CALIFORNIA
LIBRARY

ECLECTIC EDUCATIONAL SERIES.

McGUFFEY'S

FIFTH

ECLECTIC READER.

William Holmes McGuffey

REVISED EDITION.

NEW YORK ·:· CINCINNATI ·:· CHICAGO
VAN NOSTRAND REINHOLD COMPANY

M'G. REV 5TH EC.

EP 299

PREFACE.

THE plan of the revision of McGUFFEY'S FIFTH READER is the same as that pursued in the other books of the REVISED SERIES. The book has been considerably enlarged, but the new pieces have been added or substituted only after the most careful consideration, and where the advantages to be derived were assured.

It has been the object to obtain as wide a range of leading authors as possible, to present the best specimens of style, to insure interest in the subjects, to impart valuable information, and to exert a decided and healthful moral influence. Thus the essential characteristics of McGUFFEY'S READERS have been carefully kept intact.

The preliminary exercises have been retained, and are amply sufficient for drill in articulation, inflection, etc. The additional exercises on these subjects, formerly inserted between the lessons, have been omitted to make room for other valuable features of the REVISED SERIES.

A full understanding of the text is necessary in order to read it properly. As all the books of reference required for this purpose are not within the reach of the majority of pupils, full explanatory notes have been given, which, it is believed, will add greatly not only to the interest of the reading lessons, but also to their usefulness from an instructive point of view.

The definitions of the more difficult words have been given, as formerly; and the pronunciation has been indicated by diacritical marks, in conformity with the preceding books of the REVISED SERIES.

Particular attention is invited to the notices of authors. Comparatively few pupils have the opportunity of making a separate study of English and American literature, and the carefully prepared notices in the REVISED SERIES are designed, therefore, to supply as much information in regard to the leading authors as is possible in the necessarily limited space assigned.

The publishers have desired to illustrate McGUFFEY'S READERS in a manner worthy of the text and of the high favor in which they are held throughout the United States. The most celebrated designers and engravers of the country have been employed for this purpose.

It has been the privilege of the publishers to submit the REVISED SERIES to numerous eminent educators in all parts of the country. To the careful reviews and criticisms of these gentlemen is due, in a large measure, the present form of McGUFFEY'S READERS. The value of these criticisms, coming from practical sources of the highest authority, can not well be overestimated, and the publishers take this occasion to express their thanks and their indebtedness to all who have thus kindly assisted them in this work.

Especial acknowledgment is due to Messrs. Houghton, Osgood & Co. for their permission to make liberal selections from their copyright editions of many of the foremost American authors whose works they publish.

CONTENTS.

INTRODUCTORY MATTER.

SELECTIONS IN PROSE AND POETRY.

LIST OF ILLUSTRATIONS.

INTRODUCTION.

I. PRELIMINARY REMARKS.

THE great object to be accomplished in reading, as a rhetorical exercise, is to convey to the hearer, fully and clearly, the ideas and feelings of the writer.

In order to do this, it is necessary that a selection should be carefully studied by the pupil before he attempts to read it. In accordance with this view, a preliminary rule of importance is the following:

RULE I. — Before attempting to read a lesson, the learner should make himself fully acquainted with the subject as treated of in that lesson, and endeavor to make the thought and feeling and sentiments of the writer his own.

REMARK. — When he has thus identified himself with the author, he has the substance of all rules in his own mind. It is by going to nature that we find rules. The child or the savage orator never mistakes in inflection or emphasis or modulation. The best speakers and readers are those who follow the impulse of nature, or most closely imitate it as observed in others.

II. ARTICULATION.

Articulation is the utterance of the elementary sounds of a language, and of their combinations.

An **Elementary Sound** is a simple, distinct sound made by the organs of speech.

The Elementary Sounds of the English language are divided into *Vocals, Subvocals,* and *Aspirates.*

ELEMENTARY SOUNDS.

VOCALS.

Vocals are sounds which consist of pure tone only. A *diphthong* is a union of two vocals, commencing with one and ending with the other.

DIRECTION. — Put the lips, teeth, tongue, and palate in their proper position; pronounce the word in the chart forcibly, and with the falling inflection, several times in succession; then drop the subvocal or aspirate sounds which precede or follow the vocal, and repeat the vocals alone.

TABLE OF VOCALS.

Long Vocals.

ā,	as in	hāte.	ẽ,	as in	ẽrr.
â,	"	hâre.	ī,	"	pīne.
ä,	"	fär.	ō,	"	nō.
ȧ,	"	pȧss.	ū,	"	tūbe.
a̤,	"	fa̤ll.	û,	"	bûrn.
ē,	"	ēve.	o͞o,	"	co͞ol.

Short Vocals.

ă,	as in	măt.	ŏ,	as in	hŏt.
ĕ,	"	mĕt.	ŭ,	"	ŭs.
ĭ,	"	ĭt.	o͝o,	"	bo͝ok.

Diphthongs.

oi, oy, as in oil, boy.	ou, ow, as in out, now.

REMARK 1. — In this table, the short sounds, except ŭ, are nearly or quite the same in *quality* as certain of the long sounds. The difference consists chiefly in *quantity*.

REMARK 2. — The vocals are often represented by other letters or combinations of letters than those used in the table; for instance, *a* is represented by *ai* in *hail*, by *ea* in *steak*, etc.

REMARK 3. — As a general rule, the long vocals and the diphthongs should be articulated with a full, clear utterance; but the short vocals have a sharp, distinct, and almost explosive utterance.

SUBVOCALS AND ASPIRATES.

Subvocals are those sounds in which the vocalized breath is more or less obstructed.

Aspirates consist of breath only, modified by the vocal organs.

Words ending with subvocal sounds should be selected for practice on the subvocals; words beginning or ending with aspirate sounds may be used for practice on the aspirates. Pronounce these words forcibly and distinctly several times in succession; then drop the other sounds, and repeat the subvocals and aspirates alone. Let the class repeat the words and elements at first in concert, then separately.

Table of Subvocals and Aspirates.

Subvocals.			*Aspirates.*		
b,	as in	bābe.	p,	as in	răp.
d,	"	băd.	t,	"	ăt.
g̅,	"	năg̅.	k,	"	bo͝ok.
j,	"	jŭdġe.	ch,	"	rĭch.
v,	"	mo̤ve.	f,	"	līfe.
th̶,	"	wĭth̶.	th,	"	Smĭth.
z,	"	bŭzz.	s,	"	hĭss.
z,	"	ăzure (ăzh′ure).	sh,	"	rŭsh.

Remark. — These sixteen sounds make eight pairs of *cognates.* In articulating the aspirates, the vocal organs are put in the position required in the articulation of the corresponding subvocals; but the breath is expelled with some force without the utterance of any vocal sound. The pupil should first verify this by experiment, and then practice on these cognates.

The following subvocals and aspirates have no cognates.

Subvocals.

l,	as in	mĭll.	r,	as in	rṳle.
m,	"	rĭm.	r,	"	cär.
n,	"	rŭn.	w,	"	wĭn.
ng,	"	sĭng.	y,	"	yĕt.

Aspirates.

h, as in hăt. | wh, as in whĕn.

SUBSTITUTES.

Substitutes are characters used to represent sounds ordinarily represented by other characters.

TABLE OF SUBSTITUTES.

ạ	for	ŏ,	as in	whạt.	y̆	for	ĭ,	as in	hy̆mn.
ê	"	â,	"	thêre.	ç	"	s,	"	çīte.
e̱	"	ā,	"	fre̱ight.	c	"	k,	"	căp.
ï	"	ē,	"	polïçe.	çh	"	sh,	"	maçhïne.
ĩ	"	ẽ,	"	sĩr.	ch	"	k,	"	chāos.
ȯ	"	ŭ,	"	sȯn.	ġ	"	j,	"	cāġe.
o̤	"	ōō,	"	to̤.	n̲	"	ng,	"	rĭn̲k.
ọ	"	o͝o,	"	wọuld.	s̱	"	z,	"	rōs̱e.
ô	"	a̤,	"	côrn.	s	"	sh,	"	sṳre.
õ	"	û,	"	wõrk.	x̱	"	gz,	"	ex̱ămĭne.
ụ	"	o͝o,	"	pụll.	gh	"	f,	"	läugh.
ṳ	"	ōō,	"	rṳde.	ph	"	f,	"	sy̆lph.
ȳ	"	ī,	"	mȳ.	qu	"	k,	"	pïque.

qu for kw, as in quick.

FAULTS TO BE REMEDIED.

DIRECTION. — Give to each sound, to each syllable, and to each word its full, distinct, and appropriate utterance.

For the purpose of avoiding the more common errors under this head, observe the following rules:

RULE II. — Avoid the *omission* of unaccented vowels.

EXAMPLES.

INCORRECT.		CORRECT.	INCORRECT.		CORRECT.
Sep'rate	*for*	sep-*a*-rate.	Ev'dent	*for*	ev-*i*-dent.
met-ric'l	"	met-ric-*a*l.	mem'ry	"	mem-*o*-ry.
'pear	"	*a*p-pear.	'pin-ion	"	*o*-pin-ion.
com-p'tent	"	com-p*e*-tent.	pr'pose	"	pr*o*-pose.
pr'cede	"	pr*e*-cede.	gran'lar	"	gran-*u*-lar.
'spe-cial	"	*e*s-pe-cial.	par-tic'lar	"	par-tic-*u*-lar.

Rule III. — Avoid sounding *incorrectly* the unaccented vowels.

EXAMPLES.

INCORRECT.		CORRECT.	INCORRECT.		CORRECT.
Sep-*er*-ate	*for*	sep-*a*-rate.	Mem-*er*-ry	*for*	mem-*o*-ry.
met-ric-*u*l	"	met-ric-*a*l.	*u*p-pin-ion	"	*o*-pin-ion.
*u*p-pear	"	*a*p-pear.	pr*u*p-ose	"	pr*o*-pose.
com-pe*r*-tent	"	com-p*e*-tent.	gran-n*y*-lar	"	gran-*u*-lar.
d*u*m-mand	"	d*e*-mand.	par-tic-*e*-lar	"	par-tic-*u*-lar.
ob-st*ur*-nate	"	ob-st*i*-nate.	ev-*er*-dent	"	ev-*i*-dent.

Remark 1. — In correcting errors of this kind in words of more than one syllable, it is very important to avoid a fault which is the natural consequence of an effort to articulate correctly. Thus, in endeavoring to sound correctly the *a* in *met'ric-al*, the pupil is very apt to say *met-ric-al'*, accenting the last syllable instead of the first.

Remark 2. — The teacher should bear it in mind that in correcting a fault there is always danger of erring in the opposite extreme. Properly speaking, there is no danger of learning to articulate *too distinctly*, but there is danger of making the obscure sounds too prominent, and of reading in a slow, measured, and unnatural manner.

Rule IV. — Utter distinctly the terminating subvocals and aspirates.

EXAMPLES.

INCORRECT.		CORRECT.	INCORRECT.		CORRECT.
An'	*for*	an*d*.	Mos'	*for*	mos*que*.
ban'	"	ban*d*.	near-es'	"	near-es*t*.
moun'	"	moun*d*.	wep'	"	wep*t*.
mor-nin'	"	morn-in*g*.	ob-jec'	"	ob-jec*t*.
des'	"	des*k*.	sub-jec'	"	sub-jec*t*.

Remark 1. — This omission is still more likely to occur when several consonants come together.

EXAMPLES.

INCORRECT.		CORRECT.	INCORRECT.		CORRECT.
Thrus'	*for*	thrus*ts*.	Harms'	*for*	harm'*st*.
beace	"	beas*ts*.	wrongs'	"	wrong'*st*.
thinks'	"	think*st*.	twinkles'	"	twinkl'*dst*.
weps'	"	wep*tst*.	black'ns	"	black'n'*dst*.

REMARK 2.—In all cases of this kind these sounds are omitted, in the first instance, merely because they are difficult, and require care and attention for their utterance, although after a while it becomes a habit. The only remedy is to devote *that care and attention* which may be necessary. There is no other difficulty, unless there should be a defect in the organs of speech, which is not often the case.

RULE V.—Avoid blending syllables which belong to different words.

EXAMPLES.

INCORRECT.	CORRECT.
He ga-*zd*upon.	He gaze*d* upon.
Here res *ts*is *s*ed.	Here re*sts* *h*is *h*ead.
Wha*tt*is *s*is *sn*ame?	Wha*t* is *h*is *n*ame?
For *r*an*n*ins*t*antush.	Fo*r* *a*n instan*t* *h*ush.
Ther *r*is *s*a calm.	The*r*e i*s* a calm.
For tho *sth*a *tw*eep.	Fo*r* *th*ose *th*at *w*eep.
God *s*glorou *s*image.	God'*s* *g*loriou*s* image.

EXERCISES IN ARTICULATION.

This exercise and similar ones will afford valuable aid in training the organs to a distinct articulation.

Eve*r*y vice figh*ts* again*st* natu*r*e.
Folly is never plea*sed* with *its*elf.
*P*r*ide, not na*ture*, *craves* mu*ch*.
The li*ttle* *tattler* *tit*tered at th*e* te*mp*est.
Titu*s* *tak*es the pe*tul*an*t* outca*sts*.
The covetou*s* *partner* is de*stit*ute of fo*r*tune.
No one of you know*s* w*h*ere the *sh*oe pinches.
What can not be cur*ed* mu*st* be e*ndured*.
You can not catc*h* *old* bi*rds* with *ch*aff.
Neve*r* *sport* wi*th* the opini*ons* of o*thers*.
The lightni*ngs* *flashed*, *the* *th*unde*rs* *r*oa*r*ed.
*H*is *hand* in mine was fo*nd*ly *clasped*.
*The*y cu*lt*ivated *shrubs* a*nd* *pl*ants.
He sele*ct*ed his te*xts* wi*th* *gr*eat care.
His li*ps* *gr*ow *rest*less, and hi*s* *sm*ile is cu*rled* *h*alf into *scorn*.
Wi*sdom's* way*s* are way*s* of *pl*ea*sant*ness.

O *b*reeze, *th*at waf*tst* me on my way!
*Th*ou boa*st's*t *o*f what *sh*ould be thy *sh*ame.
Li*f*e's fi*tf*ul fever over, he re*sts* well.
Can*st th*ou fill his *sk*in with bar*bed* ir*ons?*
From star to star the living ligh*tnings flash.*
And *g*litter*ing* crow*ns* of *prost*rate sera*ph*im.
*Th*at *morning, th*ou *th*at *slumber'd'st* not before.
Habi*t*ual evi*ls* cha*nge* not on a sud*den.*
*Th*ou waf*t'd'*st the ri*ck*ety s*kiffs* over the *cliffs.*
Thou reef'*d'st* the ha*ggled, sh*ipwrec*ked* sai*ls.*
The ho*nest sh*epher*d's* cata*rrh.*
The heir*ess* in her di*sh*abi*lle* is *h*umorous.
The *b*rave *ch*evalier beha*ves* like a co*nserv*ative.
The lu*sc*ious notion of *ch*ampagne and *p*recious sugar

III. INFLECTIONS.

Inflections are slides of the voice upward or downward. Of these, there are two: the *rising* inflection and the *falling* inflection.

The **Rising Inflection** is that in which the voice slides *upward*, and is marked thus (ʹ); as,

Did you walkʹ? Did you walk.

The **Falling Inflection** is that in which the voice slides *downward*, and is marked thus (\`); as,

I did not walk\`. I did not walk.

Both inflections are exhibited in the following question:

Did you walkʹ or ride\`? walk or ride.

In the following examples, the first member has the *rising* and the second member the *falling* inflection:

EXAMPLES.*

Is he sick′, or is he well‵?
Did you say valor′, or value‵?
Did you say statute′, or statue‵?
Did he act properly′, or improperly‵?

In the following examples, the inflections are used in a contrary order, the first member terminating with the *falling* and the second with the *rising* inflection:

EXAMPLES.

He is well‵, not sick′.
I said value‵, not valor′.
I said statue‵, not statute′.
He acted properly‵, not improperly′.

FALLING INFLECTIONS.

Rule VI.—The falling inflection is generally proper wherever the sense is complete.

EXAMPLES.

Truth is more wonderful than fiction‵.
Men generally die as they live‵.
By industry we obtain wealth‵.

Remark.—Parts of a sentence often make complete sense in themselves, and in this case, unless qualified or restrained by the succeeding clause, or unless the contrary is indicated by some other principle, the falling inflection takes place according to the rule.

* These questions and similar ones, with their answers, should be repeatedly pronounced with their proper inflections, until the distinction between the rising and falling inflection is well understood and easily made by the learner. He will be assisted in this by emphasizing strongly the word which receives the inflection; thus, Did you RIDE′ or did you WALK‵?

EXAMPLES.

Truth is wonderful\, even more so than fiction\.

Men generally die as they live\, and by their actions we must judge of their character\.

Exception. — When a sentence concludes with a negative clause, or with a contrast or comparison (called also antithesis), the first member of which requires the falling inflection, it must close with the rising inflection. (See Rule XI, and § 2, Note.)

EXAMPLES.

No one desires to be thought a fool′.
I come to bury\ Cæsar, not to praise′ him.
He lives in England\, not in France′.

REMARK. — In bearing testimony to the general character of a man we say:

He is too honorable\ to be guilty of a vile\ act.

But if he is accused of some act of baseness, a contrast is at once instituted between his character and the specified act, and we change the inflections, and say:

He is too *honorable′* to be guilty of such′ an act.

A man may say in general terms:

I am too busy′ for projects\.

But if he is urged to embark in some particular enterprise, he will change the inflections, and say:

I am too *busy* for projects′.

In such cases, as the falling inflection is required in the former part by the principle of contrast and emphasis (as will hereafter be more fully explained), the sentence necessarily closes with the *rising* inflection.

Sometimes, also, emphasis alone seems to require the rising inflection on the concluding word. See exception to Rule VII.

STRONG EMPHASIS.

RULE VII. — Language which demands *strong emphasis* generally requires the falling inflection.

EXAMPLES.

§ 1. Command or urgent entreaty; as,

> Begone\\,
> Run\\ to your houses, fall\\ upon your knees,
> Pray\\ to the Gods to intermit the plagues.

> O, save\\ me, Hubert\\, save\\ me! My eyes are out
> Even with the fierce looks of these bloody men.

§ 2. Exclamation, especially when indicating strong emotion; as,

> O, ye Gods\\! ye Gods\\! must I endure all this?

> Hark\\! Hark\\! the horrid sound
> Hath raised up his head.

For interrogatory exclamation, see Rule X, Remark.

SERIES OF WORDS OR MEMBERS.

§ 3. A series of *words* or *members*, whether in the beginning or middle of a sentence, if it does not conclude the sentence, is called a *commencing series*, and usually requires the *rising* inflection when not emphatic.

EXAMPLES OF COMMENCING SERIES.

Wine′, beauty′, music′, pomp′, are poor expedients to heave off the load of an hour from the heir of eternity\\.

I conjure you by that which you profess,
(Howe'er you came to know it,) answer me;
Though you untie the winds and let them fight
Against the churches′; though the yeasty waves
Confound and swallow navigation′ up;
Though bladed corn be lodged, and trees blown down′;
Though castles topple on their warders' heads′;
Though palaces and pyramids do slope
Their heads to their foundations′; though the treasures
Of nature's germens tumble altogether′,
Even till destruction sicken′; answer me
To what I ask‵ you.

§ 4. A series of words or members which *concludes* a sentence is called a *concluding series*, and each member usually has the *falling* inflection.

EXAMPLE OF CONCLUDING SERIES.

They, through faith, subdued kingdoms‵, wrought righteousness‵, obtained promises‵, stopped the mouths of lions‵, quenched the violence of fire‵, escaped the edge of the sword‵, out of weakness were made strong‵, waxed valiant in fight‵, turned to flight the armies of the aliens‵.

REMARK.—When the emphasis on these words or members is not marked, they take the rising inflection, according to Rule IX.

EXAMPLES.

They are the offspring of restlessness′, vanity′, and idleness‵.
Love′, hope′, and joy′ took possession of his breast.

§ 5. When words which naturally take the rising inflection become emphatic by repetition or any other cause, they often take the falling inflection.

Exception to the Rule.—While the tendency of emphasis is decidedly to the use of the *falling inflection*, sometimes a word to which the falling inflection naturally belongs changes this, when it is emphatic, for the rising inflection.

EXAMPLES.

Three thousand ducats\`: 't is a good round *sum'*.

It is useless to point out the beauties of nature to one who is *blind'*.

Here *sum* and *blind*, according to Rule VI, would take the falling inflection, but as they are emphatic, and the object of emphasis is to draw attention to the word emphasized, this is here accomplished in part by giving an unusual inflection. Some speakers would give these words the circumflex, but it would be the *rising* circumflex, so that the sound would still terminate with the rising inflection.

RULE VIII.—Questions which *can not* be answered by *yes* or *no*, together with their answers, generally require the falling inflection.

EXAMPLES.

Where has he gone\`?	*Ans.* To New York\`.
What has he done\`?	*Ans.* Nothing\`.
Who did this\`?	*Ans.* I know not\`.
When did he go\`?	*Ans.* Yesterday\`.

REMARK.—If these questions are repeated, the inflection is changed according to the principle stated under the Exception to Rule VII.

Where did you say he had gone'?
What has he done'?
Who did this'?
When did he go'?

RISING INFLECTION.

RULE IX.—Where a pause is rendered proper by the meaning, and the sense is incomplete, the *rising* inflection is generally required.

EXAMPLES.

To endure slander and abuse with meekness′ requires no ordinary degree of self-command‵.

Night coming on′, both armies retired from the field of battle‵.

As a dog returneth to his vomit′, so a fool returneth to his folly‵.

Remark.—The person or object addressed, in ordinary conversation, comes under this head.

EXAMPLES.

Fathers′! we once again are met in council.

My lords′! and gentlemen′! we have arrived at an awful crisis.

Age′! thou art shamed.

Rome′! thou hast lost the breed of noble bloods!

Exception.—Where a word which, according to this rule, requires the rising inflection, becomes emphatic, it generally has the falling inflection; as, when a child addresses his father, he first says, Father′! but if he repeats it emphatically, he changes the inflection, and says, Father‵! Father‵! The falling inflection is also used in formal address; as, Fellow-citizens‵, Mr. President‵, etc.

EXAMPLES.

When we aim at a high standard, if we do not *attain*‵ it, we shall secure a high degree of excellence.

Those who mingle with the vicious, if they do not become *depraved*‵, will lose all delicacy of feeling.

Rule X.—Questions which *may* be answered by *yes* or *no*, generally require the *rising*, and their answers the *falling* inflection.

EXAMPLES.

Has he arrived′? Yes‵.
Will he return′? No‵.
Does the law condemn him′? It does not‵.

Exception. — If these questions are repeated emphatically, they take the falling inflection, according to Rule VII.

EXAMPLES.

Has he arrived\?
Will he return\?
Does the law condemn him\?

REMARK. — When a word or sentence is repeated as a kind of interrogatory exclamation, the rising inflection is used according to the principles of this rule.

EXAMPLES.

You ask, who would venture\ in such a cause! Who would *venture′?* Rather say, who would not\ venture all things for such an object!

He is called the friend\ of virtue. The *friend′!* ay! the enthusiastic lover\, the devoted protector\, rather.

So, also, when one receives unexpected information he exclaims, Ah′! indeed′!

REMARK. — In the above examples the words "venture," "friend," "ah," etc., may be considered as interrogatory exclamations, because if the sense were carried out it would be in the form of question; as, "Do you ask who would *venture′?*" "Do you say that he is the *friend′* of virtue?" "Is it possible′?" and thus they would receive the rising inflection according to this rule.

RISING AND FALLING INFLECTIONS.

RULE XI. — The different members of a sentence expressing comparison, or contrast, or negation and affirmation, or where the parts are united by *or* used disjunctively, require different inflections; generally the *rising* inflection in the *first* member, and the *falling* inflection in the *second* member. This order is, however, sometimes inverted.

§ 1. Comparison and contrast. This is also called antithesis.

EXAMPLES.

In all things approving ourselves as the ministers of God; by honor′, and dishonor\; by evil′ report, and good\ report; as deceivers′, and yet true\; as unknown′, and yet well\ known; as dying′, and behold we live\; as chastened′, and not killed\; as sorrowful′, yet always rejoicing\; as poor′, yet making many rich\; as having nothing′, yet possessing all\ things.

Europe was one great battlefield, where the weak struggled for freedom′, and the strong for dominion\. The king was without power′, and the nobles without principle\. They were tyrants at home′, and robbers abroad\.

§ 2. Negation and affirmation.

EXAMPLES.

He desired not to injure′ his friend, but to protect\ him.
We desire not your money′, but yourselves\.
I did not say a better′ soldier, but an elder\.

If the affirmative clause comes first, the order of the inflections is inverted.

EXAMPLES.

He desired to protect\ his friend, not to injure′ him.
We desire yourselves\, not your money′.
I said an elder\ soldier, not a better′.

The affirmative clause is sometimes understood.

We desire not your money′.
I did not say a better′ soldier.
The region beyond the grave is not a solitary′ land.

In most negative sentences standing alone, the corresponding affirmative is understood; hence the following

Remark. — Negative sentences, whether alone or connected with an affirmative clause, generally end with the rising inflection.

If such sentences are repeated emphatically, they take the falling inflection according to Rule VI.:

EXAMPLES.

We do *not*\ desire your money.
I did *not*\ say a better soldier.

§ 3. *Or* used disjunctively.

Did he behave properly′, or improperly\?
Are they living′, or dead\?
Is he rich′, or poor\?

Does God, having made his creatures, take no further′ care of them, or does he preserve and guide them\?

REMARK. — Where *or* is used conjunctively, this rule does not apply; as,

Will the law of kindness′ or of justice′ justify such conduct′?

CIRCUMFLEX.

The circumflex is a union of the rising and falling inflections. Properly speaking, there are two of these, the one called the *rising* circumflex, in which the voice slides *down* and then *up;* and the other, the *falling* circumflex, in which the voice slides *upward* and then *downward* on the same vowel. They may both be denoted by the same mark, thus, (^). The circumflex is used chiefly to indicate the emphasis of irony, of contrast, or of hypothesis.

EXAMPLES.

1. *Queen.* Hamlet, you have your father much offended.
Hamlet. Madam, yôu have my father much offended.

2. They offer us their protec′tion. Yes\, sûch protection as vûltures give to lâmbs, côvering and devôuring them.

3. I knew when seven justices could not make up a quarrel; but when the parties met themselves, one of them thought but of an *if;* as, If you said sô, then I said sô; O ho! did you say sô? So they shook hands and were sworn brothers.

REMARKS. — In the *first* example, the emphasis is that of contrast. The queen had poisoned her husband, of which she incorrectly suppòsed her son ignorant, and she blames him for treating his father-in-law with disrespect. In his reply, Hamlet contrasts her deep crime with his own slight offense, and the circumflex upon "yôu" becomes proper.

In the *second* example the emphasis is ironical. The Spaniards pretended that they would protect the Peruvians if they would submit to them, whereas it was evident that they merely desired to plunder and destroy them. Thus their protection is ironically called "sûch protection as vûltures give to lâmbs," etc.

In the *third* example, the word "so" is used hypothetically; that is, it implies a condition or supposition. It will be observed that the rising circumflex is used in the first "so," and the falling, in the second, because the first "so" must end with the rising inflection and the second with the falling inflection, according to previous rules.

MONOTONE.

When no word in a sentence receives an inflection, it is said to be read in a *monotone;* that is, in nearly the same tone throughout. This uniformity of tone is occasionally adopted, and is fitted to express solemnity or sublimity of idea, and sometimes intensity of feeling. It is used, also, when the whole sentence or phrase is emphatic. In books of elocution, when it is marked at all, it is generally marked thus (—), as in the lines following.

EXAMPLES.

Hence! loathed melancholy!
Where brooding darkness spreads her jealous wings,
And the night raven sings;
There, under ebon shades and low-browed rocks,
As ragged as thy locks,
In deep Cimmerian darkness ever dwell.

IV. ACCENT.

In every word which contains more than one syllable, one of the syllables is pronounced with a somewhat greater stress of voice than the others. This syllable is said to be *accented.* The accented syllable is distinguished by this mark (′), the same which is used in inflections.

EXAMPLES.

Love′ly,	re-turn′,	re-mem′ber,
Con′stant,	re-main′,	a-sun′der,
Mem′ber,	a-bide′,	a-ban′don,
Win′dow,	a-tone′,	rec-ol-lect′,
Ban′ner,	a-lone′,	re-em-bark′.

REMARK. — In most cases custom is the only guide for placing the accent on one syllable rather than another. Sometimes, however, the same word is differently accented in order to mark its different meanings.

EXAMPLES.

Con′jure, to practice enchantments.	Con-*jure*′, to entreat.
Gal′lant, brave.	Gal-*lant*′, a gay fellow.
Au′gust, a month.	Au-*gust*′, grand.

REMARK. — A number of words used sometimes as one part of speech, and sometimes as another, vary their accents irregularly.

EXAMPLES.

Pres′ent, the noun. *Pres*′ent, the adjective.	Pre-*sent*′, the verb.
Com′pact, the noun.	Com-*pact*′, the adjective. Com-*pact*′, the verb.

In words of more than two syllables there is often a second accent given, but more slight than the principal one, and this is called the *secondary* accent; as, *car*′a-*van*′′, *rep*′′ar-*tee*′, where the principal accent is marked (′) and the secondary (′′); so, also, this accent is obvious in *nav*′′-i-*ga*′tion, *com*′′pre-*hen*′sion, *plau*′′si-*bil*′i-ty, etc. The whole subject, however, properly belongs to dictionaries and spelling books.

V. EMPHASIS.

A word is said to be *emphasized* when it is uttered with a greater stress of voice than the other words with which it is connected.

REMARK 1.—The object of emphasis is to attract particular attention to the word upon which it is placed, indicating that the idea to be conveyed depends very much upon that word. This object, as just stated, is generally accomplished by increasing the force of utterance, but sometimes, also, by a change in the inflection, by the use of the monotone, by pause, or by uttering the words in a very *low* key. Emphatic words are often denoted by *italics*, and a still stronger emphasis by SMALL CAPITALS or CAPITALS, according to the degree of emphasis desired.

REMARK 2.—Emphasis constitutes the most important feature in reading and speaking, and, properly applied, gives life and character to language. Accent, inflection, and indeed everything yields to emphasis.

REMARK 3.—In the following examples it will be seen that *accent* is governed by it.

EXAMPLES.

What is done cannot be *un*done.
There is a difference between *giv*ing and *for*giving.
He that *de*scendèd is the same that *as*cended.

Some appear to make very little difference between *de*cency and *in*decency, *mo*rality and *im*morality, *re*ligion and *ir*religion.

REMARK 4.—There is no better illustration of the nature and importance of emphasis than the following examples. It will be observed that the meaning and proper answer of the question vary with each change of the emphasis.

EXAMPLES.

QUESTIONS.	ANSWERS.
Did *you* walk into the city yesterday?	No, my *brother* went.
Did you *walk* into the city yesterday?	No, I *rode*.
Did you walk into the *city* yesterday?	No, I went into the *country*.
Did you walk into the city *yesterday?*	No, I went *the day before.*

ABSOLUTE EMPHASIS.

Sometimes a word is emphasized simply to indicate the importance of the idea. This is called *absolute emphasis.*

EXAMPLES.

To *arms!* they *come!* the *Greek!* the *Greek!*
Woe unto you, PHARISEES! HYPOCRITES!
Days, *months*, *years*, and *ages* shall circle away.

REMARK.—In instances like the last, it is sometimes called the *emphasis of specification.*

RELATIVE EMPHASIS.

Words are often emphasized in order to exhibit the idea they express as compared or contrasted with some other idea. This is called *relative emphasis.*

EXAMPLES.

A *friend* can not be *known* in *prosperity;* an *enemy* can not be *hidden* in *adversity.*
It is much better to be *injured* than to *injure.*

REMARK.—In many instances one part only of the antithesis is expressed, the corresponding idea being understood; as,

A *friendly* eye would never see such faults.

Here the *unfriendly* eye is understood.

King Henry exclaims, while vainly endeavoring to compose himself to rest,

"How many *thousand* of my poorest *subjects*
Are at this hour *asleep!*"

Here the emphatic words *thousand, subjects*, and *asleep* are contrasted in idea with their opposites, and if the contrasted ideas were expressed it might be in this way:

While *I alone*, their *sovereign*, am doomed to *wakefulness.*

EMPHATIC PHRASE.

Sometimes several words in succession are emphasized, forming what is called an *emphatic phrase.*

EXAMPLES.

Shall I, the conqueror of Spain and Gaul, and not only of the Alpine nations but of the Alps themselves — shall I compare myself with this HALF — YEAR — CAPTAIN?

Shall we try argument? Sir, we have been trying that for the LAST TEN YEARS.

And if thou said'st I am not peer
To any lord in Scotland here,
Lowland or Highland, far or near,
Lord Angus — THOU — HAST — LIED!

EMPHATIC PAUSE.

The emphatic expression of a sentence often requires a pause where the grammatical construction authorizes none. This is sometimes called the rhetorical pause. Such pauses occur chiefly before or after an emphatic word or phrase, and sometimes both before and after it.

EXAMPLES.

Rise — fellow-men! our country — yet remains!
By that dread name we wave the sword on high,
And swear *for her — to live — with her — to die.*

But *most* — by numbers judge the poet's song:
And smooth or rough, with them is — *right or wrong.*

He said; then full before their sight
Produced the beast, and lo! — *'t was white.*

VI. MODULATION.

Modulation includes the variations of the voice. These may be classed under the heads of Pitch, Compass, Quantity, and Quality.

PITCH AND COMPASS.

If anyone will notice closely a sentence as uttered in private conversation, he will observe that very few successive words are pronounced in exactly the same key or with the same force. At the same time, however, there is a certain PITCH or *key,* which seems, on the whole, to prevail.

This *keynote,* or *governing* note, as it may be called, is that upon which the voice most frequently dwells, to which it usually returns when wearied, and upon which a sentence generally commences, and very frequently ends, while, at the same time, there is a considerable play of the voice above and below it.

This key may be high or low. It varies in different individuals, and at different times in the same individual, being governed by the nature of the subject and the emotions of the speaker. It is worthy of notice, however, that most speakers pitch their voices on a key too high.

The range of the voice above and below this note is called its COMPASS. When the speaker is animated, this range is great; but upon abstract subjects, or with a dull speaker, it is small. If, in reading or speaking, too high a note be chosen, the lungs will soon become wearied; if too low a pitch be selected, there is danger of indistinctness of utterance; and in either case there is less room for *compass* or *variety* of tone than if one be taken between the two extremes.

To secure the proper pitch and the greatest compass observe the following rule:

RULE XII.—The reader or speaker should choose that pitch in which he can feel himself most at ease, and above and below which he may have most room for variation.

REMARK 1.—Having chosen the proper keynote, he should beware of confining himself to it. This constitutes *monotony,* one of the greatest

EXERCISES.

I. DEATH OF FRANKLIN.

(To be read in a solemn tone.)

ranklin is *dead*. The genius who freed *America′*, and red a copious stream of knowledge throughout *Europe′*, is rned unto the bosom of the *Divinity*. The sage to whom *worlds′* lay claim, the man for whom *science′* and *politics* disputing, indisputably enjoyed an elevated rank in human re.

he cabinets of princes have been long in the habit of noti- the death of those who were *great′*, only in their *funeral ns*. Long hath the etiquette of *courts′*, proclaimed the ning of *hypocrisy*. *Nations′* should wear mourning for but their *benefactors*. The *representatives′* of nations d recommend to public homage′ only *those* who have been eroes of *humanity*.

II. BONAPARTE.

knew no *motive′* but *interest*; acknowledged no *criterion′* *uccess*; he worshiped no *God′* but *ambition*; and with an n devotion′, he knelt at the shrine of his idolatry\. Sub- to this, there was no *creed′* that he did not *profess*, was no *opinion′* that he did not *promulgate*: in the hope of *asty′*, he upheld the *crescent*; for the sake of a *divorce′*, he before the *cross*; the *orphan* of *St. Louis′*, he became the d *child* of the *republic*; and, with a parricidal ingrati- on the ruins both of the *throne* and the *tribune*, he reared rone of his *despotism*. is touch *crowns′ crumbled*; *beggars′ reigned*; *systems′ van-* the *wildest theories′* took the color of his *whim*; and all as *venerable*, and all that was *novel′*, changed places with idity of a *drama*. *Nature* had no *obstacle′* that he did *rmount*; *space*, no *opposition′* he did not *spurn*; and amid *Alpine rocks*,—*Arabian sands*,—or *Polar snows′*,— ned *proof* against *peril′*, and empowered with *ubiquity*.

faults in elocution. One very important instrument for giving expression and life to thought is thus lost, and the hearer soon becomes wearied and disgusted.

REMARK 2.—There is another fault of nearly equal magnitude, and of very frequent occurrence. This consists in varying the pitch and force without reference to the *sense*. A sentence is commenced with vehemence and in a high key, and the voice gradually sinks until, the breath being spent, it dies away in a whisper.

NOTE.—The power of changing the key at will is difficult to acquire, but of great importance.

REMARK 3.—The habit of *singsong*, so common in reading poetry, as it is a variation of pitch without reference to the sense, is a species of the fault above mentioned.

REMARK 4.—If the reader or speaker is guided by the *sense*, and if he gives that *emphasis*, *inflection*, and *expression* required by the *meaning*, these faults speedily disappear.

REMARK 5.—To improve the voice in these respects, practice is necessary. Commence, for example, with the lowest pitch the voice can comfortably sound, and repeat whole paragraphs and pages upon that key with gentle force. Then repeat the paragraph with increased force, taking care not to raise the pitch. Then rise one note higher, and practice on that, then another, and so on, until the highest pitch of the voice is reached. Reverse the process, and repeat as before until the lowest pitch is obtained.

NOTE.—In these and all similar exercises, be very careful not to confound pitch and force.

QUANTITY AND QUALITY.

The tones of the voice should vary also in *quantity*, or time required to utter a sound or a syllable, and in *quality*, or *expression*, according to the nature of the subject.

REMARK.—We notice a difference between the soft, insinuating tones of persuasion; the full, strong voice of command and decision; the harsh, irregular, and sometimes grating explosion of the sounds of passion; the plaintive notes of sorrow and pity; and the equable and unimpassioned flow of words in argumentative style.

The following direction, therefore, is worthy of attention:

The tones of the voice should always correspond both in *quantity* and *quality* with the nature of the subject.

EXAMPLES.

Passion and Grief.

"Come back! come back!" he cried, in grief,
"Across this stormy water,
And I'll forgive your Highland chief,
My daughter! O, my daughter!"

Plaintive.

I have lived long enough: my way of life
Is fallen into the sear, the yellow leaf:
And that which should accompany old age,
As honor, love, obedience, troops of friends,
I must not look to have.

Calm.

A very great portion of this globe is covered with water, which is called sea, and is very distinct from rivers and lakes.

Fierce Anger.

Burned Marmion's swarthy cheek like fire,
And shook his very frame for ire,
And—"This to me?" he said;
"And 'twere not for thy hoary beard,
Such hand as Marmion's had not spared
To cleave the Douglas' head!

Loud and Explosive.

"Even in thy pitch of pride,
Here, in thy hold, thy vassals near,
I tell thee thou'rt defied!
And if thou said'st I am not peer
To any lord in Scotland here,
Lowland or Highland, far or near,
Lord Angus, thou hast lied!"

REMARK 1.—In our attempt to imitate nature it is important to avoid *affectation*, for to this fault even perfect monotony is preferable.

REMARK 2.—The *strength* of the voice may be increased by practicing with different degrees of *loudness*, from a whisper to full rotundity, taking care to keep the voice on the *same key*. The same note in music may be sounded *loud* or *soft*. So also a sentence may be pronounced on the same pitch with different degrees of loudness. Having practiced with different degrees of loudness on one key, make the same experiment on another, and then on another, and so on. This will also give the learner practice in *compass*.

VII. POETIC PAUSES.

In poetry we have, in addition to othe
pauses. The object of these is simply
melody.

At the end of each line a *slight* pause
ever be the grammatical construction or
purpose of this pause is to make promine
the measure, and in rhyme to allow the
the harmony of the similar sounds.

There is, also, another important pause
the middle of each line, which is called th
ral pause. In the following lines it is m

EXAMPLES.

There are hours long departed ‖ which
Like blossoms of Eden ‖ to twine rou
And as time rushes by ‖ on the might
They may darken awhile ‖ but they

REMARK.—The cæsural pause should never b
the sense. The following lines, if melody alone
be read thus:

With fruitless la ‖ bor Clara bo
And strove to stanch ‖ the gush
The Monk with un ‖ availing ca
Exhausted all ‖ the church's pr

This manner of reading, however, would ver
proper expression of the idea. This is to be
cæsural pause yield to the sense. The above

With fruitless labor ‖ Clara bo
And strove ‖ to stanch the gu
The Monk ‖ with unavailing
Exhausted ‖ all the church's

III. HAMLET ON SEEING THE SKULL OF YORICK.

Alas, poor Yorick\! I knew him\, Horatio′; a fellow of infinite jest′, of most excellent fancy\. He hath borne me on his back′ a thousand times\; and *now′*, how abhorred my imagination is\! My gorge rises\ at it. Here hung those lips that I have kissed′, I know not how oft\. Where be your gibes\ *now?* your *gambols\?* your *songs\?* your flashes of *merriment*, that were wont to set the table on a roar\? Not *one′*, now, to mock your own grinning′? quite *chopfallen′?* Now get you to my lady's chamber\, and tell her′, let her paint *an inch thick*, to this favor′ she must come\; make her laugh at that\.

IV. DESCRIPTION OF A BATTLE.

Yet still Lord Marmion's falcon flew′
With wavering flight\, while *fiercer* grew
  Around, the battle yell.
The border slogan rent the sky\,
A *Home\!* a *Gordon\!* was the cry\;
  Loud′ were the clanging blows\;
Advanced′,—forced back\,—now low′,—now high\,
  The pennon sunk′—and rose\;
As bends the bark's mast in the gale′,
When rent are rigging\, shrouds\, and sail′,
  It wavered 'mid the foes\.
The war, that for a space did fail′,
Now trebly thundering swelled the gale\,
  And *Stanley\!* was the cry;
A light on Marmion's visage spread′,
  And fired his glazing eye\:—
With dying hand′, above his head′,
He shook the fragment of his blade′,
  And shouted′,—"*Victory\!*
Charge, Chester′, *charge\!* *On*, Stanley′, *on\!*"—
  Were the last words of Marmion.

V. LORD ULLIN'S DAUGHTER.

For the inflections and emphasis in this selection, let the pupil be guided by his own judgment.

A chieftain to the Highlands bound,
Cries, "Boatman, do not tarry!
And I'll give thee a silver pound,
To row us o'er the ferry."

"Now, who be ye would cross Loch-Gyle
This dark and stormy water?"
"Oh! I'm the chief of Ulva's isle,
And this, Lord Ullin's daughter.

"And fast before her father's men
Three days we've fled together,
For should he find us in the glen,
My blood would stain the heather.

"His horsemen hard behind us ride;
Should they our steps discover,
Then who will cheer my bonny bride,
When they have slain her lover?"

Out spoke the hardy Highland wight
"I'll go, my chief — I'm ready:
It is not for your silver bright,
But for your winsome lady:

"And, by my word! the bonny bird
In danger shall not tarry;
So, though the waves are raging white,
I'll row you o'er the ferry."

By this, the storm grew loud apace,
The water wraith was shrieking;
And, in the scowl of heaven, each face
Grew dark as they were speaking.

But still, as wilder grew the wind,
And as the night grew drearer,
Adown the glen rode armèd men,
Their trampling sounded nearer.

"Oh! haste thee, haste!" the lady cries,
"Though tempest round us gather,
I'll meet the raging of the skies,
But not an angry father."

The boat has left the stormy land,
A stormy sea before her;
When, oh! too strong for human hand,
The tempest gathered o'er her.

And still they rowed, amid the roar
Of waters fast prevailing;
Lord Ullin reached that fatal shore,
His wrath was changed to wailing.

For sore dismay through storm and shade
His child he did discover;
One lovely hand she stretched for aid,
And one was round her lover.

"Come back! come back!" he cried, in grief,
"Across this stormy water;
And I'll forgive your Highland chief,
My daughter! O, my daughter!"

'T was vain: the loud waves lashed the shore,
Return or aid preventing:
The waters wild went o'er his child,
And he was left lamenting.

— *Thomas Campbell.*

ALPHABETICAL LIST OF AUTHORS.

I. THE GOOD READER.

1. It is told of Frederick the Great, King of Prussia, that, as he was seated one day in his private room, a written petition was brought to him with the request that it should be immediately read. The King had just re-

turned from hunting, and the glare of the sun, or some other cause, had so dazzled his eyes that he found it difficult to make out a single word of the writing.

2. His private secretary happened to be absent; and the soldier who brought the petition could not read. There was a page, or favorite boy servant, waiting in the hall, and upon him the King called. The page was a son of one of the noblemen of the court, but proved to be a very poor reader.

3. In the first place, he did not articulate distinctly. He huddled his words together in the utterance, as if they were syllables of one long word, which he must get through with as speedily as possible. His pronunciation was bad, and he did not modulate his voice so as to bring out the meaning of what he read. Every sentence was uttered with a dismal monotony of voice, as if it did not differ in any respect from that which preceded it.

4. "Stop!" said the King, impatiently. "Is it an auctioneer's list of goods to be sold that you are hurrying over? Send your companion to me." Another page who stood at the door now entered, and to him the King gave the petition. The second page began by hemming and clearing his throat in such an affected manner that the King jokingly asked him whether he had not slept in the public garden, with the gate open, the night before.

5. The second page had a good share of self-conceit, however, and so was not greatly confused by the King's jest. He determined that he would avoid the mistake which his comrade had made. So he commenced reading the petition slowly and with great formality, emphasizing every word, and prolonging the articulation of every syllable. But his manner was so tedious that the King cried out, "Stop! are you reciting a lesson in the elementary sounds? Out of the room! But no: stay! Send me that little girl who is sitting there by the fountain."

6. The girl thus pointed out by the King was a daughter

of one of the laborers employed by the royal gardener; and she had come to help her father weed the flower beds. It chanced that, like many of the poor people in Prussia, she had received a good education. She was somewhat alarmed when she found herself in the King's presence, but took courage when the King told her that he only wanted her to read for him, as his eyes were weak.

7. Now, Ernestine (for this was the name of the little girl) was fond of reading aloud, and often many of the neighbors would assemble at her father's house to hear her; those who could not read themselves would come to her, also, with their letters from distant friends or children, and she thus formed the habit of reading various sorts of handwriting promptly and well.

8. The King gave her the petition, and she rapidly glanced through the opening lines to get some idea of what it was about. As she read, her eyes began to glisten, and her breast to heave. "What is the matter?" asked the King; "don't you know how to read?" "Oh, yes! sire," she replied, addressing him with the title usually applied to him: "I will now read it, if you please."

9. The two pages were about to leave the room. "Remain," said the King. The little girl began to read the petition. It was from a poor widow, whose only son had been drafted to serve in the army, although his health was delicate and his pursuits had been such as to unfit him for military life. His father had been killed in battle, and the son had a strong desire to become a portrait painter.

10. The writer told her story in a simple, concise manner, that carried to the heart a belief of its truth; and Ernestine read it with so much feeling, and with an articulation so just, in tones so pure and distinct, that when she had finished, the King, into whose eyes the tears had started, exclaimed, "Oh! now I understand what it is all about; but I might never have known, certainly I never should have felt, its meaning had I trusted to these young

gentlemen, whom I now dismiss from my service for one year, advising them to occupy their time in learning to read."

11. "As for you, my young lady," continued the King, "I know you will ask no better reward for your trouble than the pleasure of carrying to this poor widow my order for her son's immediate discharge. Let me see whether you can write as well as you can read. Take this pen, and write as I dictate." He then dictated an order, which Ernestine wrote, and he signed. Calling one of his guards, he bade him go with the girl and see that the order was obeyed.

12. How much happiness was Ernestine the means of bestowing through her good elocution, united to the happy circumstance that brought it to the knowledge of the King! First, there were her poor neighbors, to whom she could give instruction and entertainment. Then, there was the poor widow who sent the petition, and who not only regained her son, but received through Ernestine an order for him to paint the King's likeness; so that the poor boy soon rose to great distinction, and had more orders than he could attend to. Words could not express his gratitude, and that of his mother, to the little girl.

13. And Ernestine had, moreover, the satisfaction of aiding her father to rise in the world, so that he became the King's chief gardener. The King did not forget her, but had her well educated at his own expense. As for the two pages, she was indirectly the means of doing them good, also; for, ashamed of their bad reading, they commenced studying in earnest, till they overcame the faults that had offended the King. Both finally rose to distinction, one as a lawyer, and the other as a statesman; and they owed their advancement in life chiefly to their good elocution.

Definitions.—1. Pe-tĭ'tion, *a formal request.* 3. Ar-tĭe'u-lāte, *to utter the elementary sounds.* Mŏd'u-lāte, *to vary or inflect.* Mo-nŏt'o-ny, *lack of variety.* 4. Af-fĕet'ed, *unnatural and silly.*

9. Drȧft′ed, *selected by lot.* **10.** Con-çīse′, *brief and full of meaning.* **11.** Dis-chärġe′, *release.* Dĭc′tāte, *to utter so that another may write down.* **12.** Dis-tĭn̲e′tion, *honorable and notable position.* Ex-prĕss′, *to make known the feelings of.*

NOTES.—Frederick II. of Prussia (*b.* 1712, *d.* 1788), or Frederick the Great, as he was called, was one of the greatest of German rulers. He was distinguished for his military exploits, for his wise and just government, and for his literary attainments. He wrote many able works in the French language. Many pleasant anecdotes are told of this king, of which the one given in the lesson is a fair sample.

II. THE BLUEBELL.

1. THERE is a story I have heard—
A poet learned it of a bird,
And kept its music every word—

2. A story of a dim ravine,
O'er which the towering tree tops lean,
With one blue rift of sky between;

3. And there, two thousand years ago,
A little flower as white as snow
Swayed in the silence to and fro.

4. Day after day, with longing eye,
The floweret watched the narrow sky,
And fleecy clouds that floated by.

5. And through the darkness, night by night,
One gleaming star would climb the height,
And cheer the lonely floweret's sight.

6. Thus, watching the blue heavens afar,
And the rising of its favorite star,
A slow change came—but not to mar;

7. For softly o'er its petals white
There crept a blueness, like the light
Of skies upon a summer night;

8. And in its chalice, I am told,
The bonny bell was formed to hold
A tiny star that gleamed like gold.

9. Now, little people, sweet and true,
I find a lesson here for you
Writ in the floweret's bell of blue:

10. The patient child whose watchful eye
Strives after all things pure and high,
Shall take their image by and by.

DEFINITIONS.—2. Rĭft, *a narrow opening, a cleft.* 3. Swāyed, *swung.* 5. Heīght (*pro.* hīte), *an elevated place.* 7. Pĕt'al̦s, *the colored leaves of a flower.* 8. Chăl'i̦çe, *a cup or bowl.* Bŏn'ny, *beautiful.*

III. THE GENTLE HAND.

Timothy S. Arthur (*b.* 1809, *d.* 1885) was born near Newburgh, N.Y., but passed most of his life at Baltimore and Philadelphia. His opportunities for good schooling were quite limited, and he may be considered a self-educated man. He was the author of more than a hundred volumes, principally novels of a domestic and moral tone, and of many shorter tales—magazine articles, etc. "Ten Nights in a Barroom," and "Three Years in a Mantrap," are among his best known works.

1. WHEN and where it matters not now to relate—but once upon a time, as I was passing through a thinly peopled district of country, night came down upon me almost unawares. Being on foot, I could not hope to gain the village toward which my steps were directed, until a

late hour; and I therefore preferred seeking shelter and a night's lodging at the first humble dwelling that presented itself.

2. Dusky twilight was giving place to deeper shadows, when I found myself in the vicinity of a dwelling, from the small uncurtained windows of which the light shone with a pleasant promise of good cheer and comfort. The house stood within an inclosure, and a short distance from the road along which I was moving with wearied feet.

3. Turning aside, and passing through the ill-hung gate, I approached the dwelling. Slowly the gate swung on its wooden hinges, and the rattle of its latch, in closing, did not disturb the air until I had nearly reached the porch in front of the house, in which a slender girl, who had noticed my entrance, stood awaiting my arrival.

4. A deep, quick bark answered, almost like an echo, the sound of the shutting gate, and, sudden as an apparition, the form of an immense dog loomed in the doorway. At the instant when he was about to spring, a light hand was laid upon his shaggy neck, and a low word spoken.

5. "Go in, Tiger," said the girl, not in a voice of authority, yet in her gentle tones was the consciousness that she would be obeyed; and, as she spoke, she lightly bore upon the animal with her hand, and he turned away and disappeared within the dwelling.

6. "Who's that?" A rough voice asked the question; and now a heavy-looking man took the dog's place in the door.

7. "How far is it to G——?" I asked, not deeming it best to say, in the beginning, that I sought a resting place for the night.

8. "To G——!" growled the man, but not so harshly as at first. "It 's good six miles from here."

9. "A long distance; and I 'm a stranger and on foot," said I. "If you can make room for me until morning, I will be very thankful."

10. I saw the girl's hand move quickly up his arm, until it rested on his shoulder, and now she leaned to him still closer.

11. "Come in. We'll try what can be done for you." There was a change in the man's voice that made me wonder. I entered a large room, in which blazed a brisk fire. Before the fire sat two stout lads, who turned upon me their heavy eyes, with no very welcome greeting. A middle-aged woman was standing at a table, and two children were amusing themselves with a kitten on the floor.

12. "A stranger, mother," said the man who had given me so rude a greeting at the door; "and he wants us to let him stay all night."

13. The woman looked at me doubtingly for a few moments, and then replied coldly, "We don't keep a public house."

14. "I 'm aware of that, ma'am," said I; "but night has overtaken me, and it 's a long way yet to G——."

15. "Too far for a tired man to go on foot," said the master of the house, kindly, "so it 's no use talking about it, mother; we must give him a bed."

16. So unobtrusively that I scarce noticed the movement, the girl had drawn to her mother's side. What she said to her I did not hear, for the brief words were uttered in a low voice; but I noticed, as she spoke, one small, fair hand rested on the woman's hand.

17. Was there magic in that touch? The woman's repulsive aspect changed into one of kindly welcome, and she said, "Yes, it 's a long way to G——. I guess we can find a place for him."

18. Many times more during that evening, did I observe the magic power of that hand and voice — the one gentle yet potent as the other. On the next morning, breakfast being over, I was preparing to take my departure when my host informed me that if I would wait for half an hour he would give me a ride in his wagon to G——, as

business required him to go there. I was very well pleased to accept of the invitation.

19. In due time, the farmer's wagon was driven into the road before the house, and I was invited to get in. I noticed the horse as a rough-looking Canadian pony, with a certain air of stubborn endurance. As the farmer took his seat by my side, the family came to the door to see us off.

20. "Dick!" said the farmer in a peremptory voice, giving the rein a quick jerk as he spoke. But Dick moved not a step. "Dick! you vagabond! get up." And the farmer's whip cracked sharply by the pony's ear.

21. It availed not, however, this second appeal. Dick stood firmly disobedient. Next the whip was brought down upon him with an impatient hand; but the pony only reared up a little. Fast and sharp the strokes were next dealt to the number of half a dozen. The man might as well have beaten the wagon, for all his end was gained.

22. A stout lad now came out into the road, and, catching Dick by the bridle, jerked him forward, using, at the same time, the customary language on such occasions, but Dick met this new ally with increased stubbornness, planting his fore feet more firmly and at a sharper angle with the ground.

23. The impatient boy now struck the pony on the side of the head with his clinched hand, and jerked cruelly at his bridle. It availed nothing, however; Dick was not to be wrought upon by any such arguments.

24. "Don't do so, John!" I turned my head as the maiden's sweet voice reached my ear. She was passing through the gate into the road, and in the next moment had taken hold of the lad and drawn him away from the animal. No strength was exerted in this; she took hold of his arm, and he obeyed her wish as readily as if he had no thought beyond her gratification.

25. And now that soft hand was laid gently on the pony's neck, and a single low word spoken. How instantly were

the tense muscles relaxed—how quickly the stubborn air vanished!

26. "Poor Dick!" said the maiden, as she stroked his neck lightly, or softly patted it with a childlike hand. "Now, go along, you provoking fellow!" she added, in a half-chiding, yet affectionate voice, as she drew up the bridle.

27. The pony turned toward her, and rubbed his head against her arm for an instant or two; then, pricking up his ears, he started off at a light, cheerful trot, and went on his way as freely as if no silly crotchet had ever entered his stubborn brain.

28. "What a wonderful power that hand possesses!" said I, speaking to my companion, as we rode away.

29. He looked at me for a moment, as if my remark had occasioned surprise. Then a light came into his countenance, and he said briefly, "She 's good! Everybody and everything loves her."

30. Was that, indeed, the secret of her power? Was the quality of her soul perceived in the impression of her hand, even by brute beasts! The father's explanation was doubtless the true one. Yet have I ever since wondered, and still do wonder, at the potency which lay in that maiden's magic touch. I have seen something of the same power, showing itself in the loving and the good, but never to the extent as instanced in her, whom, for want of a better name, I must still call "Gentle Hand."

DEFINITIONS.—2. Vĭ-çĭn'i-ty, *neighborhood.* 16. Un-ob-trṳ'sĭve-ly, *not noticeably, modestly.* 17. Re-pŭl'sĭve, *repelling, forbidding.* 18. Pō'tent, *powerful, effective.* Hōst, *one from whom another receives food, lodging, or entertainment.* 20. Pĕr'emp-to-ry, *commanding, decisive.* 21. A-vāiled', *was of use, had effect.* 22. Al-ly', *a confederate, one who unites with another in some purpose.* 25. Tĕnse, *strained to stiffness, rigid.* Re-lăxed', *loosened.* 26. Chīd'ing, *scolding, rebuking.* 27. Crŏtch'et, *a perverse fancy, a whim.* 30. In'stançed, *mentioned as an example.*

IV. THE GRANDFATHER.

Charles G. Eastman (*b.* 1816, *d.* 1861) was born in Maine, but removed at an early age to Vermont, where he was connected with the press at Burlington, Woodstock, and Montpelier. He published a volume of poems in 1848, written in a happy lyric and ballad style, and faithfully portraying rural life in New England.

1. The farmer sat in his easy-chair
   Smoking his pipe of clay,
While his hale old wife with busy care,
   Was clearing the dinner away;
A sweet little girl with fine blue eyes,
On her grandfather's knee, was catching flies.

2. The old man laid his hand on her head,
   With a tear on his wrinkled face,
He thought how often her mother, dead,
   Had sat in the selfsame place;
As the tear stole down from his half-shut eye,
"Don't smoke!" said the child, "how it makes you cry!"

3. The house dog lay stretched out on the floor,
   Where the shade, afternoons, used to steal;
The busy old wife by the open door
   Was turning the spinning wheel,
And the old brass clock on the manteltree
Had plodded along to almost three.

4. Still the farmer sat in his easy-chair,
   While close to his heaving breast
The moistened brow and the cheek so fair
   Of his sweet grandchild were pressed;
His head bent down, on her soft hair lay;
Fast asleep were they both on that summer day.

Definitions.—1. Hāle, *healthy*. 3. Măn'tel-tree, *shelf over a fireplace*. Plŏd'ded, *went slowly*. 4. Hēav'ing, *rising and falling*.

V. A BOY ON A FARM.

Charles Dudley Warner (*b.* 1829, ——) was born at Plainfield, Mass. In 1851 he graduated at Hamilton College, and in 1856 was admitted to the bar at Philadelphia, but moved to Chicago to practice his profession. There he remained until 1860, when he became connected with the press at Hartford, Conn., and has ever since devoted himself to literature. "My Summer in a Garden," "Saunterings," and "Backlog Studies" are his best known works. The following extract is from "Being a Boy."

1. SAY what you will about the general usefulness of boys, it is my impression that a farm without a boy would very soon come to grief. What the boy does is the life of the farm. He is the factotum, always in demand, always expected to do the thousand indispensable things that nobody else will do. Upon him fall all the odds and ends, the most difficult things.

2. After everybody else is through, he has to finish up. His work is like a woman's,—perpetually waiting on others. Everybody knows how much easier it is to eat a good dinner than it is to wash the dishes afterwards. Consider what a boy on a farm is required to do,—things that must be done, or life would actually stop.

3. It is understood, in the first place, that he is to do all the errands, to go to the store, to the post office, and to carry all sorts of messages. If he had as many legs as a centiped, they would tire before night. His two short limbs seem to him entirely inadequate to the task. He would like to have as many legs as a wheel has spokes, and rotate about in the same way.

4. This he sometimes tries to do; and the people who have seen him "turning cart wheels" along the side of the road, have supposed that he was amusing himself and idling his time; he was only trying to invent a new mode of locomotion, so that he could economize his legs, and do his errands with greater dispatch.

5. He practices standing on his head, in order to accustom himself to any position. Leapfrog is one of his

methods of getting over the ground quickly. He would willingly go an errand any distance if he could leapfrog it with a few other boys.

6. He has a natural genius for combining pleasure with business. This is the reason why, when he is sent to the spring for a pitcher of water, he is absent so long; for he stops to poke the frog that sits on the stone, or, if there is a penstock, to put his hand over the spout, and squirt the water a little while.

7. He is the one who spreads the grass when the men have cut it; he mows it away in the barn; he rides the horse, to cultivate the corn, up and down the hot, weary rows; he picks up the potatoes when they are dug; he drives the cows night and morning; he brings wood and water, and splits kindling; he gets up the horse, and puts out the horse; whether he is in the house or out of it, there is always something for him to do.

8. Just before the school in winter he shovels paths; in summer he turns the grindstone. He knows where there are lots of wintergreens and sweet flags, but instead of going for them, he is to stay indoors and pare apples, and stone raisins, and pound something in a mortar. And yet, with his mind full of schemes of what he would like to do, and his hands full of occupations, he is an idle boy, who has nothing to busy himself with but school and chores!

9. He would gladly do all the work if somebody else would do the chores, he thinks; and yet I doubt if any boy ever amounted to anything in the world, or was of much use as a man, who did not enjoy the advantages of a liberal education in the way of chores.

Definitions.—1. Fac-tō'tum, *a person employed to do all kinds of work.* In-dis-pĕn'sa-ble, *absolutely necessary.* 2. Per-pĕt'u-al-ly, *continually.* 3. Cĕn'ti-pĕd, *an insect with a great number of feet.* 4. E-cŏn'o-mīze, *to save.* Dis-pătch', *diligence, haste.* 6. Pĕn'-stŏck, *a wooden tube for conducting water.* 8. Chōreṣ, *the light work of the household either within or without doors.*

VI. THE SINGING LESSON.

Jean Ingelow (*b.* 1830, *d.* 1897) was born at Boston, Lincolnshire, England. Her fame as a poetess was at once established upon the publication of her "Poems" in 1863; since which time several other volumes have appeared. The most generally admired of her poems are "Songs of Seven" and "The High Tide on the Coast of Lincolnshire." She has also written several successful novels, of which "Off the Skelligs" is the most popular. "Stories Told to a Child," "The Cumberers," "Poor Mat," "Studies for Stories," and "Mopsa, the Fairy" are also well known. Miss Ingelow resided in London, England, and spent much of her time in deeds of charity.

1. A NIGHTINGALE made a mistake;
 She sang a few notes out of tune:
Her heart was ready to break,
 And she hid away from the moon.
She wrung her claws, poor thing,
 But was far too proud to weep;
She tucked her head under her wing,
 And pretended to be asleep.

2. A lark, arm in arm with a thrush,
 Came sauntering up to the place;
The nightingale felt herself blush,
 Though feathers hid her face;
She knew they had heard her song,
 She felt them snicker and sneer;
She thought that life was too long,
 And wished she could skip a year.

3. "O nightingale!" cooed a dove;
 "O nightingale! what's the use?
You bird of beauty and love,
 Why behave like a goose?
Don't sulk away from our sight,
 Like a common, contemptible fowl;
You bird of joy and delight,
 Why behave like an owl?

4. "Only think of all you have done;
Only think of all you can do;
A false note is really fun
From such a bird as you!
Lift up your proud little crest,
Open your musical beak;
Other birds have to do their best,
You need only to speak!"

5 The nightingale shyly took
Her head from under her wing,
And, giving the dove a look,
Straightway began to sing.
There was never a bird could pass;
The night was divinely calm;
And the people stood on the grass
To hear that wonderful psalm.

6. The nightingale did not care,
She only sang to the skies;
Her song ascended there,
And there she fixed her eyes.
The people that stood below
She knew but little about;
And this tale has a moral, I know,
If you'll try and find it out.

DEFINITIONS.—2. Säun'ter-ing, *wandering idly, strolling.* Snĭck'er, *to laugh in a half-suppressed manner.* 4. Crĕst, *a tuft growing on an animal's head.* 5. Dī-vīne'ly, *in a supreme degree.* 6. Mŏr'al, *the practical lesson which anything is fitted to teach.*

NOTE.—The nightingale is a small bird, about six inches in length, with a coat of dark-brown feathers above and of grayish-white beneath. Its voice is astonishingly strong and sweet, and, when wild, it usually sings throughout the evening and night from April to the middle of summer. The bird is common in Europe, but is not found in America.

VII. DO NOT MEDDLE.

1. About twenty years ago there lived a singular gentleman in the Old Hall among the elm trees. He was about three-score years of age, very rich, and somewhat odd in many of his habits, but for generosity and benevolence he had no equal.

2. No poor cottager stood in need of comforts, which he was not ready to supply; no sick man or woman languished for want of his assistance; and not even a beggar, unless a known impostor, went empty-handed from the Hall. Like the village pastor described in Goldsmith's poem of "The Deserted Village,"

> "His house was known to all the vagrant train;
> He chid their wand'rings, but relieved their pain;
> The long-remembered beggar was his guest,
> Whose beard descending swept his aged breast."

3. Now it happened that the old gentleman wanted a boy to wait upon him at table, and to attend him in different ways, for he was very fond of young people. But much as he liked the society of the young, he had a great aversion to that curiosity in which many young people are apt to indulge. He used to say, "The boy who will peep into a drawer will be tempted to take something out of it; and he who will steal a penny in his youth will steal a pound in his manhood."

4. No sooner was it known that the old gentleman was in want of a boy than twenty applications were made for the situation; but he determined not to engage anyone until he had in some way ascertained that he did not possess a curious, prying disposition.

5. On Monday morning seven lads, dressed in their Sunday clothes, with bright and happy faces, made their appearance at the Hall, each of them desiring to obtain the situation. Now the old gentleman, being of a singular dis-

position, had prepared a room in such a way that he might easily know if any of the young people who applied were given to meddle unnecessarily with things around them, or to peep into cupboards and drawers. He took care that the lads who were then at Elm Tree Hall should be shown into this room one after another.

6. And first, Charles Brown was sent into the room, and told that he would have to wait a little. So Charles sat down on a chair near the door. For some time he was very quiet, and looked about him; but there seemed to be so many curious things in the room that at last he got up to peep at them.

7. On the table was placed a dish cover, and Charles wanted sadly to know what was under it, but he felt afraid of lifting it up. Bad habits are strong things; and, as Charles was of a curious disposition, he could not withstand the temptation of taking one peep. So he lifted up the cover.

8. This turned out to be a sad affair; for under the dish cover was a heap of very light feathers; part of the feathers, drawn up by a current of air, flew about the room, and Charles, in his fright, putting the cover down hastily, puffed the rest of them off the table.

9. What was to be done? Charles began to pick up the feathers one by one; but the old gentleman, who was in an adjoining room, hearing a scuffle, and guessing the cause of it, entered the room, to the consternation of Charles Brown, who was very soon dismissed as a boy who had not principle enough to resist even a slight temptation.

10. When the room was once more arranged, Henry Wilkins was placed there until such time as he should be sent for. No sooner was he left to himself than his attention was attracted by a plate of fine, ripe cherries. Now Henry was uncommonly fond of cherries, and he thought it would be impossible to miss one cherry among so many. He looked and longed, and longed and looked, for some

time, and just as he had got off his seat to take one, he heard, as he thought, a foot coming to the door; but no, it was a false alarm.

11. Taking fresh courage, he went cautiously and took a very fine cherry, for he was determined to take but one, and put it into his mouth. It was excellent; and then he persuaded himself that he ran no risk in taking another; this he did, and hastily popped it into his mouth.

12. Now, the old gentleman had placed a few artificial cherries at the top of the others, filled with Cayenne pepper; one of these Henry had unfortunately taken, and it made his mouth smart and burn most intolerably. The old gentleman heard him coughing, and knew very well what was the matter. The boy that would take what did not belong to him, if no more than a cherry, was not the boy for him. Henry Wilkins was sent about his business without delay, with his mouth almost as hot as if he had put a burning coal into it.

13. Rufus Wilson was next introduced into the room and left to himself; but he had not been there ten minutes before he began to move from one place to another. He was of a bold, resolute temper, but not overburdened with principle; for if he could have opened every cupboard, closet, and drawer in the house, without being found out, he would have done it directly.

14. Having looked around the room, he noticed a drawer to the table, and made up his mind to peep therein. But no sooner did he lay hold of the drawer knob than he set a large bell ringing, which was concealed under the table. The old gentleman immediately answered the summons, and entered the room.

15. Rufus was so startled by the sudden ringing of the bell, that all his impudence could not support him. He looked as though any one might knock him down with a feather. The old gentleman asked him if he had rung the bell because he wanted anything. Rufus was much con-

fused, and stammered, and tried to excuse himself, but all to no purpose, for it did not prevent him from being ordered off the premises.

16. George Jones was then shown into the room by an old steward; and being of a cautious disposition, he touched nothing, but only looked at the things about him. At last he saw that a closet door was a little open, and, thinking it would be impossible for any one to know that he had opened it a little more, he very cautiously opened it an inch farther, looking down at the bottom of the door, that it might not catch against anything and make a noise.

17. Now had he looked at the top, instead of the bottom, it might have been better for him; for to the top of the door was fastened a plug, which filled up the hole of a small barrel of shot. He ventured to open the door another inch, and then another, till, the plug being pulled out of the barrel, the leaden shot began to pour out at a strange rate. At the bottom of the closet was placed a tin pan, and the shot falling upon this pan made such a clatter that George was frightened half out of his senses.

18. The old gentleman soon came into the room to inquire what was the matter, and there he found George nearly as pale as a sheet. George was soon dismissed.

19. It now came the turn of Albert Jenkins to be put into the room. The other boys had been sent to their homes by different ways, and no one knew what the experience of the other had been in the room of trial.

20. On the table stood a small round box, with a screw top to it, and Albert, thinking it contained something curious, could not be easy without unscrewing the top; but no sooner did he do this than out bounced an artificial snake, full a yard long, and fell upon his arm. He started back, and uttered a scream which brought the old gentleman to his elbow. There stood Albert, with the bottom of the box in one hand, the top in the other, and the snake on the floor.

21. "Come, come," said the old gentleman, "one snake is quite enough to have in the house at a time; therefore, the sooner you are gone the better." With that he dismissed him, without waiting a moment for his reply.

22. William Smith next entered the room, and being left alone soon began to amuse himself in looking at the curiosities around him. William was not only curious and prying, but dishonest, too, and observing that the key was left in the drawer of a bookcase, he stepped on tiptoe in that direction. The key had a wire fastened to it, which communicated with an electrical machine, and William received such a shock as he was not likely to forget. No sooner did he sufficiently recover himself to walk, than he was told to leave the house, and let other people lock and unlock their own drawers.

23. The other boy was Harry Gordon, and though he was left in the room full twenty minutes, he never during that time stirred from his chair. Harry had eyes in his head as well as the others, but he had more integrity in his heart; neither the dish cover, the cherries, the drawer knob, the closet door, the round box, nor the key tempted him to rise from his seat; and the consequence was that, in half an hour after, he was engaged in the service of the old gentleman at Elm Tree Hall. He followed his good old master to his grave, and received a large legacy for his upright conduct in his service.

DEFINITIONS.—2. Lăn̲'g̅uished, *suffered, sank away.* Im-pŏs'-tor, *a deceiver.* 3. A-vẽr'sion, *dislike.* In-dŭlġe', *to give way to.* Pound, *a British denomination of money equal in value to about* $4.86. 4. Ap-pli-eā'tion, *the act of making a request.* 9. Cŏn-ster-nā'tion, *excessive terror, dismay.* Prĭn'çi-ple, *a right rule of conduct.* 12. Ar-ti-fĭ'cial (*pro.* är-ti-fĭsh'al), *made by art, not real.* In-tŏl'er-a-bly, *in a manner not to be borne.* 14. Sŭm'mons, *a call to appear.* 19. Ex-pē'ri-ençe, *knowledge gained by actual trial.* 23. In-tĕg̅'ri-ty, *honesty.* Lĕg̅'a-çy, *a gift, by will, of personal property.*

VIII. WORK.

Eliza Cook (*b.* 1817, *d.* 1889) was born at London. In 1837 she commenced contributing to periodicals. In 1840 the first collection of her poems was made. In 1849 she became editor of "Eliza Cook's Journal."

1. Work, work, my boy, be not afraid;
   Look labor boldly in the face;
Take up the hammer or the spade,
   And blush not for your humble place.

2. There's glory in the shuttle's song;
   There's triumph in the anvil's stroke;
There's merit in the brave and strong
   Who dig the mine or fell the oak.

3. The wind disturbs the sleeping lake,
   And bids it ripple pure and fresh;
It moves the green boughs till they make
   Grand music in their leafy mesh.

4. And so the active breath of life
   Should stir our dull and sluggard wills;
For are we not created rife
   With health, that stagnant torpor kills?

5. I doubt if he who lolls his head
   Where idleness and plenty meet,
Enjoys his pillow or his bread
   As those who earn the meals they eat.

6. And man is never half so blest
   As when the busy day is spent
So as to make his evening rest
   A holiday of glad content.

Definitions.—3. Mĕsh, *network.* 4. Rīfe, *abounding.* Stăg'nant, *inactive.* Tôr'por, *laziness, stupidity.* 5. Lŏlls, *reclines, leans.*

IX. THE MANIAC.

1. A GENTLEMAN who had traveled in Europe, relates that he one day visited the hospital of Berlin, where he saw a man whose exterior was very striking. His figure, tall and commanding, was bending with age, but more with sorrow; the few scattered hairs which remained on his temples were white almost as the driven snow, and the deepest melancholy was depicted in his countenance.

2. On inquiring who he was and what brought him there, he started, as if from sleep, and, after looking around him, began with slow and measured steps to stride the hall, repeating in a low but audible voice, "Once one is two; once one is two."

3. Now and then he would stop, and remain with his arms folded on his breast as if in contemplation, for some minutes; then again resuming his walk, he continued to repeat, "Once one is two; once one is two." His story, as our traveler understood it, is as follows:

4. Conrad Lange, collector of the revenues of the city of Berlin, had long been known as a man whom nothing could divert from the paths of honesty. Scrupulously exact in all his dealings, and assiduous in the discharge of all his duties, he had acquired the good will and esteem of all who knew him, and the confidence of the minister of finance, whose duty it is to inspect the accounts of all officers connected with the revenue.

5. On casting up his accounts at the close of a particular year, he found a deficit of ten thousand ducats. Alarmed at this discovery, he went to the minister, presented his accounts, and informed him that he did not know how it had arisen, and that he had been robbed by some person bent on his ruin.

6. The minister received his accounts, but thinking it a duty to secure a person who might probably be a defaulter,

he caused him to be arrested, and put his accounts into the hands of one of his secretaries for inspection, who returned them the day after with the information that the deficiency arose from a miscalculation; that in multiplying, Mr. Lange had said, *once one is two*, instead of once one is *one*.

7. The poor man was immediately released from confinement, his accounts returned, and the mistake pointed out. During his imprisonment, which lasted two days, he had neither eaten, drunk, nor taken any repose; and when he appeared, his countenance was as pale as death. On receiving his accounts, he was a long time silent; then suddenly awaking, as if from a trance, he repeated, "Once one is two."

8. He appeared to be entirely insensible of his situation; would neither eat nor drink, unless solicited; and took notice of nothing that passed around him. While repeating his accustomed phrase, if anyone corrected him by saying, "Once one is *one*," his attention was arrested for a moment, and he said, "Ah, right, once one *is* one;" and then resuming his walk, he continued to repeat, "Once one is two." He died shortly after the traveler left Berlin.

9. This affecting story, whether true or untrue, obviously abounds with lessons of instruction. Alas! how easily is the human mind thrown off its balance; especially when it is stayed on this world only, and has no experimental knowledge of the meaning of the injunction of Scripture, to cast all our cares upon Him who careth for us, and who heareth even the young ravens when they cry.

DEFINITIONS.—1. Ex-tē′ri-or, *outward appearance.* De-pĭct′ed, *painted, represented.* 3. Cŏn-tem-plā′tion, *continued attention of the mind to one subject.* 4. Rĕv′e-nūeș, *the annual income from taxes, public rents, etc.* Scru̥′pu-loŭs-ly, *carefully.* As-sĭd′u-oŭs, *constant in attention.* Fĭ-nănçe′, *the income of a ruler or a state.* 5. Dĕf′i-çĭt, *lack, want.* Dŭ-e̤′at, *a gold coin worth about $2.00.* 6. De-fa̤ult′er, *one who fails to account for public money intrusted to his care.* 9. Ob′vi-oŭs-ly, *plainly.* In-jŭnc′tion, *a command.*

X. ROBIN REDBREAST.

William Allingham (*b.* 1828, *d.* 1889) was born at Ballyshannon, Ireland. His father was a banker, and gave him a good education in Irish schools. He showed his literary tastes at an early date, contributing to periodicals, etc. In 1850 he published his first volume of poems; in 1854 his "Day and Night Songs" appeared, and in 1864 a poem in twelve chapters entitled "Lawrence Bloomfield in Ireland." His reputation was established chiefly through his shorter lyrics, or ballad poetry. In 1864 he received a literary pension.

1. Good-by, good-by to Summer!
For Summer 's nearly done;
The garden smiling faintly,
Cool breezes in the sun;
Our thrushes now are silent,
Our swallows flown away,—
But Robin 's here in coat of brown,
And scarlet breastknot gay.
Robin, Robin Redbreast,
O Robin dear!
Robin sings so sweetly
In the falling of the year.

2. Bright yellow, red, and orange,
The leaves come down in hosts;
The trees are Indian princes,
But soon they 'll turn to ghosts;
The leathery pears and apples
Hang russet on the bough;
It 's autumn, autumn, autumn late,
'T will soon be winter now.
Robin, Robin Redbreast,
O Robin dear!
And what will this poor Robin do?
For pinching days are near.

3. The fireside for the cricket,
   The wheat stack for the mouse,
When trembling night winds whistle
   And moan all round the house.
The frosty ways like iron,
   The branches plumed with snow,—
Alas! in winter dead and dark,
   Where can poor Robin go?
Robin, Robin Redbreast,
   O Robin dear!
And a crumb of bread for Robin,
   His little heart to cheer.

Note.—The Old World Robin here referred to is quite different in appearance and habits from the American Robin. It is only about half the size of the latter. Its prevailing color above is olive green, while the forehead, cheeks, throat, and breast are a light yellowish red. It does not migrate, but is found at all seasons throughout temperate Europe, Asia Minor, and northern Africa.

XI. THE FISH I DID N'T CATCH.

John Greenleaf Whittier was born near Haverhill, Mass., in 1807, and died at Hampton Falls, N.H., in 1892. His boyhood was passed on a farm, and he never received a classical education. In 1829 he edited a newspaper in Boston. In the following year he removed to Hartford, Conn., to assume a similar position. In 1836 he edited an antislavery paper in Philadelphia. In 1840 he removed to Amesbury, Mass. Mr. Whittier's parents were Friends, and he always held to the same faith. He wrote extensively both in prose and verse. As a poet, he ranked among those most highly esteemed and honored by his countrymen. "Snow Bound" is one of the longest and best of his poems.

1. Our bachelor uncle who lived with us was a quiet, genial man, much given to hunting and fishing; and it was one of the pleasures of our young life to accompany him on his expeditions to Great Hill, Brandy-brow Woods, the

Pond, and, best of all, to the Country Brook. We were quite willing to work hard in the cornfield or the haying lot to finish the necessary day's labor in season for an afternoon stroll through the woods and along the brook-side.

2. I remember my first fishing excursion as if it were but yesterday. I have been happy many times in my life, but never more intensely so than when I received that first fishing pole from my uncle's hand, and trudged off with him through the woods and meadows. It was a still, sweet day of early summer; the long afternoon shadows of the trees lay cool across our path; the leaves seemed greener, the flowers brighter, the birds merrier, than ever before.

3. My uncle, who knew by long experience where were the best haunts of pickerel, considerately placed me at the most favorable point. I threw out my line as I had so often seen others, and waited anxiously for a bite, moving the bait in rapid jerks on the surface of the water in imitation of the leap of a frog. Nothing came of it. "Try again," said my uncle. Suddenly the bait sank out of sight. "Now for it," thought I; "here is a fish at last."

4. I made a strong pull, and brought up a tangle of weeds. Again and again I cast out my line with aching arms, and drew it back empty. I looked at my uncle appealingly. "Try once more," he said; "we fishermen must have patience."

5. Suddenly something tugged at my line, and swept off with it into deep water. Jerking it up, I saw a fine pickerel wriggling in the sun. "Uncle!" I cried, looking back in uncontrollable excitement, "I've got a fish!" "Not yet," said my uncle. As he spoke there was a plash in the water; I caught the arrowy gleam of a scared fish shooting into the middle of the stream, my hook hung empty from the line. I had lost my prize.

6. We are apt to speak of the sorrows of childhood as trifles in comparison with those of grown-up people; but we may depend upon it the young folks don't agree with us. Our griefs, modified and restrained by reason, ex-

perience, and self-respect, keep the proprieties, and, if possible, avoid a scene; but the sorrow of childhood, unreasoning and all-absorbing, is a complete abandonment to the passion. The doll's nose is broken, and the world breaks up with it; the marble rolls out of sight, and the solid globe rolls off with the marble.

7. So, overcome with my great and bitter disappointment, I sat down on the nearest hassock, and for a time refused to be comforted, even by my uncle's assurance that there were more fish in the brook. He refitted my bait, and, putting the pole again in my hands, told me to try my luck once more.

8. "But remember, boy," he said, with his shrewd smile, "never brag of catching a fish until he is on dry ground. I've seen older folks doing that in more ways than one, and so making fools of themselves. It's no use to boast of anything until it's done, nor then, either, for it speaks for itself."

9. How often since I have been reminded of the fish that I did not catch. When I hear people boasting of a work as yet undone, and trying to anticipate the credit which belongs only to actual achievement, I call to mind that scene by the brookside, and the wise caution of my uncle in that particular instance takes the form of a proverb of universal application: "NEVER BRAG OF YOUR FISH BEFORE YOU CATCH HIM."

DEFINITIONS.—1. Gēn'ial, *cheerful.* 3. Häunts, *places frequently visited.* Con-sĭd'er-ate-ly, *with due regard to others, kindly thoughtful.* 4. Ap-pēal'ing-ly, *as though asking for aid.* 6. Mŏd'i-fied, *qualified, lessened.* Pro-prī'e-tieṣ, *fixed customs or rules of conduct.* Ab-sôrb'ing, *engaging the attention entirely.* 7. Hăs'sock, *a raised mound of turf.* 9. An-tĭç'i-pate, *to take before the proper time.* A-chiēve'ment, *performance, deed.*

XII. IT SNOWS.

Sarah Josepha Hale (*b.* 1788 ?, *d.* 1879) was born in Newport, N.H. Her maiden name was Buell. In 1814 she married David Hale, an eminent lawyer, who died in 1822. Left with five children to support, she turned her attention to literature. In 1828 she became editor of the "Ladies' Magazine." In 1837 this periodical was united with "Godey's Lady's Book," of which Mrs. Hale was literary editor for more than forty years.

1. "It snows!" cries the Schoolboy, "Hurrah!" and his shout
Is ringing through parlor and hall,
While swift as the wing of a swallow, he's out,
And his playmates have answered his call;
It makes the heart leap but to witness their joy;
Proud wealth has no pleasures, I trow,
Like the rapture that throbs in the pulse of the boy
As he gathers his treasures of snow;
Then lay not the trappings of gold on thine heirs,
While health and the riches of nature are theirs.

2. "It snows!" sighs the Imbecile, "Ah!" and his breath
Comes heavy, as clogged with a weight;
While, from the pale aspect of nature in death,
He turns to the blaze of his grate;
And nearer and nearer, his soft-cushioned chair
Is wheeled toward the life-giving flame;
He dreads a chill puff of the snow-burdened air,
Lest it wither his delicate frame;
Oh! small is the pleasure existence can give,
When the fear we shall die only proves that we live!

3. "It snows!" cries the Traveler, "Ho!" and the word
Has quickened his steed's lagging pace;
The wind rushes by, but its howl is unheard,
Unfelt the sharp drift in his face;
For bright through the tempest his own home appeared,
Ay, though leagues intervened, he can see:

There's the clear, glowing hearth, and the table prepared,
  And his wife with her babes at her knee;
Blest thought! how it lightens the grief-laden hour,
That those we love dearest are safe from its power!

4. "It snows!" cries the Belle, "Dear, how lucky!" and turns
  From her mirror to watch the flakes fall,
Like the first rose of summer, her dimpled cheek burns,
  While musing on sleigh ride and ball:
There are visions of conquests, of splendor, and mirth,
  Floating over each drear winter's day;
But the tintings of Hope, on this storm-beaten earth,
  Will melt like the snowflakes away.
Turn, turn thee to Heaven, fair maiden, for bliss;
That world has a pure fount ne'er opened in this.

5. "It snows!" cries the Widow, "O God!" and her sighs
  Have stifled the voice of her prayer;
Its burden ye'll read in her tear-swollen eyes,
  On her cheek sunk with fasting and care.
'T is night, and her fatherless ask her for bread,
  But "He gives the young ravens their food,"
And she trusts till her dark hearth adds horror to dread,
  And she lays on her last chip of wood.
Poor sufferer! that sorrow thy God only knows;
'T is a most bitter lot to be poor when it snows.

Definitions.—1. Trōw, *to think, to believe.* Trăp'pings, *ornaments.* 2. Im'be-çile, *one who is feeble either in body or mind.* 3. In-ter-vēned', *were situated between.* 4. Mūs'ing, *thinking in an absent-minded way.* Cŏn'quests, *triumphs, successes.* Tĭnt'ings, *slight colorings.* 5. Stī'fled, *choked, suppressed.*

Remark.—Avoid reading this piece in a monotonous style. Try to express the actual feeling of each quotation; and enter into the descriptions with spirit.

XIII. RESPECT FOR THE SABBATH REWARDED.

1. In the city of Bath, not many years since, lived a barber who made a practice of following his ordinary occupation on the Lord's day. As he was on the way to his morning's employment, he happened to look into some place of worship just as the minister was giving out his text--"Remember the Sabbath day, to keep it holy." He listened long enough to be convinced that he was constantly breaking the laws of God and man by shaving and dressing his customers on the Lord's day. He became uneasy, and went with a heavy heart to his Sabbath task.

2. At length he took courage, and opened his mind to his minister, who advised him to give up Sabbath work, and worship God. He replied that beggary would be the consequence. He had a flourishing trade, but it would almost all be lost. At length, after many a sleepless night spent in weeping and praying, he was determined to cast all his care upon God, as the more he reflected, the more his duty became apparent.

3. He discontinued his Sabbath work, went constantly and early to the public services of religion, and soon enjoyed that satisfaction of mind which is one of the rewards of doing our duty, and that peace which the world can neither give nor take away. The consequences he foresaw actually followed. His genteel customers left him, and he was nicknamed "Puritan" or "Methodist." He was obliged to give up his fashionable shop, and, in the course of years, became so reduced as to take a cellar under the old market house and shave the poorer people.

4. One Saturday evening, between light and dark, a stranger from one of the coaches, asking for a barber, was directed by the hostler to the cellar opposite. Coming in hastily, he requested to be shaved quickly, while they changed horses, as he did not like to violate the Sabbath.

This was touching the barber on a tender chord. He burst into tears; asked the stranger to lend him a half-penny to buy a candle, as it was not light enough to shave him with safety. He did so, revolving in his mind the extreme poverty to which the poor man must be reduced.

5. When shaved, he said, "There must be something extraordinary in your history, which I have not now time to hear. Here is half a crown for you. When I return, I will call and investigate your case. What is your name?" "William Reed," said the astonished barber. "William Reed?" echoed the stranger: "William Reed? by your dialect you are from the West." "Yes, sir, from Kingston, near Taunton." "William Reed from Kingston, near Taunton? What was your father's name?" "Thomas." "Had he any brother?" "Yes, sir, one, after whom I was named; but he went to the Indies, and, as we never heard from him, we supposed him to be dead."

6. "Come along, follow me," said the stranger, "I am going to see a person who says his name is William Reed, of Kingston, near Taunton. Come and confront him. If you prove to be indeed he who you say you are, I have glorious news for you. Your uncle is dead, and has left an immense fortune, which I will put you in possession of when all legal doubts are removed."

7. They went by the coach; saw the pretended William Reed, and proved him to be an impostor. The stranger, who was a pious attorney, was soon legally satisfied of the barber's identity, and told him that he had advertised him in vain. Providence had now thrown him in his way in a most extraordinary manner, and he had great pleasure in transferring a great many thousand pounds to a worthy man, the rightful heir of the property. Thus was man's extremity God's opportunity. Had the poor barber possessed one half-penny, or even had credit for a candle, he might have remained unknown for years; but he trusted God, who never said, "Seek ye my face," in vain.

Definitions.—2. Ap-pâr'ent, *clear, plain.* 3. Gen-teel', *fashionable, elegant.* Re-dūçed', *brought to poverty.* 4. Vī'o-lāte, *to break, to profane.* 5. In-vĕs'ti-gāte, *to inquire into with care.* Dī'a-leet, *a local form of speech.* 6. Con-frŏnt', *to face, to stand before.* 7. At-tor'ney (*pro.* at-tûr'nỹ), *a lawyer.* I-dĕn'ti-ty, *the condition of being the same as something claimed.* Trans-fẽr'ring, *making over the possession of.* Ex-trĕm'i-ty, *greatest need.* Op-por-tū'-ni-ty, *favorable time.*

XIV. THE SANDS O' DEE.

Charles Kingsley (*b.* 1819, *d.* 1875) was born at Holne, Devonshire, England. He took his bachelor's degree at Cambridge in 1842, and soon after entered the Church. His writings are quite voluminous, including sermons, lectures, novels, fairy tales, and poems, published in book form, besides numerous miscellaneous sermons and magazine articles. He was an earnest worker for bettering the condition of the working classes, and this object was the basis of most of his writings. As a lyric poet he has gained a high place. The "Saint's Tragedy" and "Andromeda" are the most pretentious of his poems, and "Alton Locke" and "Hypatia" are his best known novels.

1. "O Mary, go and call the cattle home,
 And call the cattle home,
 And call the cattle home,
 Across the sands o' Dee!"
The western wind was wild and dank with foam,
 And all alone went she.

2. The creeping tide came up along the sand,
 And o'er and o'er the sand,
 And round and round the sand,
 As far as eye could see;
The blinding mist came down and hid the land—
 And never home came she.

3. Oh, is it weed, or fish, or floating hair?—
A tress o' golden hair,
O' drowned maiden's hair,
Above the nets at sea.
Was never salmon yet that shone so fair
Among the stakes on Dee.

4. They rowed her in across the rolling foam,
The cruel, crawling foam,
The cruel, hungry foam,
To her grave beside the sea;
But still the boatmen hear her call the cattle home,
Across the sands o' Dee.

NOTES.—*The Sands o' Dee.* The Dee is a river of Scotland, noted for its salmon fisheries.

O' is a contraction for *of*, commonly used by the Scotch.

REMARK.—The first three lines of each stanza deserve special attention in reading. The final words are nearly or quite the same, but the expression of each line should vary. The piece should be read in a low key and with a pure, musical tone.

XV. SELECT PARAGRAPHS.

1. O GIVE thanks unto the Lord; call upon his name; make known his deeds among the people. Sing unto him; sing psalms unto him; talk ye of all his wondrous works. Glory ye in his holy name; let the heart of them rejoice that seek the Lord. Remember his marvelous works that he hath done; his wonders, and the judgments of his mouth.

2. O Lord, our Lord, how excellent is thy name in all the earth! who hast set thy glory above the heavens. When I consider thy heavens, the work of thy fingers; the

moon and the stars which thou hast ordained; what is man, that thou art mindful of him? and the son of man, that thou visitest him? For thou hast made him a little lower than the angels, and hast crowned him with glory and honor. Thou madest him to have dominion over the work of thy hands; thou hast put all things under his feet. O Lord, our Lord, how excellent is thy name in all the earth!

3. I will say of the Lord, He is my refuge and my fortress, my God; in him will I trust. Because he hath set his love upon me, therefore will I deliver him: I will set him on high, because he hath known my name. He shall call upon me, and I will answer him; I will be with him in trouble; I will deliver him, and honor him. With long life will I satisfy him, and show him my salvation.

4. O come, let us sing unto the Lord, let us heartily rejoice in the strength of our salvation. Let us come before his presence with thanksgiving, and show ourselves glad in him with psalms. For the Lord is a great God, and a great King above all gods. O worship the Lord in the beauty of holiness; let the whole earth stand in awe of him. For he cometh, for he cometh, to judge the earth; and with righteousness to judge the world, and the people with his truth.

5. Oh that men would praise the Lord for his goodness, and for his wonderful works to the children of men! They that go down to the sea in ships, that do business in great waters; these see the works of the Lord, and his wonders in the deep. For he commandeth, and raiseth the stormy wind, which lifteth up the waves thereof. They mount up to the heaven; they go down again to the depths; their soul is melted because of trouble; they reel to and fro, and stagger like a drunken man, and are at their wit's end. Then they cry unto the Lord in their trouble, and he bringeth them out of their distresses. He maketh the storm a calm, so that the waves thereof are still. Then

are they glad because they be quiet; so he bringeth them unto their desired haven. Oh that men would praise the Lord for his goodness, and for his wonderful works to the children of men!

6. The Lord is my shepherd; I shall not want. He maketh me to lie down in green pastures; he leadeth me beside the still waters. He restoreth my soul; he leadeth me in the paths of righteousness for his name's sake. Yea, though I walk through the valley of the shadow of death, I will fear no evil; for thou art with me: thy rod and thy staff, they comfort me. Thou preparest a table before me in the presence of mine enemies; thou anointest my head with oil; my cup runneth over. Surely, goodness and mercy shall follow me all the days of my life; and I will dwell in the house of the Lord forever.

—*Bible.*

DEFINITIONS.—1. Mär′vel-oŭs, *wonderful.* 2. Or-dāined′, *appointed, established.* Do-mĭn′ion (*pro.* do-mĭn′yŭn), *supreme power.* 5. Hā ven, *a harbor, a place where ships can lie in safety.*

XVI. THE CORN SONG.

1. HEAP high the farmer's wintry hoard!
 Heap high the golden corn!
No richer gift has Autumn poured
 From out her lavish horn!

2. Let other lands, exulting, glean
 The apple from the pine,
The orange from its glossy green,
 The cluster from the vine;

3. We better love the hardy gift
   Our rugged vales bestow,
To cheer us, when the storm shall drift
   Our harvest fields with snow.

4. Through vales of grass and meads of flowers
   Our plows their furrows made,
While on the hills the sun and showers
   Of changeful April played.

5. We dropped the seed o'er hill and plain,
   Beneath the sun of May,
And frightened from our sprouting grain
   The robber crows away.

6. All through the long, bright days of June,
   Its leaves grew green and fair,
And waved in hot midsummer's noon
   Its soft and yellow hair.

7. And now, with Autumn's moonlit eves,
   Its harvest time has come;
We pluck away the frosted leaves
   And bear the treasure home.

8. There, richer than the fabled gift
   Apollo showered of old,
Fair hands the broken grain shall sift,
   And knead its meal of gold.

9. Let vapid idlers loll in silk,
   Around their costly board;
Give us the bowl of samp and milk,
   By homespun beauty poured!

10. Where'er the wide old kitchen hearth
 Sends up its smoky curls,
Who will not thank the kindly earth
 And bless our farmer girls!

11. Then shame on all the proud and vain,
 Whose folly laughs to scorn
The blessing of our hardy grain,
 Our wealth of golden corn!

12. Let earth withhold her goodly root;
 Let mildew blight the rye,
Give to the worm the orchard's fruit,
 The wheat field to the fly:

13. But let the good old crop adorn
 The hills our fathers trod;
Still let us, for his golden corn,
 Send up our thanks to God!

From Whittier's "Songs of Labor."

DEFINITIONS.—1. Hōard, *a large quantity of anything laid up.* Lăv'ish, *profuse.* 4. Mēads, *meadows.* 9. Văp'id, *spiritless, dull.* Sămp, *bruised corn cooked by boiling.*

NOTE.—8. According to the ancient fable, *Apollo*, the god of music, sowed the isle of Delos, his birthplace, with golden flowers, by the music of his lyre.

XVII. THE VENOMOUS WORM.

John Russell (*b.* 1793, *d.* 1863) graduated at Middlebury College, Vt., in 1818. He was at one time editor of the "Backwoodsman," published at Grafton, Ill., and later of the "Louisville Advocate." He was the author of many tales of western adventure and of numerous essays, sketches, etc. His language is clear, chaste, and classical; his style concise, vigorous, and sometimes highly ornate.

1. Who has not heard of the rattlesnake or copperhead? An unexpected sight of either of these reptiles will make even the lords of creation recoil; but there is a species of worm, found in various parts of this country, which conveys a poison of a nature so deadly that, compared with it, even the venom of the rattlesnake is harmless. To guard our readers against this foe of human kind is the object of this lesson.

2. This worm varies much in size. It is frequently an inch in diameter, but, as it is rarely seen except when coiled, its length can hardly be conjectured. It is of a dull lead color, and generally lives near a spring or small stream of water, and bites the unfortunate people who are in the habit of going there to drink. The brute creation it never molests. They avoid it with the same instinct that teaches the animals of India to shun the deadly cobra.

3. Several of these reptiles have long infested our settlements, to the misery and destruction of many of our fellow-citizens. I have, therefore, had frequent opportunities of being the melancholy spectator of the effects produced by the subtile poison which this worm infuses.

4. The symptoms of its bite are terrible. The eyes of the patient become red and fiery, his tongue swells to an immoderate size, and obstructs his utterance; and delirium of the most horrid character quickly follows. Sometimes, in his madness, he attempts the destruction of his nearest friends.

5. If the sufferer has a family, his weeping wife and helpless infants are not unfrequently the objects of his

frantic fury. In a word, he exhibits, to the life, all the detestable passions that rankle in the bosom of a savage; and such is the spell in which his senses are locked, that no sooner has the unhappy patient recovered from the paroxysm of insanity occasioned by the bite, than he seeks out the destroyer for the sole purpose of being bitten again.

6. I have seen a good old father, his locks as white as snow, his step slow and trembling, beg in vain of his only son to quit the lurking place of the worm. My heart bled when he turned away; for I knew the fond hope that his son would be the "staff of his declining years," had supported him through many a sorrow.

7. Youths of America, would you know the name of this reptile? It is called the WORM OF THE STILL.

DEFINITIONS.—1. Rĕp′tīleṣ, *animals that crawl, as snakes, lizards, etc.* Re-coil′, *to start back, to shrink from.* 2. Cō′bra, *a highly venomous reptile inhabiting the East Indies.* In-fĕst′ed, *troubled, annoyed.* 3. Sŭb′tīle, *acute, piercing.* In-fūṣ′eṣ, *introduces.* 4. Ob-strŭcts′, *hinders.* De-lĭr′i-ŭm, *a wandering of the mind.* 5. Răn̲′kle, *to rage.* Păr′ox-ȳṣm, *a fit, a convulsion.* 7. Wõrm, *a spiral metallic pipe used in distilling liquors.* Stĭll, *a vessel used in distilling or making liquors.*

XVIII. THE FESTAL BOARD.

1. COME to the festal board to-night,
   For bright-eyed beauty will be there,
Her coral lips in nectar steeped,
   And garlanded her hair.

2. Come to the festal board to-night,
   For there the joyous laugh of youth
Will ring those silvery peals, which speak
   Of bosom pure and stainless truth.

3. Come to the festal board to-night,
   For friendship, there, with stronger chain,
Devoted hearts already bound
   For good or ill, will bind again.

I went.

4. Nature and art their stores outpoured;
   Joy beamed in every kindling glance;
Love, friendship, youth, and beauty smiled;
   What could that evening's bliss enhance?

We parted.

5. And years have flown; but where are now
   The guests who round that table met?
Rises their sun as gloriously
   As on the banquet's eve it set?

6. How holds the chain which friendship wove?
   It broke; and soon the hearts it bound
Were widely sundered; and for peace,
   Envy and strife and blood were found.

7. The merriest laugh which then was heard
   Has changed its tones to maniac screams,
As half-quenched memory kindles up
   Glimmerings of guilt in feverish dreams.

8. And where is she whose diamond eyes
   Golconda's purest gems outshone?
Whose roseate lips of Eden breathed?
   Say, where is she, the beauteous one?

9. Beneath yon willow's drooping shade,
   With eyes now dim, and lips all pale,
She sleeps in peace. Read on her urn,
   "*A broken heart.*" This tells her tale.

10. And where is he, that tower of strength,
Whose fate with hers for life was joined?
How beats his heart, once honor's throne?
How high has soared his daring mind?

11. Go to the dungeon's gloom to-night;
His wasted form, his aching head,
And all that now remains of him,
Lies, shuddering, on a felon's bed.

12. Ask you of all these woes the cause?
The festal board, the enticing bowl,
More often came, and reason fled,
And maddened passions spurned control.

13. Learn wisdom, then. The frequent feast
Avoid; for there, with stealthy tread
Temptation walks, to lure you on,
Till death, at last, the banquet spread.

14. And shun, oh shun, the enchanted cup!
Though now its draught like joy appears,
Ere long it will be fanned by sighs,
And sadly mixed with blood and tears.

DEFINITIONS. — 1. Fĕs′tal, *mirthful, joyous.* Gär′land-ed, *adorned with wreaths of flowers.* 3. De-vōt′ed, *solemnly set apart.* 4. En-hànçe′, *increase.* 6. Sŭn′dered, *separated.* 7. Glĭm′mer-ingṣ, *faint views, glimpses.* 8. Rō′ṣe-ate, *blooming, rosy.* 11. Fĕl′on, *a public criminal.* 12. En-tīç′ing, *attracting to evil.* Spûrned, *rejected with disdain.* 13. Lūre, *to attract, to entice.* 14. En-chànt′ed, *affected with enchantment, bewitched.*

NOTES. — 8. *Golconda* is an ancient city and fortress of India, formerly renowned for its diamonds. They were merely cut and polished there, however, being generally brought from Parteall, a city farther south.

XIX. HOW TO TELL BAD NEWS.

Mr. H. and the Steward.

Mr. H. HA! Steward, how are you, my old boy? How do things go on at home?

Steward. Bad enough, your honor; the magpie 's dead.

H. Poor Mag! So he 's gone. How came he to die?

S. Overeat himself, sir.

H. Did he? A greedy dog; why, what did he get he liked so well?

S. Horseflesh, sir; he died of eating horseflesh.

H. How came he to get so much horseflesh?

S. All your father's horses, sir.

H. What! are they dead, too?

S. Ay, sir; they died of overwork.

H. And why were they overworked, pray?

S. To carry water, sir.

H. To carry water! and what were they carrying water for?

S. Sure, sir, to put out the fire.

H. Fire! what fire?

S. O, sir, your father's house is burned to the ground.

H. My father's house burned down! and how came it set on fire?

S. I think, sir, it must have been the torches.

H. Torches! what torches?

S. At your mother's funeral.

H. My mother dead!

S. Ah, poor lady! she never looked up, after it.

H. After what?

S. The loss of youı father.

H. My father gone, too?

S. Yes, poor gentleman! he took to his bed as soon as he heard of it.

H. Heard of what?

S. The bad news, sir, and please your honor.

H. What! more miseries! more bad news!

S. Yes, sir; your bank has failed, and your credit is lost, and you are not worth a shilling in the world. I made bold, sir, to wait on you about it, for I thought you would like to hear the news.

XX. THE BATTLE OF BLENHEIM.

Robert Southey (*b.* 1774, *d.* 1843) was born in Bristol, England. He entered Balliol College, Oxford, in 1793. In 1804 he established himself permanently at Greta Hall, near Keswick, Cumberland, in the "Lake Country," where he enjoyed the friendship and society of Wordsworth and Coleridge, other poets of the "Lake School." He was appointed poet laureate in 1813, and received a pension of £300 a year from the government in 1835. Mr. Southey was a voluminous writer in both prose and verse. As a poet, he can not be placed in the first rank, although some of his minor poems are very happy in thought and expression. Among his most noted poetical works are "Joan of Arc," "Thalaba the Destroyer," "Madoc," "Roderick," and the "Curse of Kehama."

1. It was a summer evening,
Old Kaspar's work was done,
And he, before his cottage door,
Was sitting in the sun;
And by him sported on the green,
His little grandchild Wilhelmine.

2. She saw her brother Peterkin
Roll something large and round,
Which he beside the rivulet,
In playing there, had found;
He came to ask what he had found,
That was so large, and smooth, and round.

3. Old Kaspar took it from the boy,
   Who stood expectant by;
And then the old man shook his head,
   And, with a natural sigh,
"'T is some poor fellow's skull," said he,
"Who fell in the great victory.

4. "I find them in the garden,
   For there's many hereabout;
And often when I go to plow,
   The plowshare turns them out;
For many thousand men," said he,
"Were slain in that great victory."

5. "Now tell us what 't was all about,"
   Young Peterkin he cries;
While little Wilhelmine looks up
   With wonder-waiting eyes;
"Now tell us all about the war,
And what they killed each other for."

6. "It was the English," Kaspar cried,
   "Who put the French to rout,
But what they killed each other for,
   I could not well make out;
But everybody said," quoth he,
"That 't was a famous victory:

7. "My father lived at Blenheim then,
   Yon little stream, hard by;
They burnt his dwelling to the ground,
   And he was forced to fly;
So, with his wife and child he fled,
Nor had he where to rest his head.

8. "With fire and sword, the country round
Was wasted, far and wide;
And many a nursing mother then,
And newborn baby died;
But things like that, you know, must be
At every famous victory.

9. "They say it was a shocking sight
After the field was won;
For many thousand bodies here
Lay rotting in the sun:
But things like that, you know, must be
After a famous victory.

10. "Great praise the Duke of Marlboro' won,
And our young prince, Eugene."
"Why, 't was a very wicked thing!"
Said little Wilhelmine.
"Nay, nay, my little girl!" quoth he,
"It was a famous victory.

11. "And everybody praised the Duke
Who this great fight did win."
"But what good came of it at last?"
Quoth little Peterkin.
"Why, that I can not tell," said he,
"But 't was a glorious victory."

Notes.—The Battle of Blenheim, in the "War of the Spanish Succession," was fought August 13, 1704, near Blenheim, in Bavaria, between the French and Bavarians, on one side, and an allied army under the great English general, the Duke of Marlborough, and Eugene, Prince of Savoy, on the other. The latter won a decisive victory: 10,000 of the defeated army were killed and wounded, and 13,000 were taken prisoners.

XXI. "I PITY THEM."

1. A POOR man once undertook to emigrate from Castine, Me., to Illinois. When he was attempting to cross a river in New York, his horse broke through the rotten timbers of the bridge, and was drowned. He had but this one animal to convey all his property and his family to his new home.

2. His wife and children were almost miraculously saved from sharing the fate of the horse; but the loss of this poor animal was enough. By its aid the family, it may be said, had lived and moved; now they were left helpless in a land of strangers, without the ability to go on or return, without money or a single friend to whom to appeal. The case was a hard one.

3. There were a great many who "passed by on the other side." Some even laughed at the predicament in which the man was placed; but by degrees a group of people began to collect, all of whom pitied him.

4. Some pitied him a great deal, and some did not pity him very much, because, they said, he might have known better than to try to cross an unsafe bridge, and should have made his horse swim the river. Pity, however, seemed rather to predominate. Some pitied the man, and some the horse; all pitied the poor, sick mother and her six helpless children.

5. Among this pitying party was a rough son of the West, who knew what it was to migrate some hundreds of miles over new roads to locate a destitute family on a prairie. Seeing the man's forlorn situation, and looking around on the bystanders, he said, "All of you seem to pity these poor people very much, but I would beg leave to ask each of you how much."

6. "There, stranger," continued he, holding up a ten-dollar bill, "there is the amount of my pity; and if others

will do as I do, you may soon get another pony. God bless you." It is needless to state the effect that this active charity produced. In a short time the happy emigrant arrived at his destination, and he is now a thriving farmer, and a neighbor to him who was his "friend in need, and a friend indeed."

DEFINITIONS.—1. Em'i-grāte, *to remove from one country or state to another for the purpose of residence, to migrate.* 2. Mi-răc'u-loŭs-ly, *as if by miracle, wonderfully.* A-bĭl'i-ty, *power, capability.* 3. Pre-dĭc'a-ment, *condition, plight.* 4. Pre-dŏm'i-nāte, *to prevail, to rule.* 5. Lō'cāte, *to place.* Dĕs'ti-tūte, *needy, poor.* 6. Dĕs-ti-nā'tion, *end of a journey.* Thrīv'ing, *prosperous through industry, economy, and good management.*

XXII. AN ELEGY ON MADAM BLAIZE.

Oliver Goldsmith (*b.* 1728, *d.* 1774) was born at Pallas, or Pallasmore, in the parish of Forney, Ireland. He received his education at several schools, at Trinity College, Dublin, at Edinburgh, and at Leyden. He spent some time in wandering over continental Europe, often in poverty and want. In 1756 he became a resident of London, where he made the acquaintance of several celebrated men, among whom were Dr. Johnson and Sir Joshua Reynolds. His writings are noted for their purity, grace, and fluency. His fame as a poet is secured by "The Traveler," and "The Deserted Village;" as a dramatist, by "She Stoops to Conquer;" and as a novelist, by "The Vicar of Wakefield." His reckless extravagance always kept him in financial difficulty, and he died heavily in debt. His monument is in Westminster Abbey.

1. Good people all, with one accord,
   Lament for Madam Blaize,
Who never wanted a good word—
   From those who spoke her praise.

2. The needy seldom passed her door,
   And always found her kind;
She freely lent to all the poor—
   Who left a pledge behind.

3. She strove the neighborhood to please,
   With manner wondrous winning:
She never followed wicked ways—
   Unless when she was sinning.

4. At church, in silks and satin new,
   With hoop of monstrous size,
She never slumbered in her pew—
   But when she shut her eyes.

5. Her love was sought, I do aver,
   By twenty beaux and more;
The king himself has followed her—
   When she has walked before.

6. But now, her wealth and finery fled,
   Her hangers-on cut short all,
Her doctors found, when she was dead—
   Her last disorder mortal.

7. Let us lament, in sorrow sore;
   For Kent Street well may say,
That, had she lived a twelvemonth more—
   She had not died to-day.

DEFINITIONS. — 1. Ac-côrd′, *agreement of opinion, consent.* 2. Plĕdġe, *personal property delivered to another as a security for a debt.* 6. Hăng′erṣ-ŏn, *followers.* Môr′tal, *destructive to life.*

XXIII. KING CHARLES II. AND WILLIAM PENN.

King Charles. WELL, friend William! I have sold you a noble province in North America; but still, I suppose you have no thoughts of going thither yourself?

Penn. Yes, I have, I assure thee, friend Charles; and I am just come to bid thee farewell.

K. C. What! venture yourself among the savages of North America! Why, man, what security have you that you will not be in their war kettle in two hours after setting foot on their shores?

P. The best security in the world.

K. C. I doubt that, friend William; I have no idea of any security against those cannibals but in a regiment of good soldiers, with their muskets and bayonets. And mind, I tell you beforehand, that, with all my good will for you and your family, to whom I am under obligations, I will not send a single soldier with you.

P. I want none of thy soldiers, Charles: I depend on something better than thy soldiers.

K. C. Ah! what may that be?

P. Why, I depend upon themselves; on the working of their own hearts; on their notions of justice; on their moral sense.

K. C. A fine thing, this same moral sense, no doubt; but I fear you will not find much of it among the Indians of North America.

P. And why not among them as well as others?

K. C. Because if they had possessed any, they would not have treated my subjects so barbarously as they have done.

P. That is no proof of the contrary, friend Charles. Thy subjects were the aggressors. When thy subjects first went to North America, they found these poor people the fondest and kindest creatures in the world. Every day they would watch for them to come ashore, and hasten to meet them, and feast them on the best fish, and venison, and corn, which were all they had. In return for this hospitality of the *savages*, as we call them, thy subjects, termed *Christians*, seized on their country and rich hunting grounds for farms for themselves. Now, is it to be wondered at, that these much-injured people should have been driven to desperation by such injustice; and that, burning with revenge, they should have committed some excesses?

K. C. Well, then, I hope you will not complain when they come to treat you in the same manner.

P. I am not afraid of it.

K. C. Ah! how will you avoid it? You mean to get their hunting grounds, too, I suppose?

P. Yes, but not by driving these poor people away from them.

K. C. No, indeed? How then will you get their lands?

P. I mean to buy their lands of them.

K. C. Buy their lands of them? Why, man, you have already bought them of me!

P. Yes, I know I have, and at a dear rate, too; but I did it only to get thy good will, not that I thought thou hadst any right to their lands.

K. C. How, man? no right to their lands?

P. No, friend Charles, no right; no right at all: what right hast thou to their lands?

K. C. Why, the right of discovery, to be sure; the right which the Pope and all Christian kings have agreed to give one another.

P. The right of discovery? A strange kind of right, indeed. Now suppose, friend Charles, that some canoe load of these Indians, crossing the sea, and discovering this island of Great Britain, were to claim it as their own, and set it up for sale over thy head, what wouldst thou think of it?

K. C. Why—why—why—I must confess, I should think it a piece of great impudence in them.

P. Well, then, how canst thou, a Christian, and a Christian prince, too, do that which thou so utterly condemnest in these people whom thou callest savages? And suppose, again, that these Indians, on thy refusal to give up thy island of Great Britain, were to make war on thee, and, having weapons more destructive than thine, were to destroy many of thy subjects, and drive the rest away—wouldst thou not think it horribly cruel?

K. C. I must say, friend William, that I should; how can I say otherwise?

P. Well, then, how can I, who call myself a Christian, do what I should abhor even in the heathen? No. I will not do it. But I will buy the right of the proper owners, even of the Indians themselves. By doing this, I shall imitate God himself in his justice and mercy, and thereby insure his blessing on my colony, if I should ever live to plant one in North America.

—*Mason L. Weems.*

Definitions. — Căn′ni-bals, *human beings that eat human flesh.* Rĕg′i-ment, *a body of troops, consisting usually of ten companies.* Ag-grĕss′ors, *those who first commence hostilities.* Vĕn′i-son (*pro.* vĕn′ĭ-zn, or vĕn′zn), *the flesh of deer.* Ex-çĕss′es, *misdeeds, evil acts.* Con-dĕmn′est (*pro.* kon-dĕm′est), *censure, blame.*

Notes. — Charles II. was king of England from A.D. 1660 to 1685. William Penn (*b.* 1644, *d.* 1718) was a noted Englishman who belonged to the sect of Friends. He came to America in 1682, and founded the province which is now the state of Pennsylvania. He purchased the lands from the Indians, who were so impressed with the justice and good will of Penn and his associates, that the Quaker dress often served as a sure protection when other settlers were trembling for their lives.

XXIV. WHAT I LIVE FOR.

1. I live for those who love me,
   Whose hearts are kind and true;
For the heaven that smiles above me,
   And awaits my spirit, too;
For all human ties that bind me,
For the task my God assigned me,
For the bright hopes left behind me,
   And the good that I can do.

2. I live to learn their story,
   Who suffered for my sake;
To emulate their glory,
   And follow in their wake;
Bards, patriots, martyrs, sages,
The noble of all ages,
Whose deeds crown History's pages,
   And Time's great volume make.

3. I live to hail that season,
 By gifted minds foretold,
When man shall live by reason,
 And not alone by gold;
When man to man united,
And every wrong thing righted,
The whole world shall be lighted
 As Eden was of old.

4. I live for those who love me,
 For those who know me true;
For the heaven that smiles above me,
 And awaits my spirit, too;
For the cause that needs assistance,
For the wrongs that need resistance,
For the future in the distance,
 And the good that I can do.

Definitions.—1. As-sīgned′ (*pro.* as-sīnd′), *allotted, marked out.* 2. Em′-u-lāte, *to strive to equal or excel, to rival.* Wāke, *the track left by a vessel in the water; hence, figuratively, in the train of.* Bard, *a poet.* Mär′tyr, *one who sacrifices what is of great value to him for the sake of principle.* Sāge, *a wise man.* 3. Hāil, *to salute.*

XXV. THE RIGHTEOUS NEVER FORSAKEN.

1. It was Saturday night, and the widow of the Pine Cottage sat by her blazing fagots, with her five tattered children at her side, endeavoring by listening to the artlessness of their prattle to dissipate the heavy gloom that pressed upon her mind. For a year, her own feeble hand had provided for her helpless family, for she had no supporter: she thought of no friend in all the wide, unfriendly world around.

2. But that mysterious Providence, the wisdom of whose ways is above human comprehension, had visited her with wasting sickness, and her little means had become exhausted. It was now, too, midwinter, and the snow lay heavy and deep through all the surrounding forests, while storms still seemed gathering in the heavens, and the driving wind roared amid the neighboring pines, and rocked her puny mansion.

3. The last herring smoked upon the coals before her; it was the only article of food she possessed, and no wonder her forlorn, desolate state brought up in her lone bosom all the anxieties of a mother when she looked upon her children: and no wonder, forlorn as she was, if she suffered the heart swellings of despair to rise, even though she knew that He, whose promise is to the widow and to the orphan, can not forget his word.

4. Providence had many years before taken from her her eldest son, who went from his forest home to try his fortune on the high seas, since which she had heard no tidings of him; and in her latter time had, by the hand of death, deprived her of the companion and staff of her earthly pilgrimage, in the person of her husband. Yet to this hour she had upborne; she had not only been able to provide for her little flock, but had never lost an opportunity of ministering to the wants of the miserable and destitute.

5. The indolent may well bear with poverty while the ability to gain sustenance remains. The individual who has but his own wants to supply may suffer with fortitude the winter of want; his affections are not wounded, his heart is not wrung. The most desolate in populous cities may hope, for charity has not quite closed her hand and heart, and shut her eyes on misery.

6. But the industrious mother of helpless and depending children, far from the reach of human charity, has none of these to console her. And such a one was the widow of

the Pine Cottage; but as she bent over the fire, and took up the last scanty remnant of food to spread before her children, her spirits seemed to brighten up, as by some sudden and mysterious impulse, and Cowper's beautiful lines came uncalled across her mind:

> "Judge not the Lord by feeble sense,
> But trust him for his grace;
> Behind a frowning Providence
> He hides a smiling face."

7. The smoked herring was scarcely laid upon the table, when a gentle rap at the door, and the loud barking of a dog, attracted the attention of the family. The children flew to open it, and a weary traveler, in tattered garments and in apparently indifferent health, entered, and begged a lodging and a mouthful of food. Said he: "It is now twenty-four hours since I tasted bread." The widow's heart bled anew, as under a fresh complication of distresses; for her sympathies lingered not around her fireside. She hesitated not even now; rest, and a share of all she had, she proffered to the stranger. "We shall not be forsaken," said she, "or suffer deeper for an act of charity."

8. The traveler drew near the board, but when he saw the scanty fare, he raised his eyes toward heaven with astonishment: "And is this all your store?" said he; "and a share of this do you offer to one you know not? then never saw I charity before! But, madam," said he, continuing, "do you not wrong your children by giving a part of your last mouthful to a stranger?"

9. "Ah," said the poor widow—and the tear-drops gushed into her eyes as she said it—"I have a boy, a darling son, somewhere on the face of the wide world, unless Heaven has taken him away, and I only act toward you as I would that others should act toward him. God, who sent manna from heaven, can provide for us as he did for Israel; and how should I this night offend him, if my son should be a wanderer, destitute as you, and he should have provided

for him a home, even poor as this, were I to turn you unrelieved away!"

10. The widow ended, and the stranger, springing from his seat, clasped her in his arms. "God indeed has provided your son a home, and has given him wealth to reward the goodness of his benefactress: my mother! oh, my mother!" It was her long lost son, returned to her bosom from the Indies. He had chosen that disguise that he might the more completely surprise his family; and never was surprise more perfect, or followed by a sweeter cup of joy.

DEFINITIONS. — 1. Făg'ots, *bundles of sticks used for fuel.* Prăt'tle, *trifling talk.* Dĭs'si-pāte, *to scatter.* 2. Pū'ny, *small and weak.* 4. Pĭl'grim-aġe, *a journey.* 5. Sŭs'te-nançe, *that which supports life.* Fôr'ti-tūde, *resolute endurance.* 7. In-dĭf'fer-ent, *neither very good nor very bad.* Cŏm-pli-cā'tion, *entanglement.* Sy̆m'pa-thieș, *compassion.* Prŏf'fered, *offered to give.* 9. Măn'nȧ, *food miraculously provided by God for the Israelites.*

XXVI. ABOU BEN ADHEM.

James Henry Leigh Hunt (*b.* 1784, *d.* 1859) was the son of a West Indian, who married an American lady, and practiced law in Philadelphia until the Revolution; being a Tory, he then returned to England, where Leigh Hunt was born. The latter wrote many verses while yet a boy, and in 1801 his father published a collection of them, entitled "Juvenilia." For many years he was connected with various newspapers, and, while editor of the "Examiner," was imprisoned for two years for writing disrespectfully of the prince regent. While in prison he was visited frequently by the poets Byron, Moore, Lamb, Shelley, and Keats; and there wrote "The Feast of the Poets," "The Descent of Liberty, a Mask," and "The Story of Rimini," which immediately gave him a reputation as a poet. His writings include various translations, dramas, novels, collections of essays, and poems.

1. ABOU BEN ADHEM (may his tribe increase!)
Awoke one night from a deep dream of peace,
And saw within the moonlight in his room,
Making it rich and like a lily in bloom,
An angel writing in a book of gold.

2. Exceeding peace had made Ben Adhem bold;
And to the presence in the room he said,
"What writest thou?" The vision raised its head,
And, with a look made of all sweet accord,
Answered, "The names of those who love the Lord."

3. "And is mine one?" said Abou. "Nay, not so,"
Replied the angel. Abou spoke more low,
But cheerly still; and said, "I pray thee, then,
Write me as one that loves his fellow-men."

4. The angel wrote, and vanished. The next night
It came again, with a great wakening light,
And showed the names whom love of God had blessed;
And, lo! Ben Adhem's name led all the rest.

NOTE.—The above selection is written in imitation of an oriental fable.

XXVII. LUCY FORESTER.

John Wilson (*b.* 1785, *d.* 1854), better known as "Christopher North," was a celebrated author, poet, and critic, born at Paisley, Scotland, and educated at the University of Glasgow and at Oxford. In 1808 he moved to Westmoreland, England, where he formed one of the "Lake School" of poets. While at Oxford he gained a prize for a poem on "Painting, Poetry, and Architecture." In 1820 he became Professor of Moral Philosophy in the University of Edinburgh, which position he retained until 1851. He gained his greatest reputation as the chief author of "Noctes Ambrosianæ," essays contributed to Blackwood's Magazine between 1822 and 1825. Among his poems may be mentioned "The Isle of Palms" and the "City of the Plague." This selection is adapted from "The Foresters," a tale of Scottish life.

1. LUCY was only six years old, but bold as a fairy; she had gone by herself a thousand times about the braes, and often upon errands to houses two or three miles distant. What had her parents to fear? The footpaths were all firm, and led to no places of danger, nor are infants themselves incautious when alone in their pastimes. Lucy went

singing into the low woods, and singing she reappeared on the open hillside. With her small white hand on the rail, she glided along the wooden bridge, or tripped from stone to stone across the shallow streamlet.

2. The creature would be away for hours, and no fear be felt on her account by anyone at home; whether she had gone, with her basket on her arm, to borrow some articles of household use from a neighbor, or, merely for her own solitary delight, had wandered off to the braes to play among the flowers, coming back laden with wreaths and garlands.

3. The happy child had been invited to pass a whole day, from morning to night, at Ladyside (a farmhouse about two miles off) with her playmates the Maynes; and she left home about an hour after sunrise.

4. During her absence, the house was silent but happy, and, the evening being now far advanced, Lucy was expected home every minute, and Michael, Agnes, and Isabel, her father, mother, and aunt, went to meet her on the way. They walked on and on, wondering a little, but in no degree alarmed till they reached Ladyside, and heard the cheerful din of the children within, still rioting at the close of the holiday. Jacob Mayne came to the door, but, on their kindly asking why Lucy had not been sent home before daylight was over, he looked painfully surprised, and said that she had not been at Ladyside.

5. Within two hours, a hundred persons were traversing the hills in all directions, even at a distance which it seemed most unlikely that poor Lucy could have reached. The shepherds and their dogs, all the night through, searched every nook, every stony and rocky place, every piece of taller heather, every crevice that could conceal anything alive or dead, but no Lucy was there.

6. Her mother, who for a while seemed inspired with supernatural strength, had joined in the search, and with a quaking heart looked into every brake, or stopped and

listened to every shout and halloo reverberating among the hills, intent to seize upon some tone of recognition or discovery. But the moon sank; and then the stars, whose increased brightness had for a short time supplied her place, all faded away; and then came the gray dawn of the morning, and then the clear brightness of the day,—and still Michael and Agnes were childless.

7. "She has sunk into some mossy or miry place," said Michael, to a man near him, into whose face he could not look, "a cruel, cruel death to one like her! The earth on which my child walked has closed over her, and we shall never see her more!"

8. At last, a man who had left the search, and gone in a direction toward the highroad, came running with something in his arms toward the place where Michael and others were standing beside Agnes, who lay, apparently exhausted almost to dying, on the sward. He approached hesitatingly; and Michael saw that he carried Lucy's bonnet, clothes, and plaid.

9. It was impossible not to see some spots of blood upon the frill that the child had worn around her neck. "Murdered! murdered!" was the one word whispered or ejaculated all around; but Agnes heard it not; for, worn out by that long night of hope and despair, she had fallen asleep, and was, perhaps, seeking her lost Lucy in her dreams.

10. Isabel took the clothes, and, narrowly inspecting them with eye and hand, said, with a fervent voice that was heard even in Michael's despair, "No, Lucy is yet among the living. There are no marks of violence on the garments of the innocent; no murderer's hand has been here. These blood spots have been put there to deceive. Besides, would not the murderer have carried off these things? For what else would he have murdered her? But, oh! foolish despair! What speak I of? For, wicked as the world is—ay! desperately wicked—there is not, on

all the surface of the wide earth, a hand that would murder our child! Is it not plain as the sun in the heaven, that Lucy has been stolen by some wretched gypsy beggar?"

11. The crowd quietly dispersed, and horse and foot began to scour the country. Some took the highroads, others all the bypaths, and many the trackless hills. Now that they were in some measure relieved from the horrible belief that the child was dead, the worst other calamity seemed nothing, for hope brought her back to their arms.

12. Agnes had been able to walk home to Bracken-Braes, and Michael and Isabel sat by her bedside. All her strength was gone, and she lay at the mercy of the rustle of a leaf, or a shadow across the window. Thus hour after hour passed, till it was again twilight. "I hear footsteps coming up the brae," said Agnes, who had for some time appeared to be slumbering; and in a few moments the voice of Jacob Mayne was heard at the outer door.

13. Jacob wore a solemn expression of countenance, and he seemed, from his looks, to bring no comfort. Michael stood up between him and his wife, and looked into his heart. Something there seemed to be in his face that was not miserable. "If he has heard nothing of my child," thought Michael, "this man must care little for his own fireside." "Oh, speak, speak," said Agnes; "yet why need you speak? All this has been but a vain belief, and Lucy is in heaven."

14. "Something like a trace of her has been discovered; a woman, with a child that did not look like a child of hers, was last night at Clovenford, and left it at the dawning." "Do you hear that, my beloved Agnes?" said Isabel; "she will have tramped away with Lucy up into Ettrick or Yarrow; but hundreds of eyes will have been upon her; for these are quiet but not solitary glens; and the hunt will be over long before she has crossed down

upon Hawick. I knew that country in my young days. What say you, Mr. Mayne? There is the light of hope in your face." "There is no reason to doubt, ma'am, that it was Lucy. Everybody is sure of it. If it was my own Rachel, I should have no fear as to seeing her this blessed night."

15. Jacob Mayne now took a chair, and sat down, with even a smile upon his countenance. "I may tell you now, that Watty Oliver knows it was your child, for he saw her limping along after the gypsy at Galla-Brigg; but, having no suspicion, he did not take a second look at her,—but one look is sufficient, and he swears it was bonny Lucy Forester."

16. Aunt Isabel, by this time, had bread and cheese and a bottle of her own elder-flower wine on the table. "You have been a long and hard journey, wherever you have been, Mr. Mayne; take some refreshment;" and Michael asked a blessing.

17. Jacob saw that he might now venture to reveal the whole truth. "No, no, Mrs. Irving, I am over happy to eat or to drink. You are all prepared for the blessing that awaits you. Your child is not far off; and I myself, for it is I myself that found her, will bring her by the hand, and restore her to her parents."

18. Agnes had raised herself up in her bed at these words, but she sank gently back on her pillow; aunt Isabel was rooted to her chair; and Michael, as he rose up, felt as if the ground were sinking under his feet. There was a dead silence all around the house for a short space, and then the sound of many voices, which again by degrees subsided. The eyes of all then looked, and yet feared to look, toward the door.

19. Jacob Mayne was not so good as his word, for he did not bring Lucy by the hand to restore her to her parents; but dressed again in her own bonnet and gown, and her own plaid, in rushed their own child, by herself,

with tears and sobs of joy, and her father laid her within her mother's bosom.

Definitions. — 1. Brāe, *shelving ground, a declivity or slope of a hill.* Pas'tīmes, *sports, plays.* 4. Rī'ot-ing, *romping.* 5. Hĕath'er, *an evergreen shrub bearing beautiful flowers, used in Great Britain for making brooms, etc.* 6. In-spīred', *animated, enlivened.* Sū-per-năt'u-ral, *more than human.* Brāke, *a place overgrown with shrubs and brambles.* Re-vẽr'ber-āt-ing, *resounding, echoing.* In-tĕnt', *having the mind closely fixed.* 8. Plăid (*pro.* plăd), *a striped or checked overgarment worn by the Scotch.* 9. E-jăc'u-lāt-ed, *exclaimed.* 11. Seour, *to pass over swiftly and thoroughly.*

Note. — The scene of this story is laid in Scotland, and many of the words employed, such as *brae, brake, heather,* and *plaid,* are but little used except in that country.

XXVIII. THE REAPER AND THE FLOWERS.

Henry Wadsworth Longfellow (*b.* 1807, *d.* 1882), the son of Hon. Stephen Longfellow, an eminent lawyer, was born in Portland, Maine. He graduated at Bowdoin College in 1825. After spending four years in Europe, he was Professor of Modern Languages and Literature at Bowdoin till 1835, when he was appointed to the chair of Modern Languages and Belles-lettres in Harvard University. He resigned his professorship in 1854, after which time he resided in Cambridge, Mass. Longfellow wrote many original works both in verse and prose, and made several translations, the most famous of which is that of the works of Dante. His poetry is always chaste and elegant, showing traces of careful scholarship in every line. The numerous and varied editions of his poems are evidences of their popularity.

1. There is a Reaper whose name is Death,
   And, with his sickle keen,
He reaps the bearded grain at a breath,
   And the flowers that grow between.

2. "Shall I have naught that is fair?" saith he;
 "Have naught but the bearded grain?
Though the breath of these flowers is sweet to me,
 I will give them all back again."

3. He gazed at the flowers with tearful eyes,
 He kissed their drooping leaves;
It was for the Lord of Paradise
 He bound them in his sheaves.

4. "My Lord has need of these flowerets gay,"
 The Reaper said, and smiled;
"Dear tokens of the earth are they,
 Where he was once a child.

5. "They shall all bloom in the fields of light,
 Transplanted by my care,
And saints, upon their garments white,
 These sacred blossoms wear."

6. And the mother gave in tears and pain
 The flowers she most did love;
She knew she should find them all again
 In the fields of light above.

7. O, not in cruelty, not in wrath,
 The Reaper came that day,
'T was an angel visited the green earth,
 And took the flowers away.

DEFINITIONS.—3. Shēaveş, *bundles of grain*. 4. Tō'ken (*pro.* tō'kn), *a souvenir, that which is to recall some person, thing, or event.* 5. Trans-plănt'ed, *removed, and planted in another place.*

XXIX. THE TOWN PUMP.

Nathaniel Hawthorne (*b.* 1804, *d.* 1864) was born in Salem, Mass. He graduated at Bowdoin College in 1825. His earliest literary productions, written for periodicals, were published in two volumes — the first in 1837, the second in 1842 — under the title of "Twice-Told Tales." "Mosses from an Old Manse," another series of tales and sketches, was published in 1845. From 1846 to 1850 he was surveyor of the port of Salem. In 1852 he was appointed United States consul for Liverpool. After holding this office four years, he traveled for some time on the continent. His most popular works are "The Scarlet Letter," a work showing a deep knowledge of human nature, "The House of the Seven Gables," "The Blithedale Romance," and "The Marble Faun," an Italian romance, which is regarded by many as the best of his works. Being of a modest and retiring disposition, Mr. Hawthorne avoided publicity. Most of his works are highly imaginative. As a prose writer he has no superior among American authors. He died at Plymouth, N. H., while on a visit to the White Mountains for his health.

[SCENE. — *The corner of two principal streets. The Town Pump talking through its nose.*]

1. NOON, by the north clock! Noon, by the east! High noon, too, by those hot sunbeams which fall, scarcely aslope, upon my head, and almost make the water bubble and smoke in the trough under my nose. Truly, we public characters have a tough time of it! And among all the town officers, chosen at the yearly meeting, where is he that sustains, for a single year, the burden of such manifold duties as are imposed, in perpetuity, upon the Town Pump?

2. The title of town treasurer is rightfully mine, as guardian of the best treasure the town has. The overseers of the poor ought to make me their chairman, since I provide bountifully for the pauper, without expense to him that pays taxes. I am at the head of the fire department, and one of the physicians of the board of health. As a keeper of the peace, all water drinkers confess me equal to the constable. I perform some of the duties of the town clerk, by promulgating public notices, when they are pasted on my front.

3. To speak within bounds, I am chief person of the municipality, and exhibit, moreover, an admirable pattern to my brother officers by the cool, steady, upright, downright, and impartial discharge of my business, and the constancy with which I stand to my post. Summer or winter, nobody seeks me in vain; for all day long I am seen at the busiest corner, just above the market, stretching out my arms to rich and poor alike; and at night I hold a lantern over my head, to show where I am, and to keep people out of the gutters.

4. At this sultry noontide, I am cupbearer to the parched populace, for whose benefit an iron goblet is chained to my waist. Like a dramseller on the public square, on a muster day, I cry aloud to all and sundry, in my plainest accents, and at the very tiptop of my voice. "Here it is, gentlemen! Here is the good liquor! Walk up, walk up, gentlemen, walk up, walk up! Here is the superior stuff! Here is the unadulterated ale of father Adam! better than Cognac, Hollands, Jamaica, strong beer, or wine of any price; here it is, by the hogshead or the single glass, and not a cent to pay. Walk up, gentlemen, walk up and help yourselves!"

5. It were a pity if all this outcry should draw no customers. Here they come. A hot day, gentlemen. Quaff and away again, so as to keep yourselves in a nice, cool sweat. You, my friend, will need another cupful to wash the dust out of your throat, if it be as thick there as it is on your cowhide shoes. I see that you have trudged half a score of miles to-day, and, like a wise man, have passed by the taverns, and stopped at the running brooks and well curbs. Otherwise, betwixt heat without and fire within, you would have been burnt to a cinder, or melted down to nothing at all—in the fashion of a jellyfish.

6. Drink, and make room for that other fellow, who seeks my aid to quench the fiery fever of last night's potations, which he drained from no cup of mine. Welcome, most

rubicund sir! You and I have been strangers hitherto; nor, to confess the truth, will my nose be anxious for a closer intimacy, till the fumes of your breath be a little less potent.

7. Mercy on you, man! The water absolutely hisses down your red-hot gullet, and is converted quite into steam in the miniature Tophet, which you mistake for a stomach. Fill again, and tell me, on the word of an honest toper, did you ever, in cellar, tavern, or any other kind of dramshop, spend the price of your children's food for a swig half so delicious? Now, for the first time these ten years, you know the flavor of cold water. Good-by; and whenever you are thirsty, recollect that I keep a constant supply at the old stand.

8. Who next? Oh, my little friend, you are just let loose from school, and come hither to scrub your blooming face, and drown the memory of certain taps of the ferule, and other schoolboy troubles, in a draught from the Town Pump. Take it, pure as the current of your young life; take it, and may your heart and tongue never be scorched with a fiercer thirst than now.

9. There, my dear child, put down the cup, and yield your place to this elderly gentleman, who treads so tenderly over the paving stones that I suspect he is afraid of breaking them. What! he limps by without so much as thanking me, as if my hospitable offers were meant only for people who have no wine cellars.

10. Well, well, sir, no harm done, I hope! Go, draw the cork, tip the decanter; but when your great toe shall set you a-roaring, it will be no affair of mine. If gentlemen love the pleasant titillation of the gout, it is all one to the Town Pump. This thirsty dog, with his red tongue lolling out, does not scorn my hospitality, but stands on his hind legs, and laps eagerly out of the trough. See how lightly he capers away again! Jowler, did your worship ever have the gout?

11. Your pardon, good people! I must interrupt my stream of eloquence, and spout forth a stream of water to replenish the trough for this teamster and his two yoke of oxen, who have come all the way from Staunton, or

somewhere along that way. No part of my business gives me more pleasure than the watering of cattle. Look! how rapidly they lower the watermark on the sides of the trough, till their capacious stomachs are moistened with a gallon or two apiece, and they can afford time to breathe, with sighs of calm enjoyment! Now they roll their quiet eyes around the brim of their monstrous drinking vessel. An ox is your true toper.

12. I hold myself the grand reformer of the age. From my spout, and such spouts as mine, must flow the stream that shall cleanse our earth of a vast portion of its crime and anguish, which have gushed from the fiery fountains of the still. In this mighty enterprise, the cow shall be my great confederate. Milk and water!

13. Ahem! Dry work this speechifying, especially to all unpracticed orators. I never conceived till now what toil the temperance lecturers undergo for my sake. Do, some kind Christian, pump a stroke or two, just to wet my whistle. Thank you, sir. But to proceed.

14. The Town Pump and the Cow! Such is the glorious partnership that shall finally monopolize the whole business of quenching thirst. Blessed consummation! Then Poverty shall pass away from the land, finding no hovel so wretched where her squalid form may shelter itself. Then Disease, for lack of other victims, shall gnaw his own heart and die. Then Sin, if she do not die, shall lose half her strength.

15. Then there will be no war of households. The husband and the wife, drinking deep of peaceful joy, a calm bliss of temperate affections, shall pass hand in hand through life, and lie down, not reluctantly, at its protracted close. To them the past will be no turmoil of mad dreams, nor the future an eternity of such moments as follow the delirium of a drunkard. Their dead faces shall express what their spirits were, and are to be, by a lingering smile of memory and hope.

16. Drink, then, and be refreshed! The water is as pure and cold as when it slaked the thirst of the red hunter, and flowed beneath the aged bough, though now this gem of the wilderness is treasured under these hot stones, where no shadow falls, but from the brick buildings. But, still is this fountain the source of health, peace, and happiness, and I behold, with certainty and joy, the approach of the period when the virtues of cold water, too little valued since our father's days, will be fully appreciated and recognized by all.

DEFINITIONS. — 1. Pĕr-pe-tū'i-ty, *endless duration.* 2. Pro-mŭl'-gāt-ing, *announcing.* 3. Mu-nĭç-i-păl'i-ty, *a division of a country or of a city.* 4. Mŭs'ter dāy, *parade day.* Sŭn'dry, *several.* Un-a-dŭl'ter-āt-ed, *pure, unmixed.* Co'gnac (*pro.* Kōn'yak), *a French brandy.* 6. Po-tā'tions, *drinkings.* Ru'bi-cund, *inclining to redness.* 7. Tō'phet, *the infernal regions.* 10. Tĭt-il-lā'tion, *tickling.* 11. Re-plĕn'ish, *to fill again.* 14. Mo-nŏp'o-līze, *to obtain the whole.* Cŏn-sum-mā'tion, *completion, termination.* Squal id, *filthy.* 15. Pro-trăct'ed, *delayed.* 16. Slāked, *quenched.*

XXX. GOOD NIGHT.

Samuel Griswold Goodrich (*b.* 1793, *d.* 1860) was born in Ridgefield, Conn. Mr. Goodrich is best known as "Peter Parley," under which assumed name he commenced the publication of a series of juvenile works about 1827. He edited "Parley's Magazine" from 1841 to 1854. He was appointed United States consul for Paris in 1848, and held that office four years. He was a voluminous writer, and his works are interesting and popular. His "Recollections of a Lifetime" was published in 1857, and "Peter Parley's Own Story" the year after his death.

1. THE sun has sunk behind the hills,
   The shadows o'er the landscape creep;
A drowsy sound the woodland fills,
   As nature folds her arms to sleep:
      Good night — good night.

2. The chattering jay has ceased his din,
The noisy robin sings no more;
The crow, his mountain haunt within,
Dreams 'mid the forest's surly roar:
Good night—good night.

3. The sunlit cloud floats dim and pale;
The dew is falling soft and still,
The mist hangs trembling o'er the vale,
And silence broods o'er yonder mill:
Good night—good night.

4. The rose, so ruddy in the light,
Bends on its stem all rayless now;
And by its side a lily white,
A sister shadow, seems to bow:
Good night—good night.

5. The bat may wheel on silent wing,
The fox his guilty vigils keep,
The boding owl his dirges sing;
But love and innocence will sleep:
Good night—good night.

XXXI. AN OLD-FASHIONED GIRL.

Louisa May Alcott (*b.* 1833, *d.* 1888) was born at Germantown, Pa., of New England parentage. Her parents afterwards returned to New England, and most of her life was spent in Concord, Mass. During the Civil War she went to Washington and nursed the wounded and sick until her own health gave way. As a child she used to write stories for the amusement of her playmates, and in 1857 published her first book, "Flower Fables." Her first novel, "Moods," appeared in 1865. "Little Women," published in 1868, is a picture of her own home life. "An Old-Fashioned Girl," from which this extract is adapted, was published in 1870, and is one of her most popular books.

1. POLLY hoped the "dreadful boy" (Tom) would not be present; but he was, and stared at her all dinner time in a most trying manner.

2. Mr. Shaw, a busy-looking gentleman, said, "How do you do, my dear? Hope you'll enjoy yourself;" and then appeared to forget her entirely. Mrs. Shaw, a pale, nervous woman, greeted her little guest kindly, and took care that she wanted for nothing.

3. Madam Shaw, a quiet old lady, with an imposing cap, exclaimed, on seeing Polly, "Bless my heart! the image of her mother — a sweet woman — how is she, dear?" and kept peering at the newcomer over her glasses till, between Madam and Tom, poor Polly lost her appetite.

4. Her cousin Fanny chatted like a magpie, and little Maud fidgeted, till Tom proposed to put her under the big dish cover, which produced such an explosion that the young lady was borne screaming away by the much-enduring nurse.

5. It was, altogether, an uncomfortable dinner, and Polly was very glad when it was over. They all went about their own affairs; and, after doing the honors of the house, Fan was called to the dressmaker, leaving Polly to amuse herself in the great drawing-room.

6. Polly was glad to be alone for a few minutes; and, having examined all the pretty things about her, began to walk up and down over the soft, flowery carpet, humming

to herself, as the daylight faded, and only the ruddy glow of the fire filled the room.

7. Presently Madam came slowly in, and sat down in her armchair, saying, "That's a fine old tune; sing it to me, my dear. I have n't heard it this many a day."

8. Polly did n't like to sing before strangers, for she had no teaching but such as her busy mother could give her; but she had been taught the utmost respect for old people, and, having no reason for refusing, she directly went to the piano and did as she was bid.

9. "That's the sort of music it's a pleasure to hear. Sing some more, dear," said Madam, in her gentle way, when she had done.

10. Pleased with this praise, Polly sang away in a fresh little voice that went straight to the listener's heart and nestled there. The sweet old tunes that one is never tired of were all Polly's store. The more she sung, the better she did it; and when she wound up with "A Health to King Charlie," the room quite rung with the stirring music made by the big piano and the little maid.

11. "That's a jolly tune! Sing it again, please," cried Tom's voice; and there was Tom's red head bobbing up over the high back of the chair where he had hidden himself.

12. It gave Polly quite a turn, for she thought no one was hearing her but the old lady dozing by the fire. "I can't sing any more; I'm tired," she said, and walked away to Madam in the other room. The red head vanished like a meteor, for Polly's tone had been decidedly cool.

13. The old lady put out her hand, and, drawing Polly to her knee, looked into her face with such kind eyes that Polly forgot the impressive cap, and smiled at her confidently; for she saw that her simple music had pleased her listener, and she felt glad to know it.

14. "You mus'n't mind my staring, dear," said Madam, softly pinching her rosy cheek, "I haven't seen a little girl for so long, it does my old eyes good to look at you."

Polly thought that a very odd speech, and could n't help saying, "Are n't Fan and Maud little girls, too?"

15. "Oh, dear, no! not what I call little girls. Fan has been a young lady this two years, and Maud is a spoiled baby. Your mother 's a very sensible woman, my child."

16. "What a queer old lady!" thought Polly; but she said "Yes 'm," respectfully, and looked at the fire. "You don't understand what I mean, do you?" asked Madam, still holding her by the chin. "No 'm; not quite."

17. "Well, dear, I 'll tell you. In my day, children of fourteen and fifteen did n't dress in the height of the fashion; go to parties as nearly like those of grown people as it 's possible to make them; lead idle, giddy, unhealthy lives, and get *blasé* at twenty. We were little folks till eighteen or so; worked and studied, dressed and played, like children; honored our parents; and our days were much longer in the land than now, it seems to me."

18. The old lady appeared to forget Polly, at the end of her speech; for she sat patting the plump little hand that lay in her own, and looking up at a faded picture of an old gentleman with a ruffled shirt and a queue. "Was he your father, Madam?"

19. "Yes, my dear; my honored father. I did up his frills to the day of his death; and the first money I ever earned, was five dollars which he offered as a prize to whichever of his six girls would lay the handsomest darn in his silk stockings."

20. "How proud you must have been!" cried Polly, leaning on the old lady's knee with an interested face.

21. "Yes; and we all learned to make bread, and cook, and wore little chintz gowns, and were as gay and hearty as kittens. All lived to be grandmothers; and I 'm the last—seventy next birthday, my dear, and not worn out yet; though daughter Shaw is an invalid at forty."

22. "That 's the way I was brought up, and that 's why

Fan calls me old-fashioned, I suppose. Tell more about your papa, please; I like it," said Polly.

23. "Say, 'father.' We never called him papa; and if one of my brothers had addressed him as 'governor,' as boys now do, I really think he'd have him cut off with a shilling."

DEFINITIONS. — 3. Im-pōṣ′ing, *having the power of exciting attention and feeling, impressive.* 4. Măg′pīe, *a noisy, mischievous bird, common in Europe and America.* 12. Văn′ished, *disappeared.* Mē′te-or, *a shooting star.* 13. Cŏn′fi-dent-ly, *with trust.* 17. Blȧ-ṣé (*pro.* blȧ-za′), *a French word meaning surfeited, rendered incapable of further enjoyment.* 21. In′va-lĭd, *a person who is sickly.*

XXXII. MY MOTHER'S HANDS.

1. SUCH beautiful, beautiful hands!
They're neither white nor small;
And you, I know, would scarcely think
That they are fair at all.
I've looked on hands whose form and hue
A sculptor's dream might be;
Yet are those aged, wrinkled hands
More beautiful to me.

2. Such beautiful, beautiful hands!
Though heart were weary and sad,
Those patient hands kept toiling on,
That the children might be glad.
I always weep, as, looking back
To childhood's distant day,
I think how those hands rested not
When mine were at their play.

3. Such beautiful, beautiful hands!
They're growing feeble now,
For time and pain have left their mark
On hands and heart and brow.

Alas! alas! the nearing time,
  And the sad, sad day to me,
When 'neath the daisies, out of sight,
  These hands will folded be.

4. But oh! beyond this shadow land,
  Where all is bright and fair,
I know full well these dear old hands
  Will palms of victory bear;
Where crystal streams through endless years
  Flow over golden sands,
And where the old grow young again,
  I'll clasp my mother's hands.

XXXIII. THE DISCONTENTED PENDULUM.

Jane Taylor (*b.* 1783, *d.* 1824) was born in London. Her mother was a writer of some note. In connection with her sister Ann, Jane Taylor wrote several juvenile works of more than ordinary excellence. Among them were "Hymns for Infant Minds" and "Original Poems." Besides these, she wrote "Display, a Tale," "Essays in Rhyme," and "Contributions of QQ." Her writings are graceful, and often contain a useful moral.

1. An old clock that had stood for fifty years in a farmer's kitchen, without giving its owner any cause of complaint, early one summer's morning, before the family was stirring, suddenly stopped. Upon this, the dial plate (if we may credit the fable) changed countenance with alarm; the hands made a vain effort to continue their course; the wheels remained motionless with surprise; the weights hung speechless; and each member felt disposed to lay the blame on the others. At length the dial instituted a formal inquiry as to the cause of the stagnation, when hands, wheels, weights, with one voice, protested their innocence.

2. But now a faint tick was heard below from the pendulum, who spoke thus: "I confess myself to be the sole cause of the present stoppage; and I am willing, for the

general satisfaction, to assign my reasons. The truth is, that I am tired of ticking." Upon hearing this, the old clock became so enraged that it was upon the very point of striking. "Lazy wire!" exclaimed the dial plate, holding up its hands.

3. "Very good!" replied the pendulum; "it is vastly easy for you, Mistress Dial, who have always, as everybody knows, set yourself up above me, — it is vastly easy for you, I say, to accuse other people of laziness! you who have had nothing to do all your life but to stare people in the face, and to amuse yourself with watching all that goes on in the kitchen. Think, I beseech you, how you would like to be shut up for life in this dark closet, and to wag backward and forward year after year, as I do."

4. "As to that," said the dial, "is there not a window in your house on purpose for you to look through?" "For all that," resumed the pendulum, "it is very dark here; and, although there is a window, I dare not stop even for an instant to look out at it. Besides, I am really tired of my way of life; and, if you wish, I'll tell you how I took this disgust at my employment. I happened, this morning, to be calculating how many times I should have to tick in the course of only the next twenty-four hours; perhaps some one of you above there can give me the exact sum."

5. The minute hand, being quick at figures, presently replied, "Eighty-six thousand four hundred times." "Exactly so," replied the pendulum. "Well, I appeal to you all, if the very thought of this was not enough to fatigue anyone; and when I began to multiply the strokes of one day by those of months and years, really it was no wonder if I felt discouraged at the prospect. So, after a great deal of reasoning and hesitation, thinks I to myself, I'll stop."

6. The dial could scarcely keep its countenance during this harangue; but, resuming its gravity, thus replied: "Dear Mr. Pendulum, I am really astonished that such

a useful, industrious person as yourself should have been seized by this sudden weariness. It is true, you have done a great deal of work in your time; so have we all, and are likely to do; which, although it may fatigue us to think of, the question is, whether it will fatigue us to do. Would you now do me the favor to give about half a dozen strokes to illustrate my argument?"

7. The pendulum complied, and ticked six times at its usual pace. "Now," resumed the dial, "may I be allowed to inquire if that exertion is at all fatiguing or disagreeable to you?" "Not in the least," replied the pendulum; "it is not of six strokes that I complain, nor of sixty, but of millions."

8. "Very good," replied the dial; "but recollect that, although you may think of a million of strokes in an instant, you are required to execute but one; and that, however often you may hereafter have to swing, a moment will always be given you to swing in." "That consideration staggers me, I confess," said the pendulum. "Then I hope," resumed the dial plate, "that we shall all return to our duty immediately; for the maids will lie in bed if we stand idling thus."

9. Upon this, the weights, who had never been accused of light conduct, used all their influence in urging him to proceed; when, as if with one consent, the wheels began to turn, the hands began to move, the pendulum began to swing, and, to its credit, ticked as loud as ever; while a red beam of the rising sun, that streamed through a hole in the kitchen, shining full upon the dial plate, it brightened up as if nothing had been the matter.

10. When the farmer came down to breakfast that morning, upon looking at the clock, he declared that his watch had gained half an hour in the night.

Definitions. — 1. In'sti-tūt-ed, *commenced, began.* Pro-tĕst'ed, *solemnly declared.* 4. Căl'eu-lāt-ing, *reckoning, computing.* 5. Prŏs'-peet, *anticipation, that to which one looks forward.* 6. Ha-răngue' (*pro.* ha-răng′), *speech.* Il-lŭs′trāte, *to make clear, to exemplify.* 7. Ex-ẽr′tion (*pro.* egz-ẽr′shun), *effort.* 8. Ex′e-cūte, *to complete, to finish.* Con-sĭd-er-ā′tion, *reason.*

XXXIV. THE DEATH OF THE FLOWERS.

William Cullen Bryant (*b.* 1794, *d.* 1878) was born in Cummington, Mass. He entered Williams College at the age of sixteen, but was honorably dismissed at the end of two years. At the age of twenty-one he was admitted to the bar, and practiced his profession successfully for nine years. In 1826 he removed to New York, and became connected with the "Evening Post"—a connection which continued to the time of his death. His residence for more than thirty of the last years of his life was at Roslyn, Long Island. He visited Europe several times; and in 1849 he continued his travels into Egypt and Syria.

In all his poems, Mr. Bryant exhibits a remarkable love for, and a careful study of, nature. His language, both in prose and verse, is always chaste, correct, and elegant. "Thanatopsis," perhaps the best known of all his poems, was written when he was but nineteen. His excellent translations of the "Iliad" and the "Odyssey" of Homer, and some of his best poems, were written after he had passed the age of seventy. He retained his powers and his activity till the close of his life.

1. The melancholy days are come,
   The saddest of the year,
Of wailing winds, and naked woods,
   And meadows brown and sear.
Heaped in the hollows of the grove
   The autumn leaves lie dead;
They rustle to the eddying gust,
   And to the rabbit's tread.
The robin and the wren are flown,
   And from the shrubs the jay,
And from the wood top calls the crow
   Through all the gloomy day.

2. Where are the flowers, the fair young flowers,
   That lately sprang and stood
In brighter light and softer airs,
   A beauteous sisterhood?

Alas! they all are in their graves;
  The gentle race of flowers
Are lying in their lowly beds
  With the fair and good of ours.
The rain is falling where they lie;
  But the cold November rain
Calls not from out the gloomy earth
  The lovely ones again.

3. The windflower and the violet,
  They perished long ago,
And the brier rose and the orchis died
  Amid the summer's glow;
But on the hill, the golden-rod,
  And the aster in the wood,
And the yellow sunflower by the brook,
  In autumn beauty stood,
Till fell the frost from the clear, cold heaven,
  As falls the plague on men,
And the brightness of their smile was gone
  From upland, glade, and glen,

4 And now, when comes the calm, mild day,
  As still such days will come,
To call the squirrel and the bee
  From out their winter home;
When the sound of dropping nuts is heard,
  Though all the trees are still,
And twinkle in the smoky light
  The waters of the rill,
The south wind searches for the flowers
  Whose fragrance late he bore,
And sighs to find them in the wood
  And by the stream no more.

5. And then I think of one, who in
  Her youthful beauty died,

The fair, meek blossom that grew up
  And faded by my side.
In the cold, moist earth we laid her,
  When the forest cast the leaf,
And we wept that one so lovely
  Should have a life so brief;
Yet not unmeet it was that one,
  Like that young friend of ours,
So gentle and so beautiful,
  Should perish with the flowers.

Definitions.—1. Wāil′ing, *lamenting, mourning.* Sēar, *dry, withered.* 3. Glāde, *an open place in the forest.* Glĕn, *a valley, a dale.* 4. Un-meet′, *improper, unfitting.*

XXXV. THE THUNDERSTORM.

Washington Irving (*b.* 1783, *d.* 1859). This distinguished author, whose works have enriched American literature, was born in the city of New York. He had an ordinary school education, and began his literary career at the age of nineteen, by writing for a paper published by his brother. His first book, "Salmagundi," was published in 1807. Two years later he published "Knickerbocker's History of New York." In 1815 he sailed for Europe, and remained abroad seventeen years, during which time he wrote several of his works. From 1842 to 1846 he was minister to Spain. The last years of his life were passed at "Sunnyside," near Tarrytown, N.Y. He was never married. "The Life of Washington," his last work, was completed in the same year in which he died. Mr. Irving's works are characterized by humor, chaste sentiment, and elegance and correctness of expression. The following selection is from "Dolph" in "Bracebridge Hall."

1. In the second day of the voyage, they came to the Highlands. It was the latter part of a calm, sultry day, that they floated gently with the tide between these stern mountains. There was that perfect quiet which prevails over nature in the languor of summer heat. The turning of a plank, or the accidental falling of an oar, on deck, was echoed from the mountain side and reverberated along the shores; and, if by chance the captain gave a shout of

command, there were airy tongues that mocked it from every cliff.

2. Dolph gazed about him, in mute delight and wonder, at these scenes of nature's magnificence. To the left, the Dunderberg reared its woody precipices, height over height, forest over forest, away into the deep summer sky. To the right, strutted forth the bold promontory of Antony's Nose, with a solitary eagle wheeling about it; while beyond, mountain succeeded to mountain, until they seemed to lock their arms together and confine this mighty river in their embraces.

3. In the midst of this admiration, Dolph remarked a pile of bright, snowy clouds peering above the western heights. It was succeeded by another, and another, each seemingly pushing onward its predecessor, and towering, with dazzling brilliancy, in the deep blue atmosphere; and now muttering peals of thunder were faintly heard rolling behind the mountains. The river, hitherto still and glassy, reflecting pictures of the sky and land, now showed a dark ripple at a distance, as the wind came creeping up it. The fishhawks wheeled and screamed, and sought their nests on the high, dry trees; the crows flew clamorously to the crevices of the rocks; and all nature seemed conscious of the approaching thunder gust.

4. The clouds now rolled in volumes over the mountain tops; their summits still bright and snowy, but the lower parts of an inky blackness. The rain began to patter down in broad and scattered drops; the wind freshened, and curled up the waves; at length, it seemed as if the bellying clouds were torn open by the mountain tops, and complete torrents of rain came rattling down. The lightning leaped from cloud to cloud, and streamed quivering against the rocks, splitting and rending the stoutest forest trees. The thunder burst in tremendous explosions; the peals were echoed from mountain to mountain; they crashed upon Dunderberg, and then rolled up the long

defile of the Highlands, each headland making a new echo, until old Bull Hill seemed to bellow back the storm.

5. For a time the scudding rack and mist and the sheeted rain almost hid the landscape from the sight. There was a fearful gloom, illumined still more fearfully by the streams of lightning which glittered among the raindrops. Never had Dolph beheld such an absolute warring of the elements; it seemed as if the storm was tearing and rending its way through the mountain defile, and had brought all the artillery of heaven into action.

DEFINITIONS.—1. Lăn̲′ḡuor (*pro.* lăng′gwẽr), *exhaustion of strength, dullness.* 3. Re-märked′, *noticed, observed.* Prĕd-e-çĕs′-sor, *the one going immediately before.* Clăm′or-oŭs-ly, *with a loud noise.* 4. Bĕl′ly-ing, *swelling out.* De-fīle′, *a long, narrow pass.* 5. Răck, *thin, flying, broken clouds.* El′e-ments, *a term usually including fire, water, earth, and air.*

NOTES.—1. *The Highlands* are a mountainous region in New York, bordering the Hudson River above Peekskill.

2. The *Dunderberg* and *Antony's Nose* are names of two peaks of the Highlands.

4. *Bull Hill,* also called Mt. Taurus, is 15 miles farther north.

XXXVI. APRIL DAY.

Caroline Anne Southey (*b* 1786, *d.* 1854), the second wife of Southey the poet, and better known as Caroline Bowles, was born near Lymington, Hampshire, England. Her first work, "Ellen Fitzarthur," a poem, was published in 1820; and for more than twenty years her writings were published anonymously. In 1839 she was married to Mr. Southey, and survived him over ten years. Her poetry is graceful in expression, and full of tenderness, though somewhat melancholy. The following extract first appeared in 1822 in a collection entitled, "The Widow's Tale, and other Poems."

1. ALL day the low-hung clouds have dropped
  Their garnered fullness down;
All day that soft, gray mist hath wrapped
  Hill, valley, grove, and town.

2. There has not been a sound to-day
   To break the calm of nature;
Nor motion, I might almost say,
   Of life or living creature;

3. Of waving bough, or warbling bird,
   Or cattle faintly lowing;
I could have half believed I heard
   The leaves and blossoms growing.

4. I stood to hear—I love it well—
   The rain's continuous sound;
Small drops, but thick and fast they fell,
   Down straight into the ground.

5. For leafy thickness is not yet
   Earth's naked breast to screen,
Though every dripping branch is set
   With shoots of tender green.

6. Sure, since I looked, at early morn,
   Those honeysuckle buds
Have swelled to double growth; that thorn
   Hath put forth larger studs.

7. That lilac's cleaving cones have burst,
   The milk-white flowers revealing;
Even now upon my senses first
   Methinks their sweets are stealing.

8. The very earth, the steamy air,
   Is all with fragrance rife!
And grace and beauty everywhere
   Are flushing into life.

9. Down, down they come, those fruitful stores,
Those earth-rejoicing drops!
A momentary deluge pours,
Then thins, decreases, stops.

10. And ere the dimples on the stream
Have circled out of sight,
Lo! from the west a parting gleam
Breaks forth of amber light.

* * * * * * *

11. But yet behold—abrupt and loud,
Comes down the glittering rain;
The farewell of a passing cloud,
The fringes of its train.

Definitions.—1. Gär′nered, *laid up, treasured.* 6. Stŭds, *knobs, buds.* 7. Clēav′ing, *dividing.* 10. Dĭm′ples, *small depressions.* Am′ber, *the color of amber, yellow.*

XXXVII. THE TEA ROSE.

1. There it stood, in its little green vase, on a light ebony stand in the window of the drawing-room. The rich satin curtains, with their costly fringes, swept down on either side of it, and around it glittered every rare and fanciful trifle which wealth can offer to luxury, and yet that simple rose was the fairest of them all. So pure it looked, its white leaves just touched with that delicious, creamy tint peculiar to its kind: its cup so full, so per-

fect, its head bending, as if it were sinking and melting away in its own richness.—Oh! when did ever man make anything to equal the living, perfect flower!

2. But the sunlight that streamed through the window

revealed something fairer than the rose — a young lady reclining on an ottoman, who was thus addressed by her livelier cousin: "I say, cousin, I have been thinking what you are to do with your pet rose when you go to New York; as, to our consternation, you are determined to do. You know it would be a sad pity to leave it with such a scatter-brain as I am. I love flowers, indeed, — that is, I like a regular bouquet, cut off and tied up, to carry to a party; but as to all this tending and fussing which is needful to keep them growing, I have no gifts in that line."

3. "Make yourself easy as to that, Kate," said Florence, with a smile; "I have no intention of calling upon your talents; I have an asylum in view for my favorite."

4. "Oh, then you know just what I was going to say. Mrs. Marshall, I presume, has been speaking to you; she was here yesterday, and I was quite pathetic upon the subject; telling her the loss your favorite would sustain, and so forth; and she said how delighted she would be to have it in her greenhouse; it is in such a fine state now, so full of buds. I told her I knew you would like to give it to her; you are so fond of Mrs. Marshall, you know."

5. "Now, Kate, I am sorry, but I have otherwise engaged."

"Whom can it be to? you have so few intimates here."

"Oh, it is only one of my odd fancies."

"But do tell me, Florence."

"Well, cousin, you know the little pale girl to whom we give sewing?"

6. "What! little Mary Stephens? How absurd, Florence! This is just another of your motherly, old-maidish ways; dressing dolls for poor children, making bonnets, and knitting socks for all the little dirty babies in the neighborhood. I do believe you have made more calls in those two vile, ill-smelling alleys behind our house than ever you have in Chestnut Street, though you know every-

body is half dying to see you; and now, to crown all, you must give this choice little bijou to a seamstress girl, when one of your most intimate friends, in your own class, would value it so highly. What in the world can people in their circumstances want with flowers?"

7. "Just the same as I do," replied Florence, calmly. "Have you not noticed that the little girl never comes without looking wistfully at the opening buds? And don't you remember, the other morning she asked me so prettily if I would let her mother come and see it, she was so fond of flowers?"

8. "But, Florence, only think of this rare flower standing on a table with ham, eggs, cheese, and flour, and stifled in that close little room, where Mrs. Stephens and her daughter manage to wash, iron, and cook."

9. "Well, Kate, and if I were obliged to live in one coarse room, and wash, and iron, and cook, as you say; if I had to spend every moment of my time in toil, with no prospect from my window but a brick wall and a dirty lane, such a flower as this would be untold enjoyment to me."

10. "Pshaw, Florence; all sentiment! Poor people have no time to be sentimental. Besides, I don't believe it will grow with them; it is a greenhouse flower, and used to delicate living."

11. "Oh, as to that, a flower never inquires whether its owner is rich or poor; and poor Mrs. Stephens, whatever else she has not, has sunshine of as good quality as this that streams through our window. The beautiful things that God makes are his gifts to all alike. You will see that my fair rose will be as well and cheerful in Mrs. Stephens's room as in ours."

12. "Well, after all, how odd! When one gives to poor people, one wants to give them something useful — a bushel of potatoes, a ham, and such things."

13. "Why, certainly, potatoes and ham must be supplied;

but, having ministered to the first and most craving wants, why not add any other little pleasures or gratifications we may have it in our power to bestow? I know there are many of the poor who have fine feeling and a keen sense of the beautiful, which rusts out and dies because they are too hard pressed to procure it any gratification. Poor Mrs. Stephens, for example; I know she would enjoy birds, and flowers, and music as much as I do. I have seen her eye light up as she looked upon these things in our drawing-room, and yet not one beautiful thing can she command. From necessity, her room, her clothing, — all she has, must be coarse and plain. You should have seen the almost rapture she and Mary felt when I offered them my rose."

14. "Dear me! all this may be true, but I never thought of it before. I never thought that these hard-working people had any ideas of *taste!*"

15. "Then why do you see the geranium or rose so carefully nursed in the old cracked teapot in the poorest room, or the morning-glory planted in a box and twined about the window? Do not these show that the human heart yearns for the beautiful in all ranks of life? You remember, Kate, how our washerwoman sat up a whole night, after a hard day's work, to make her first baby a pretty dress to be baptized in." "Yes, and I remember how I laughed at you for making such a tasteful little cap for it."

16. "True, Kate, but I think the look of perfect delight with which the poor woman regarded her baby in its new dress and cap was something quite worth creating; I do believe she could not have felt more grateful if I had sent her a barrel of flour."

17. "Well, I never thought before of giving anything to the poor but what they really needed, and I have always been willing to do that when I could without going far out of my way."

18. "Ah! cousin, if our heavenly Father gave to us after this mode, we should have only coarse, shapeless piles of

provisions lying about the world, instead of all this beautiful variety of trees, and fruits, and flowers."

19. "Well, well, cousin, I suppose you are right, but have mercy on my poor head; it is too small to hold so many new ideas all at once, so go on your own way;" and the little lady began practicing a waltzing step before the glass with great satisfaction.

DEFINITIONS.—2. Ot′to-man, *a stuffed seat without a back.* 3. A-sȳ′lum, *a place of refuge and protection.* 4. Pa-thĕt′ie, *moving to pity or grief.* 6. Bi-jọu′ (*pro.* be-zhōō′, *a jewel.* Cĩr′eum-stănç-eş, *condition in regard to worldly property.* 10. Sĕn-ti-mĕnt′al, *showing an excess of sentiment or feeling.* 13. Com-mȧnd′, *to claim.* Răp′-ture, *extreme joy or pleasure, ecstasy.* 14. Tāste, *the faculty of discerning beauty or whatever forms excellence.* 15. Yẽarnş, *longs, is eager.*

XXXVIII. THE CATARACT OF LODORE.

1. "How does the water
Come down at Lodore?"
My little boy asked me
  Thus once on a time;
And, moreover, he tasked me
  To tell him in rhyme.

2. Anon at the word,
There first came one daughter,
And then came another,
  To second and third
The request of their brother,
And to hear how the water
  Comes down at Lodore,
  With its rush and its roar,
    As many a time
  They had seen it before.

3. So I told them in rhyme,
For of rhymes I had store,
And 't was in my vocation
For their recreation
That so I should sing;
Because I was Laureate
To them and the King.

4. From its sources which well
In the tarn on the fell;
From its fountains
In the mountains,
Its rills and its gills;
Through moss and through brake,
It runs and it creeps
For a while, till it sleeps
In its own little lake.

5. And thence at departing,
Awakening and starting,
It runs through the reeds,
And away it proceeds,
Through meadow and glade,
In sun and in shade,
And through the wood shelter,
Among crags in its flurry,
Helter-skelter,
Hurry-skurry.

6. Here it comes sparkling,
And there it lies darkling;
Now smoking and frothing
Its tumult and wrath in,
Till, in this rapid race
On which it is bent,
It reaches the place
Of its steep descent.

7. The cataract strong
Then plunges along,
Striking and raging
As if a war waging
Its caverns and rocks among;

8. Rising and leaping,
Sinking and creeping,
Swelling and sweeping,
Showering and springing,
Flying and flinging,
Writhing and ringing,
Eddying and whisking,
Spouting and frisking,
Turning and twisting,
Around and around
With endless rebound;
Smiting and fighting,
A sight to delight in;
Confounding, astounding,
Dizzying, and deafening the ear with its sound

9. Collecting, projecting,
Receding and speeding,
And shocking and rocking,
And darting and parting,
And threading and spreading,
And whizzing and hissing,
And dripping and skipping,
And hitting and splitting,
And shining and twining,
And rattling and battling,
And shaking and quaking,
And pouring and roaring,
And waving and raving,
And tossing and crossing,

And guggling and struggling,
And heaving and cleaving,
And moaning and groaning,
And glittering and frittering,
And gathering and feathering,
And whitening and brightening,
And quivering and shivering,
And hurrying and skurrying,
And thundering and floundering;

10. Dividing and gliding and sliding,
And falling and brawling and sprawling,
And driving and riving and striving,
And sprinkling and twinkling and wrinkling;

11. And thumping and plumping and bumping and jumping,
And dashing and flashing and splashing and clashing;
And so never ending, but always descending,
Sounds and motions forever and ever are blending,
All at once and all o'er, with a mighty uproar,
And this way the water comes down at Lodore.

—*Abridged from Southey.*

DEFINITIONS.—4. Tärn, *a small lake among the mountains.* Fĕll (provincial English), *a stony hill.* Gĭlls (provincial English), *brooks.* 10. Brawl'ing, *roaring.* Rīv'ing, *splitting.*

NOTES.—1. *Lodore* is a cascade on the banks of Lake Derwentwater, in Cumberland, England, near where Southey lived.

3. *Laureate.* The term probably arose from a custom in the English universities of presenting a laurel wreath to graduates in rhetoric and versification. In England the poet laureate's office is filled by appointment of the lord chamberlain. The salary is quite small, and the office is valued chiefly as one of honor.

This lesson is peculiarly adapted for practice on the difficult sound *ing.*

XXXIX. THE BOBOLINK.

1. The happiest bird of our spring, however, and one that rivals the European lark in my estimation, is the boblincoln, or bobolink as he is commonly called. He arrives at that choice portion of our year which, in this latitude, answers to the description of the month of May so often given by the poets. With us it begins about the middle of May, and lasts until nearly the middle of June. Earlier than this, winter is apt to return on its traces, and to blight the opening beauties of the year; and later than this, begin the parching, and panting, and dissolving heats of summer. But in this genial interval, Nature is in all her freshness and fragrance: "the rains are over and gone, the flowers appear upon the earth, the time of the singing of birds is come, and the voice of the turtle is heard in the land."

2. The trees are now in their fullest foliage and brightest verdure; the woods are gay with the clustered flowers of the laurel; the air is perfumed with the sweetbrier and the wild rose; the meadows are enameled with clover blossoms; while the young apple, peach, and the plum begin to swell, and the cherry to glow among the green leaves.

3. This is the chosen season of revelry of the bobolink. He comes amid the pomp and fragrance of the season; his life seems all sensibility and enjoyment, all song and sunshine. He is to be found in the soft bosoms of the freshest and sweetest meadows, and is most in song when the clover is in blossom. He perches on the topmost twig of a tree, or on some long, flaunting weed, and, as he rises and sinks with the breeze, pours forth a succession of rich, tinkling notes, crowding one upon another, like the outpouring melody of the skylark, and possessing the same rapturous character.

4. Sometimes he pitches from the summit of a tree, be-

gins his song as soon as he gets upon the wing, and flutters tremulously down to the earth, as if overcome with ecstasy at his own music. Sometimes he is in pursuit of his mate; always in full song, as if he would win her by his melody; and always with the same appearance of intoxication and delight. Of all the birds of our groves and meadows, the bobolink was the envy of my boyhood. He crossed my path in the sweetest weather, and the sweetest season of the year, when all nature called to the fields, and the rural feeling throbbed in every bosom; but when I, luckless urchin! was doomed to be mewed up, during the livelong day, in a schoolroom.

5. It seemed as if the little varlet mocked at me as he flew by in full song, and sought to taunt me with his happier lot. Oh, how I envied him! No lessons, no task, no school; nothing but holiday, frolic, green fields, and fine weather. Had I been then more versed in poetry, I might have addressed him in the words of Logan to the cuckoo:

"Sweet bird, thy bower is ever green,
Thy sky is ever clear;
Thou hast no sorrow in thy song,
No winter in thy year.

"Oh, could I fly, I'd fly with thee!
We'd make, with joyful wing,
Our annual visit o'er the globe,
Companions of the spring."

6. Further observation and experience have given me a different idea of this feathered voluptuary, which I will venture to impart for the benefit of my young readers, who may regard him with the same unqualified envy and admiration which I once indulged. I have shown him only as I saw him at first, in what I may call the poetical part of his career, when he, in a manner, devoted himself to elegant pursuits and enjoyments, and was a bird of music, and song, and taste, and sensibility, and refinement. While

this lasted he was sacred from injury; the very schoolboy would not fling a stone at him, and the merest rustic would pause to listen to his strain.

7. But mark the difference. As the year advances, as the clover blossoms disappear, and the spring fades into summer, he gradually gives up his elegant tastes and habits, doffs his poetical suit of black, assumes a russet, dusty garb, and sinks to the gross enjoyment of common vulgar birds. His notes no longer vibrate on the ear; he is stuffing himself with the seeds of the tall weeds on which he lately swung and chanted so melodiously. He has become a *bon vivant*, a *gourmand:* with him now there is nothing like the "joys of the table." In a little while he grows tired of plain, homely fare, and is off on a gastronomic tour in quest of foreign luxuries.

8. We next hear of him, with myriads of his kind, banqueting among the reeds of the Delaware, and grown corpulent with good feeding. He has changed his name in traveling. Boblincoln no more, he is the reedbird now, the much-sought-for tidbit of Pennsylvanian epicures, the rival in unlucky fame of the ortolan! Wherever he goes, pop! pop! pop! every rusty firelock in the country is blazing away. He sees his companions falling by thousands around him. Does he take warning and reform? Alas! not he. Again he wings his flight. The rice swamps of the south invite him. He gorges himself among them almost to bursting; he can scarcely fly for corpulency. He has once more changed his name, and is now the famous ricebird of the Carolinas. Last stage of his career: behold him spitted, with dozens of his corpulent companions, and served up, a vaunted dish, on some southern table.

9. Such is the story of the bobolink; once spiritual, musical, admired, the joy of the meadows, and the favorite bird of spring; finally, a gross little sensualist, who expiates his sensuality in the larder. His story contains a moral

worthy the attention of all little birds and little boys; warning them to keep to those refined and intellectual pursuits which raised him to so high a pitch of popularity during the early part of his career, but to eschew all tendency to that gross and dissipated indulgence which brought this mistaken little bird to an untimely end.

— *From Irving's "Birds of Spring."*

DEFINITIONS.—2. En-ăm'eled, *coated with a smooth, glossy surface*. 3. Sĕn-si-bĭl'i-ty, *feeling*. 4. Mewed, *shut up*. 5. Vär'let, *a rascal*. Vẽrsed, *familiar, practiced*. 6. Vo-lŭp'tu-a-ry, *one who makes his bodily enjoyment his chief object*. 7. Bon vi-vant (French, *pro.* bôɴ ve-väɴ'), *one who lives well*. Gour-mand (French, *pro.* gōōr'mäɴ), *a glutton*. Găs-tro-nŏm'ie, *relating to the science of good eating*. 8. Côr'pu-lent, *fleshy, fat*. Ep'i-eūre, *one who indulges in the luxuries of the table*. Väunt'ed, *boasted*. 9. Ex'pi-ātes, *atones for*. Lärd'er, *a pantry*. Es-chew', *to shun*.

NOTES.—5. *John Logan* (*b.* 1748, *d.* 1788). A Scotch writer of note. His writings include dramas, poetry, history, and essays.

8. The *ortolan* is a small bird, abundant in southern Europe, Cyprus, and Japan. It is fattened for the table, and is considered a great delicacy.

XL. ROBERT OF LINCOLN.

1. MERRILY swinging on brier and weed,
   Near to the nest of his little dame,
Over the mountain side or mead,
   Robert of Lincoln is telling his name:
      "Bobolink, bobolink,
         Spink, spank, spink,
Snug and safe is that nest of ours.
Hidden among the summer flowers.
         Chee, chee, chee."

2. Robert of Lincoln is gaily dressed,
   Wearing a bright black wedding coat:
White are his shoulders, and white his crest,
   Hear him call in his merry note:
      "Bobolink, bobolink,
      Spink, spank, spink,
Look what a nice new coat is mine;
Sure, there was never a bird so fine.
            Chee, chee, chee."

3. Robert of Lincoln's Quaker wife,
   Pretty and quiet, with plain brown wings,
Passing at home a patient life,
   Broods in the grass while her husband sings:
      "Bobolink, bobolink,
      Spink, spank, spink,
Brood, kind creature; you need not fear
Thieves and robbers while I am here.
            Chee, chee, chee."

4. Modest and shy as a nun is she,
   One weak chirp is her only note;
Braggart and prince of braggarts is he,
   Pouring boasts from his little throat:
      "Bobolink, bobolink,
      Spink, spank, spink,
Never was I afraid of man,
Catch me, cowardly knaves, if you can.
            Chee, chee, chee."

5. Six white eggs on a bed of hay,
   Flecked with purple, a pretty sight!
There as the mother sits all day,
   Robert is singing with all his might:
      "Bobolink, bobolink,
      Spink, spank, spink,

Nice good wife that never goes out,
Keeping house while I frolic about.
Chee, chee, chee."

6. Soon as the little ones chip the shell,
Six wide mouths are open for food;
Robert of Lincoln bestirs him well,
Gathering seeds for the hungry brood.
"Bobolink, bobolink,
Spink, spank, spink,
This new life is likely to be
Hard for a gay young fellow like me.
Chee, chee, chee."

7. Robert of Lincoln at length is made
Sober with work, and silent with care;
Off is his holiday garment laid,
Half forgotten that merry air:
"Bobolink, bobolink,
Spink, spank, spink,
Nobody knows but my mate and I
Where our nest and our nestlings lie.
Chee, chee, chee."

8. Summer wanes; the children are grown;
Fun and frolic no more he knows;
Robert of Lincoln's a humdrum crone;
Off he flies, and we sing as he goes:
"Bobolink, bobolink,
Spink, spank, spink,
When you can pipe that merry old strain,
Robert of Lincoln, come back again.
Chee, chee, chee."

— *William Cullen Bryant.*

XLI. REBELLION IN MASSACHUSETTS STATE PRISON.

1. A MORE impressive exhibition of moral courage, opposed to the wildest ferocity under the most appalling circumstances, was never seen than that which was witnessed by the officers of our state prison, in the rebellion which occurred some years since.

2. Three convicts had been sentenced, under the rules of the prison, to be whipped in the yard, and, by some effort of one of the other prisoners, a door had been opened at midday communicating with the great dining hall and, through the warden's lodge, with the street.

3. The dining hall was long, dark, and damp, from its situation near the surface of the ground; and in this all the prisoners assembled, with clubs and such other tools as they could seize in passing through the workshops.

4. Knives, hammers, and chisels, with every variety of such weapons, were in the hands of the ferocious spirits, who are drawn away from their encroachments on society, forming a congregation of strength, vileness, and talent that can hardly be equaled on earth, even among the famed brigands of Italy.

5. Men of all ages and characters, guilty of every variety of infamous crime, dressed in the motley and peculiar garb of the institution, and displaying the wild and demoniac appearance that always pertains to imprisoned wretches, were gathered together for the single purpose of preventing the punishment which was to be inflicted on the morrow upon their comrades.

6. The warden, the surgeon, and some other officers of the prison were there at the time, and were alarmed at the consequences likely to ensue from the conflict necessary to restore order. They huddled together, and could scarcely be said to consult, as the stoutest among them lost all presence of mind in overwhelming fear. The news

rapidly spread through the town, and a subordinate officer, of the most mild and kind disposition, hurried to the scene, and came calm and collected into the midst of the officers. The most equable-tempered and the mildest man in the government was in this hour of peril the firmest.

7. He instantly dispatched a request to Major Wainright, commander of the marines stationed at the Navy Yard, for assistance, and declared his purpose to enter into the hall and try the force of firm demeanor and persuasion upon the enraged multitude.

8. All his brethren exclaimed against an attempt so full of hazard, but in vain. They offered him arms, a sword and pistols, but he refused them, and said that he had no fear, and, in case of danger, arms would do him no service; and alone, with only a little rattan, which was his usual walking stick, he advanced into the hall to hold parley with the selected, congregated, and enraged villains of the whole commonwealth.

9. He demanded their purpose in thus coming together with arms, in violation of the prison laws. They replied that they were determined to obtain the remission of the punishment of their three comrades. He said it was impossible; the rules of the prison must be obeyed, and they must submit.

10. At the hint of submission they drew a little nearer together, prepared their weapons for service, and, as they were dimly seen in the further end of the hall by those who observed from the gratings that opened up to the day, a more appalling sight can not be conceived, nor one of more moral grandeur, than that of the single man standing within their grasp, and exposed to be torn limb from limb instantly if a word or look should add to the already intense excitement.

11. That excitement, too, was of a most dangerous kind. It broke not forth in noise and imprecations, but was seen only in the dark looks and the strained nerves that showed

a deep determination. The officer expostulated. He reminded them of the hopelessness of escape; that the town was alarmed, and that the government of the prison would submit to nothing but unconditional surrender. He said that all those who would go quietly away should be forgiven for this offense; but that if every prisoner were killed in the contest, power enough would be obtained to enforce the regulations of the prison.

12. They replied that they expected that some would be killed,—that death would be better than such imprisonment; and, with that look and tone which bespeak an indomitable purpose, they declared that not a man should leave the hall alive till the flogging was remitted. At this period of the discussion their evil passions seemed to be more inflamed, and one or two offered to destroy the officer, who still stood firmer and with a more temperate pulse than did his friends, who saw from above, but could not avert, the danger that threatened him.

13. Just at this moment, and in about fifteen minutes from the commencement of the tumult, the officer saw the feet of the marines, on whose presence alone he relied for succor, filing by the small upper lights. Without any apparent anxiety, he had repeatedly turned his attention to their approach; and now he knew that it was his only time to escape, before the conflict became, as was expected, one of the most dark and dreadful in the world.

14. He stepped slowly backward, still urging them to depart before the officers were driven to use the last resort of firearms. When within three or four feet of the door, it was opened, and closed instantly again as he sprang through, and was thus unexpectedly restored to his friends.

15. Major Wainright was requested to order his men to fire down upon the convicts through the little windows, first with powder and then with ball, till they were willing to retreat; but he took a wiser as well as a bolder course, relying upon the effect which firm determination would have

upon men so critically situated. He ordered the door to be again opened, and marched in at the head of twenty or thirty men, who filed through the passage, and formed at the end of the hall opposite to the crowd of criminals huddled together at the other.

16. He stated that he was empowered to quell the rebellion, that he wished to avoid shedding blood, but that he would not quit that hall alive till every convict had returned to his duty. They seemed balancing the strength of the two parties, and replied that some of them were ready to die, and only waited for an attack to see which was the more powerful; swearing that they would fight to the last, unless the punishment was remitted, for they would not submit to any such punishment in the prison. Major Wainright ordered his marines to load their pieces, and, that they might not be suspected of trifling, each man was made to hold up to view the bullet which he afterward put in his gun.

17. This only caused a growl of determination, and no one blenched or seemed disposed to shrink from the foremost exposure. They knew that their number would enable them to bear down and destroy the handful of marines after the first discharge, and before their pieces could be reloaded. Again they were ordered to retire; but they answered with more ferocity than ever. The marines were ordered to take their aim so as to be sure and kill as many as possible. Their guns were presented, but not a prisoner stirred, except to grasp more firmly his weapon.

18. Still desirous to avoid such a tremendous slaughter as must have followed the discharge of a single gun, Major Wainright advanced a step or two, and spoke even more firmly than before, urging them to depart. Again, and while looking directly into the muzzles of the guns which they had seen loaded with ball, they declared their intention "to fight it out." This intrepid officer then took out his watch, and told his men to hold their pieces aimed at

the convicts, but not to fire till they had orders; then, turning to the prisoners, he said: "You must leave this hall; I give you three minutes to decide; if at the end of that time a man remains, he shall be shot dead."

19. No situation of greater interest than this can be conceived. At one end of the hall, a fearful multitude of the most desperate and powerful men in existence, waiting for the assault; at the other, a little band of disciplined men, waiting with arms presented, and ready, upon the least motion or sign, to begin the carnage; and their tall and imposing commander, holding up his watch to count the lapse of three minutes, given as the reprieve to the lives of hundreds. No poet or painter can conceive a spectacle of more dark and terrible sublimity; no human heart can conceive a situation of more appalling suspense.

20. For two minutes not a person nor a muscle moved; not a sound was heard in the unwonted stillness of the prison, except the labored breathings of the infuriated wretches, as they began to pant between fear and revenge: at the expiration of two minutes, during which they had faced the ministers of death with unblenching eyes, two or three of those in the rear, and nearest the further entrance, went slowly out; a few more followed the example, dropping out quietly and deliberately: and before half of the last minute was gone, every man was struck by the panic, and crowded for an exit, and the hall was cleared, as if by magic.

21. Thus the steady firmness of moral force and the strong effect of determination, acting deliberately, awed the most savage men, and suppressed a scene of carnage, which would have instantly followed the least precipitancy or exertion of physical force.

—*J. T. Buckingham.*

"It may be that more lofty courage dwells
In one weak heart which braves an adverse fate
Than does in his whose soul indignant swells,
Warmed by the fight, or cheered through high debate."

Definitions.—2. Wạrd'en, *a keeper, one who guards.* 4. En-erōach'ment, *unlawful intrusion on the rights of others.* Brĭg'andş, *robbers, those who live by plunder.* 5. Mŏt'ley, *composed of various colors.* De-mō'ni-ae, *devil-like.* 6. Sub-ôr'di-nate, *inferior in power.* 7. Ma-rineş', *soldiers that serve on board of ships.* De-mēan'or, *behavior, deportment.* 8. Pär'ley, *conversation or conference with an enemy.* 9. Re-mĭs'sion (*pro.* re-mĭsh'un), *pardon of transgression.* 11. Im-pre-eā'tionş, *curses, prayers for evil.* Ex-pŏs'tu-lāt-ed, *reasoned earnestly.* 12. In-dŏm'i-ta-ble, *that can not be subdued or tamed.* 17. Blĕnched, *gave way, shrunk.* 18. In-trĕp'id, *fearless.* 19. Re-priēve', *a delay of punishment.* 21. Pre-çĭp'i-tan-çy, *headlong hurry.*

XLII. FAITHLESS NELLY GRAY.

Thomas Hood (*b.* 1798, *d.* 1845) was the son of a London bookseller. After leaving school he undertook to learn the art of an engraver, but soon turned his attention to literature. In 1821 he became sub-editor of the "London Magazine." Hood is best known as a humorist; but some of his poems are full of the tenderest pathos; and a gentle, humane spirit pervades even his lighter productions. He was poor, and during the last years of his life suffered much from ill health. Some of his most humorous pieces were written on a sick bed.

1. Ben Battle was a soldier bold,
And used to war's alarms;
But a cannon ball took off his legs,
So he laid down his arms!

2. Now, as they bore him off the field,
Said he, "Let others shoot,
For here I leave my second leg,
And the Forty-second Foot!"

3. The army surgeons made him limbs;
Said he, "They 're only pegs:
But there's as wooden members quite,
As represent my legs!"

4. Now Ben, he loved a pretty maid,
Her name was Nelly Gray;
So he went to pay her his *devoirs*,
When he'd devoured his pay.

5. But when he called on Nelly Gray,
She made him quite a scoff;
And when she saw his wooden legs,
Began to take them off!

6. "O Nelly Gray! O Nelly Gray!
Is this your love so warm?
The love that loves a scarlet coat
Should be more uniform!"

7. Said she, "I loved a soldier once,
For he was blithe and brave;
But I will never have a man
With both legs in the grave!

8. "Before you had these timber toes,
Your love I did allow,
But then, you know, you stand upon
Another footing now!"

9. "O false and fickle Nelly Gray!
I know why you refuse:
Though I've no feet—some other man
Is standing in my shoes!

10. "I wish I ne'er had seen your face;
But, now, a long farewell!
For you will be my death;—alas!
You will not be my NELL!"

11. Now when he went from Nelly Gray,
His heart so heavy got,
And life was such a burden grown,
It made him take a knot!

12. So round his melancholy neck,
A rope he did entwine,
And for the second time in life,
Enlisted in the Line!

13. One end he tied around a beam,
And then removed his pegs,
And, as his legs were off, of course
He soon was off his legs.

14. And there he hung till he was dead
As any nail in town:
For, though distress had cut him up,
It could not cut him down!

DEFINITIONS.—4. De-voirs′ (French, *pro.* dĕ-vwôr′), *respects, compliments.* 5. Scŏff, *an object of ridicule.* 6. U′ni-form (adj.), *consistent,* (noun) *military dress.* 7. Blīthe, *merry, gay.*

NOTES.—2. *Forty-second Foot.* Infantry in the army is spoken of as "the foot," and the "Forty-second Foot" means the Forty-second Regiment of Infantry.

3. *Members.* Persons elected to Parliament in Great Britain are called "Members," and are said to *represent* those who elect them.

12. *The Line* is another name for the regular infantry.

XLIII. THE GENEROUS RUSSIAN PEASANT.

1. Let Vergil sing the praises of Augustus, genius celebrate merit, and flattery extol the talents of the great. "The short and simple annals of the poor" engross my pen; and while I record the history of Flor Silin's virtues, though I speak of a poor peasant, I shall describe a noble man. I ask no eloquence to assist me in the task; modest worth rejects the aid of ornament to set it off.

2. It is impossible, even at this distant period, to reflect without horror on the miseries of that year known in Lower Volga by the name of the "Famine Year." I remember the summer, whose scorching heats had dried up all the fields, and the drought had no relief but from the tears of the ruined farmer.

3. I remember the cold, comfortless autumn, and the despairing rustics, crowding round their empty barns, with folded arms and sorrowful countenances, pondering on their misery, instead of rejoicing, as usual, at the golden harvest. I remember the winter which succeeded, and I reflect with agony on the miseries it brought with it. Whole families left their homes to become beggars on the highway.

4. At night the canopy of heaven served them as their only shelter from the piercing winds and bitter frost. To describe these scenes would be to harm the feelings of my readers; therefore, to my tale. In those days I lived on an estate not far from Simbirsk; and, though but a child, I have not forgotten the impression made on my mind by the general calamity.

5. In a village adjoining lived Flor Silin, a poor, laboring peasant,—a man remarkable for his assiduity and the skill and judgment with which he cultivated his lands. He was blessed with abundant crops; and his means being

larger than his wants, his granaries, even at this time, were full of corn. The dry year coming on had beggared all the village except himself. Here was an opportunity to grow rich. Mark how Flor Silin acted. Having called the poorest of his neighbors about him, he addressed them in the following manner:

6. "My friends, you want corn for your subsistence. God has blessed me with abundance. Assist in thrashing out a quantity, and each of you take what he wants for his family." The peasants were amazed at this unexampled generosity; for sordid propensities exist in the village as well as in the populous city.

7. The fame of Flor Silin's benevolence having reached other villages, the famished inhabitants presented themselves before him, and begged for corn. This good creature received them as brothers; and, while his store remained, afforded all relief. At length, his wife, seeing no end to the generosity of his noble spirit, reminded him how necessary it would be to think of their own wants, and hold his lavish hand before it was too late. "It is written in the Scripture," said he, "'Give, and it shall be given unto you.'"

8. The following year Providence listened to the prayers of the poor, and the harvest was abundant. The peasants who had been saved from starving by Flor Silin now gathered around him.

9. "Behold," said they, "the corn you lent us. You saved our wives and children. We should have been famished but for you; may God reward you; he only can; all we have to give is our corn and grateful thanks." "I want no corn at present, my good neighbors," said he; "my harvest has exceeded all my expectations; for the rest, thank heaven: I have been but an humble instrument."

10. They urged him in vain. "No," said he, "I shall not accept your corn. If you have superfluities, share them

among your poor neighbors, who, being unable to sow their fields last autumn, are still in want; let us assist them, my dear friends; the Almighty will bless us for it." "Yes," replied the grateful peasants, "our poor neighbors shall have this corn. They shall know it is to you that they owe this timely succor, and join to teach their children the debt of gratitude due to your benevolent heart." Silin raised his tearful eyes to heaven. An angel might have envied him his feelings.

—*Nikolai Karamzin.*

Definitions.—1. Ex-tŏl′, *to elevate by praise.* An′nals, *history of events.* En-grōss′, *to occupy wholly.* El′o-quençe, *the power of speaking well.* 2. Drought (*pro.* drout), *want of rain or water.* 4. Es-tāte′, *property in land.* 5. Grăn′a-ry, *a storehouse for grain.* 6. Sub-sĭst′ençe, *means of support.* Pro-pĕn′si-ties, *bent of mind, inclination.* 10. Sū-per-flū′i-ties, *greater quantities than are wanted.* Sŭc′cor, *aid, help.*

Notes.—1. *Vergil* was the greatest of Roman poets. He was born in the year 70 B.C., and died 19 B.C.

Augustus Cæsar was emperor of Rome in the latter portion of Vergil's life, and received many compliments in the verses of his friend the poet.

2. *Lower Volga* is a district in eastern Russia, bordering on the Caspian Sea, and takes its name from the river Volga.

4. *Simbirsk* is a town of eastern Russia, on the Volga.

XLIV. FORTY YEARS AGO.

1. I've wandered to the village, Tom,
   I've sat beneath the tree,
Upon the schoolhouse playground,
   That sheltered you and me;
But none were left to greet me, Tom,
   And few were left to know,
Who played with me upon the green,
   Just forty years ago.

2. The grass was just as green, Tom,
   Barefooted boys at play
Were sporting, just as we did then,
   With spirits just as gay.
But the master sleeps upon the hill,
   Which, coated o'er with snow,
Afforded us a sliding place,
   Some forty years ago.

3. The old schoolhouse is altered some;
   The benches are replaced
By new ones very like the same
   Our jackknives had defaced.
But the same old bricks are in the wall,
   The bell swings to and fro;
Its music 's just the same, dear Tom,
   'T was forty years ago.

4. The spring that bubbled 'neath the hill,
   Close by the spreading beech,
Is very low; 't was once so high
   That we could almost reach;
And kneeling down to take a drink,
   Dear Tom, I started so,
To think how very much I 've changed
   Since forty years ago.

5. Near by that spring, upon an elm,
   You know, I cut your name,
Your sweetheart's just beneath it, Tom;
   And you did mine the same.
Some heartless wretch has peeled the bark;
   'T was dying sure, but slow,
Just as that one whose name you cut
   Died forty years ago.

6. My lids have long been dry, Tom,
   But tears came in my eyes:
I thought of her I loved so well,
   Those early broken ties.
I visited the old churchyard,
   And took some flowers to strew
Upon the graves of those we loved
   Just forty years ago.

7. Some are in the churchyard laid,
   Some sleep beneath the sea;
And none are left of our old class
   Excepting you and me.
And when our time shall come, Tom,
   And we are called to go,
I hope we 'll meet with those we loved
   Some forty years ago.

XLV. MRS. CAUDLE'S LECTURE.

Douglas Jerrold (*b.* 1803, *d.* 1857) was born in London. A midshipman's appointment was obtained for him, but he quit the naval service in a few years. He was then apprenticed to a printer. By improving his leisure hours he made himself master of several languages, and formed the habit of expressing his thoughts in writing. An essay on the opera of Der Freischütz was his first published literary production. Before he was twenty-one years of age, he wrote "Black-eyed Susan," one of the most popular dramas of modern times. Several other popular plays followed this. He was a regular contributor to the London "Punch," from the second number, and edited, at different times, several papers and magazines. As a humorist, he occupies the first rank. The most noted of his works are his plays, and "Mrs. Caudle's Curtain Lectures," "Saint Giles and Saint James," "Bubbles of a Day," and "Chronicles of Clovernook."

1. WELL, Mr. Caudle, I hope you're in a little better temper than you were this morning. There, you need n't begin to whistle: people don't come to bed to whistle. But it's like you; I can't speak that you don't try to insult me. Once, I used to say you were the best creature living: now, you get quite a fiend. *Do* let you rest? No, I won't let you rest. It's the only time I have to talk to you, and you *shall* hear me. I'm put upon all day long: it's very hard if I can't speak a word at night; besides, it is n't often I open my mouth, goodness knows!

2. Because *once* in your lifetime your shirt wanted a button, you must almost swear the roof off the house. You *did n't* swear? Ha, Mr. Caudle! you don't know what you do when you're in a passion. You were not in a passion, wer'n't you? Well, then, I don't know what a passion is; and I think I ought by this time. I've lived long enough with you, Mr. Caudle, to know that.

3. It's a pity you hav'n't something worse to complain of than a button off your shirt. If you'd *some* wives, you would, I know. I'm sure I'm never without a needle and thread in my hand; what with you and the children, I'm made a perfect slave of. And what's my

thanks? Why, if once in your life a button's off your shirt — what do you cry "*oh*" at? I say once, Mr. Caudle; or twice, or three times, at most. I'm sure, Caudle, no man's buttons in the world are better looked after than yours. I only wish I'd kept the shirts you had when you were first married! I should like to know where were your buttons then?

4. Yes, it *is* worth talking of! But that's how you always try to put me down. You fly into a rage, and then if I only try to speak, you won't hear me. That's how you men always will have all the talk to yourselves: a poor woman is n't allowed to get a word in. A nice notion you have of a wife, to suppose she's nothing to think of but her husband's buttons. A pretty notion, indeed, you have of marriage. Ha! if poor women only knew what they had to go through! — what with buttons, and one thing and another, — they'd never tie themselves up, — no, not to the best man in the world, I'm sure. What would they do, Mr. Caudle? — Why, do much better without you, I'm certain.

5. And it's my belief, after all, that the button was n't off the shirt; it's my belief that you pulled it off that you might have something to talk about. Oh, you're aggravating enough, when you like, for anything! All I know is, it's very odd that the button should be off the shirt; for I'm sure no woman's a greater slave to her husband's buttons than I am. I only say it's very odd.

6. However, there's one comfort; it can't last long. I'm worn to death with your temper, and sha' n't trouble you a great while. Ha! you may laugh! And I dare say you would laugh! I've no doubt of it! That's your love; that's your feeling! I know that I'm sinking every day, though I say nothing about it. And when I'm gone we shall see how your second wife will look after your buttons! You'll find out the difference then.

Yes, Caudle, you 'll think of me then; for then, I hope, you 'll never have a blessed button to your back.

7. No, I 'm not a vindictive woman, Mr. Caudle: nobody ever called me that but you. What do you say? *Nobody ever knew so much of me?* That 's nothing at all to do with it. Ha! I would n't have your aggravating temper, Caudle, for mines of gold. It 's a good thing I 'm not as worrying as you are, or a nice house there 'd be between us. I only wish you 'd had a wife that *would* have talked to you! Then you 'd have known the difference. But you impose upon me because, like a poor fool, I say nothing. I should be ashamed of myself, Caudle.

8. And a pretty example you set as a father! You 'll make your boys as bad as yourself. Talking as you did all breakfast time about your buttons! and of a Sunday morning, too! And you call yourself a Christian! I should like to know what your boys will say of you when they grow up! And all about a paltry button off one of your wristbands! A decent man would n't have mentioned it. *Why don't I hold my tongue?* Because I *won't* hold my tongue. I 'm to have my peace of mind destroyed — I 'm to be worried into my grave for a miserable shirt button, and I 'm to hold my tongue! Oh! but that 's just like you men!

9. But I know what I 'll do for the future. Every button you have may drop off, and I won't so much as put a thread to 'em. And I should like to know what you 'll do then! Oh, *you must get somebody else to sew 'em,* must you? That 's a pretty threat for a husband to hold out to his wife! And to *such* a wife as I 've been, too: such a slave to your buttons, as I may say. *Somebody else to sew 'em?* No, Caudle, no; not while I 'm alive! When I 'm dead — and, with what I have to bear, there 's no knowing how soon that may be — when I 'm dead, I say — oh! what a brute you must be to snore so!

10. *You're not snoring?* Ha! that 's what you always

say; but that's nothing to do with it. You must get somebody else to sew 'em, must you? Ha! I should n't wonder. Oh, no! I should be surprised at nothing now! Nothing at all! It's what people have always told me it would come to; and now the buttons have opened my eyes! But the whole world shall know of your cruelty, Mr. Caudle. After the wife I've been to you. Caudle, you've a heart like a hearthstone, you have!

DEFINITIONS.—5. Ag̅'g̅ra-vāt-ing, *provoking, irritating.* 6. Sĭn̲k'-ing, *failing in strength.* 7. Vin-dĭe'tĭve, *revengeful.* 8. Pa̤l'try, *mean, contemptible.*

XLVI. THE VILLAGE BLACKSMITH.

1. UNDER a spreading chestnut tree
   The village smithy stands;
The smith, a mighty man is he,
   With large and sinewy hands;
And the muscles of his brawny arms
   Are strong as iron bands.

2. His hair is crisp, and black, and long,
   His face is like the tan;
His brow is wet with honest sweat,
   He earns whate'er he can,
And looks the whole world in the face,
   For he owes not any man.

3. Week in, week out, from morn till night,
   You can hear his bellows blow;
You can hear him swing his heavy sledge,
   With measured beat and slow,
Like a sexton ringing the village bell,
   When the evening sun is low.

4. And children coming home from school
   Look in at the open door;
They love to see the flaming forge,
   And hear the bellows roar,
And catch the burning sparks that fly
   Like chaff from a threshing floor.

5. He goes on Sunday to the church,
   And sits among his boys;
He hears the parson pray and preach,
   He hears his daughter's voice
Singing in the village choir,
   And it makes his heart rejoice.

6. It sounds to him like her mother's voice
   Singing in Paradise!
He needs must think of her once more,
   How in the grave she lies;
And with his hard, rough hand he wipes
   A tear out of his eyes.

7. Toiling, rejoicing, sorrowing,
   Onward through life he goes;
Each morning sees some task begin,
   Each evening sees its close;
Something attempted, something done,
   Has earned a night's repose.

8. Thanks, thanks to thee, my worthy friend,
   For the lesson thou hast taught!
Thus at the flaming forge of life
   Our fortunes must be wrought;
Thus on its sounding anvil shaped
   Each burning deed and thought!

— *Longfellow.*

XLVII. THE RELIEF OF LUCKNOW.

[From a letter to the "London Times," by a lady, the wife of an officer at Lucknow.]

1. On every side death stared us in the face; no human skill could avert it any longer. We saw the moment approach when we must bid farewell to earth, yet without feeling that unutterable horror which must have been experienced by the unhappy victims at Cawnpore. We were resolved rather to die than to yield, and were fully persuaded that in twenty-four hours all would be over. The engineer had said so, and all knew the worst. We women strove to encourage each other, and to perform the light duties which had been assigned to us, such as conveying orders to the batteries, and supplying the men with provisions, especially cups of coffee, which we prepared day and night.

2. I had gone out to try to make myself useful, in company with Jessie Brown, the wife of a corporal in my husband's regiment. Poor Jessie had been in a state of restless excitement all through the siege, and had fallen away visibly within the last few days. A constant fever consumed her, and her mind wandered occasionally, especially that day, when the recollections of home seemed powerfully present to her. At last, overcome with fatigue, she lay down on the ground, wrapped up in her plaid. I sat beside her, promising to awaken her when, as she said, her "father should return from the plowing."

3. She fell at length into a profound slumber, motionless and apparently breathless, her head resting in my lap. I myself could no longer resist the inclination to sleep, in spite of the continual roar of the cannon. Suddenly I was aroused by a wild, unearthly scream close to my ear; my companion stood upright beside me, her arms raised, and her head bent forward in the attitude of listening.

4. A look of intense delight broke over her countenance; she grasped my hand, drew me toward her, and exclaimed: "Dinna ye hear it? dinna ye hear it? Ay. I'm no dreaming: it's the slogan o' the Highlanders! We're saved! we're saved!" Then flinging herself on her knees, she thanked God with passionate fervor. I felt utterly bewildered; my English ears heard only the roar of artillery, and I thought my poor Jessie was still raving; but she darted to the batteries, and I heard her cry incessantly to the men, "Courage! courage! Hark to the slogan—to the Macgregor, the grandest of them a'! Here's help at last!"

5. To describe the effect of these words upon the soldiers would be impossible. For a moment they ceased firing, and every soul listened with intense anxiety. Gradually, however, there arose a murmur of bitter disappointment, and the wailing of the women, who had flocked to the spot, burst out anew as the colonel shook his head. Our dull Lowland ears heard only the rattle of the musketry. A few moments more of this deathlike suspense, of this agonizing hope, and Jessie, who had again sunk on the ground, sprang to her feet, and cried in a voice so clear and piercing that it was heard along the whole line, "Will ye no believe it noo? The slogan has ceased, indeed, but the Campbells are comin'! D' ye hear? d' ye hear?"

6. At that moment all seemed indeed to hear the voice of God in the distance, when the pibroch of the Highlanders brought us tidings of deliverance; for now there was no longer any doubt of the fact. That shrill, penetrating, ceaseless sound, which rose above all other sounds, could come neither from the advance of the enemy nor from the work of the sappers. No, it was indeed the blast of the Scottish bagpipes, now shrill and harsh, as threatening vengeance on the foe, then in softer tones, seeming to promise succor to their friends in need.

7. Never, surely, was there such a scene as that which

followed. Not a heart in the residency of Lucknow but bowed itself before God. All, by one simultaneous impulse, fell upon their knees, and nothing was heard but bursting sobs and the murmured voice of prayer. Then all arose, and there rang out from a thousand lips a great shout of joy, which resounded far and wide, and lent new vigor to that blessed pibroch.

8. To our cheer of "God save the Queen," they replied by the well-known strain that moves every Scot to tears, "Should auld acquaintance be forgot." After that, nothing else made any impression on me. I scarcely remember what followed. Jessie was presented to the general on his entrance into the fort, and at the officers' banquet her health was drunk by all present, while the pipers marched around the table playing once more the familiar air of "Auld Lang Syne."

Definitions. — 1. A-vẽrt′, *to turn aside.* En-ġi-neer′, *an officer in the army, who designs and constructs defensive and offensive works.* 2. Siēġe, *the setting of an army around a fortified place to compel its surrender.* 3. Pro-found′, *deep.* 4. Slō′ḡan, *the war cry or gathering word of a Highland clan in Scotland.* Fẽr′vor, *intensity of feeling.* 6. Pï′broch, *a wild, irregular species of music belonging to the Highlands of Scotland; it is performed on a bagpipe.* Săp′perş, *men employed in making an approach to a fortified place by digging.* 7. Rĕş′i-den-çy, *the official dwelling of a government officer in India.* Sī-mul-tā′ne-oŭs, *happening at the same time.*

Notes. — *Lucknow*, a city in the British possession of India. In 1857 there was a mutiny of the native troops, and the British garrison of 1700 men was besieged by 10,000 mutineers. After twelve weeks' siege, fresh British troops forced an entrance, and the town was held until relieved three weeks later by the arrival of Sir Colin Campbell, as above described.

1. *Cawnpore*, also a city of India, near Lucknow, which was besieged during the mutiny. After surrendering, the English, two thirds of whom were women and children, were treacherously massacred.

4. The inhabitants of the northern part of Scotland are called *Highlanders;* those of the southern part, *Lowlanders.* The dialect of the former is very peculiar, as shown in the language of Jessie Brown; as, *dinna* for *did not, a'* for *all, no* for *not, noo* for *now, auld* for *old. Macgregor* and *Campbell* are names of Highland clans or families.

Whittier's poem, "The Pipes at Lucknow," and Robert T. S. Lowell's "The Relief of Lucknow," are descriptive of this same incident.

XLVIII. THE SNOWSTORM.

James Thomson (*b.* 1700, *d.* 1748) was born at Ednam, in the shire of Roxburgh, Scotland. He was educated at the University of Edinburgh, and afterwards studied for the ministry, but in a short time changed his plans and devoted himself to literature. His early poems are quite insignificant, but "The Seasons," from which the following selection is taken, and the "Castle of Indolence," are masterpieces of English poetry.

1. Through the hushed air the whitening shower descends,
At first thin wavering; till at last the flakes
Fall broad and wide and fast, dimming the day,
With a continual flow. The cherished fields
Put on their winter robe of purest white.
'T is brightness all: save where the new snow melts
Along the mazy current.

2. Low the woods
Bow their hoar head; and ere the languid sun
Faint from the west emits its evening ray,
Earth's universal face, deep-hid and chill,
Is one wild dazzling waste, that buries wide
The works of man.

3. Drooping, the laborer ox
Stands covered o'er with snow, and then demands
The fruit of all his toil. The fowls of heaven,
Tamed by the cruel season, crowd around
The winnowing store, and claim the little boon
Which Providence assigns them.

4. One alone,
The Redbreast, sacred to the household gods,
Wisely regardful of the embroiling sky,
In joyless fields and thorny thickets leaves
His shivering mates, and pays to trusted man
His annual visit.

5. Half-afraid, he first
Against the window beats; then, brisk, alights
On the warm hearth; then, hopping o'er the floor,
Eyes all the smiling family askance,
And pecks, and starts, and wonders where he is;
Till, more familiar grown, the table crumbs
Attract his slender feet.

6. The foodless wilds
Pour forth their brown inhabitants. The hare,
Though timorous of heart, and hard beset
By death in various forms, dark snares and dogs,
And more unpitying men, the garden seeks,
Urged on by fearless want. The bleating kind
Eye the bleak heaven, and next the glistening earth,
With looks of dumb despair; then, sad dispersed,
Dig for the withered herb through heaps of snow

7. Now, shepherds, to your helpless charge be kind,
Baffle the raging year, and fill their pens
With food at will; lodge them below the storm,
And watch them strict; for from the bellowing east,
In this dire season, oft the whirlwind's wing
Sweeps up the burden of whole wintry plains
In one wide waft, and o'er the hapless flocks,
Hid in the hollow of two neighboring hills,
The billowy tempest 'whelms; till, upward urged,
The valley to a shining mountain swells,
Tipped with a wreath high-curling in the sky

DEFINITIONS.—1. Mā'zy, *winding.* 2. Hōar, *white or grayish white.* E-mĭts', *sends forth, throws out.* 3. Wĭn'now-ing, *separating chaff from grain by means of wind.* Bo͞on, *a gift.* 4. Em-broil'ing, *throwing into disorder or contention.* 5. A-skănçe', *sideways.* 6. Wīlds, *woods, forests.* Be-sĕt', *hemmed in on all sides so that escape is difficult.* 7. Dīre, *dreadful, terrible.* Wạft, *a current of wind.* Whĕlms', *covers completely.*

NOTE.—4. *Household gods.* An allusion to the belief of the ancient Romans in the *Penates* — certain gods who were supposed to protect the household and all connected with it. The idea here expressed is, that the Redbreast was secure from harm.

XLIX. BEHIND TIME.

1. A RAILROAD train was rushing along at almost lightning speed. A curve was just ahead, beyond which was a station where two trains usually met. The conductor was late,—so late that the period during which the up train was to wait had nearly elapsed; but he hoped yet to pass the curve safely. Suddenly a locomotive dashed into sight right ahead. In an instant there was a collision. A shriek, a shock, and fifty souls were in eternity; and all because an engineer had been behind time.

2. A great battle was going on. Column after column had been precipitated for eight hours on the enemy posted along the ridge of a hill. The summer sun was sinking in the west; reënforcements for the obstinate defenders were already in sight; it was necessary to carry the position with one final charge, or everything would be lost.

3. A powerful corps had been summoned from across the country, and if it came up in season all would yet be well. The great conqueror, confident in its arrival, formed his reserve into an attacking column, and ordered them to charge the enemy. The whole world knows the result. Grouchy failed to appear; the imperial guard was beaten

back; and Waterloo was lost. Napoleon died a prisoner at St. Helena because one of his marshals was behind time.

4. A leading firm in commercial circles had long struggled against bankruptcy. As it had large sums of money in California, it expected remittances by a certain day, and if they arrived, its credit, its honor, and its future prosperity would be preserved. But week after week elapsed without bringing the gold. At last came the fatal day on which the firm had bills maturing to large amounts. The steamer was telegraphed at daybreak; but it was found, on inquiry, that she brought no funds, and the house failed. The next arrival brought nearly half a million to the insolvents, but it was too late; they were ruined because their agent, in remitting, had been behind time.

5. A condemned man was led out for execution. He had taken human life, but under circumstances of the greatest provocation, and public sympathy was active in his behalf. Thousands had signed petitions for a reprieve; a favorable answer had been expected the night before, and though it had not come, even the sheriff felt confident that it would yet arrive. Thus the morning passed without the appearance of the messenger.

6. The last moment was up. The prisoner took his place, the cap was drawn over his eyes, the bolt was drawn, and a lifeless body swung revolving in the wind. Just at that moment a horseman came into sight, galloping down hill, his steed covered with foam. He carried a packet in his right hand, which he waved frantically to the crowd. He was the express rider with the reprieve; but he came too late. A comparatively innocent man had died an ignominious death because a watch had been five minutes too late, making its bearer arrive behind time.

7. It is continually so in life. The best laid plans, the most important affairs, the fortunes of individuals, the weal of nations, honor, happiness, life itself, are daily sacrificed, because somebody is "behind time." There are men who

always fail in whatever they undertake, simply because they are "behind time." There are others who put off reformation year after year, till death seizes them, and they perish unrepentant, because forever "behind time."

DEFINITIONS.—1. Col-lĭ'ṣion, *the act of striking together violently.* 2. Pre-çĭp'i-tāt-ed, *urged on violently.* Rē-en-fōrçe'ments, *additional troops.* 3. Cōrps (*pro.* kōr), *a body of troops.* Re-ṣẽrve', *a select body of troops held back in case of special need for their services.* 4. Băn̲k'rupt-çy, *inability to pay all debts, insolvency.* Re-mĭt'tanç-eṣ, *money, drafts, etc., sent from a distance.* Ma-tūr'ing, *approaching the time fixed for payment.* 5. Prŏv-o-eā'tion, *that which causes anger.* 6. Ig̅-no-mĭn'i-oŭs, *infamous.* 7. Wēal, *prosperity, happiness.*

NOTES.—3. *Emmanuel Grouchy* was one of Napoleon's marshals at the battle of Waterloo, fought in 1815, between the French under Napoleon, and the English, Dutch, and German troops under Wellington.

Napoleon Bonaparte (*b.* 1769, *d.* 1821) was born on the island of Corsica. At school he was "studious, well-behaved, and distinguished in mathematical studies." In 1785 he was commissioned as a sublieutenant in the army. From this obscure position he raised himself to the head of the army, and in 1804 was elected emperor of the French. He is almost universally acknowledged to have been the greatest general the world has known.

L. THE OLD SAMPLER.

1. OUT of the way, in a corner
   Of our dear old attic room,
Where bunches of herbs from the hillside
   Shake ever a faint perfume,
An oaken chest is standing,
   With hasp and padlock and key,
Strong as the hands that made it
   On the other side of the sea.

2. When the winter days are dreary,
And we 're out of heart with life,
Of its crowding cares aweary,
And sick of its restless strife,
We take a lesson in patience
From the attic corner dim,
Where the chest still holds its treasures,
A warder faithful and grim.

3. Robes of an antique fashion,
Linen and lace and silk,
That time has tinted with saffron,
Though once they were white as milk;
Wonderful baby garments,
'Broidered with loving care
By fingers that felt the pleasure,
As they wrought the ruffles fair;

4. A sword, with the red rust on it,
That flashed in the battle tide,
When from Lexington to Yorktown
Sorely men's souls were tried;
A plumed chapeau and a buckle,
And many a relic fine,
And, all by itself, the sampler,
Framed in with berry and vine.

5. Faded the square of canvas,
And dim is the silken thread,
But I think of white hands dimpled,
And a childish, sunny head;
For here in cross and in tent stitch,
In a wreath of berry and vine,
She worked it a hundred years ago,
"Elizabeth, Aged Nine."

6. In and out in the sunshine,
   The little needle flashed,
And in and out on the rainy day,
   When the merry drops down plashed,
As close she sat by her mother,
   The little Puritan maid,
And did her piece in the sampler,
   While the other children played.

7. You are safe in the beautiful heaven,
   "Elizabeth, aged nine;"
But before you went you had troubles
   Sharper than any of mine.
Oh, the gold hair turned with sorrow
   White as the drifted snow.

And your tears dropped here where I'm standing,
  On this very plumed *chapeau.*

8. When you put it away, its wearer
  Would need it nevermore,
By a sword thrust learning the secrets
  God keeps on yonder shore;
And you wore your grief like glory,
  You could not yield supine,
Who wrought in your patient childhood,
  "Elizabeth, Aged Nine."

9. Out of the way, in a corner,
With hasp and padlock and key,
Stands the oaken chest of my fathers
That came from over the sea;
And the hillside herbs above it
Shake odors fragrant and fine,
And here on its lid is a garland
To "Elizabeth, aged nine."

10. For love is of the immortal,
And patience is sublime,
And trouble a thing of every day,
And touching every time;
And childhood sweet and sunny,
And womanly truth and grace,
Ever can light life's darkness
And bless earth's lowliest place.

— *Mrs. M. E. Sangster.*

Definitions. — 2. Wạrd′er, *a keeper, a guard.* 3. An-tïque′, *old, ancient.* Săf′fron, *a deep yellow.* 4. Cha-peau′, *a hat.* 8. Su-pīne′, *listless.* 10. Im-môr′tal, *undying.*

Notes. — 6. *Puritan.* The Puritans were a religious sect who fled from persecution in England, and afterwards settled the most of New England.

A *sampler* is a needlework pattern; a species of fancywork formerly much in vogue.

LI. THE GOODNESS OF GOD.

1. Bless the Lord, O my soul! O Lord, my God, thou art very great; thou art clothed with honor and majesty: who coverest thyself with light as with a garment; who stretchest out the heavens like a curtain; who layeth the

beams of his chambers in the waters; who maketh the clouds his chariot; who walketh upon the wings of the wind; who maketh his angels spirits, his ministers a flaming fire; who laid the foundations of the earth, that it should not be removed forever.

2. Thou coveredst it with the deep as with a garment: the waters stood above the mountains. At thy rebuke they fled; at the voice of thy thunder they hasted away. They go up by the mountains; they go down by the valleys unto the place which thou hast founded for them. Thou hast set a bound which they may not pass over; that they turn not again to cover the earth.

3. He sendeth the springs into the valleys, which run among the hills. They give drink to every beast of the field; the wild asses quench their thirst. By them shall the fowls of the heaven have their habitation, which sing among the branches. He watereth the hills from his chambers; the earth is satisfied with the fruit of thy works.

4. He caused the grass to grow for the cattle, and herb for the service of man, that he may bring forth food out of the earth; and wine that maketh glad the heart of man, and oil to make his face to shine, and bread which strengtheneth man's heart.

5. The trees of the Lord are full of sap; the cedars of Lebanon, which he hath planted, where the birds make their nests: as for the stork, the fir trees are her house. The high hills are a refuge for the wild goats, and the rocks for the conies.

6. He appointed the moon for seasons; the sun knoweth his going down. Thou makest darkness, and it is night, wherein all the beasts of the forest do creep forth. The young lions roar after their prey, and seek their meat from God. The sun ariseth, they gather themselves together, and lay them down in their dens. Man goeth forth unto his work, and to his labor until the evening.

7. O Lord, how manifold are thy works! in wisdom hast thou made them all: the earth is full of thy riches. So is this great and wide sea, wherein are things creeping innumerable, both small and great beasts. There go the ships: there is that leviathan, whom thou hast made to play therein. These wait all upon thee, that thou mayest give them their meat in due season.

8. That thou givest them they gather; thou openest thine hand, they are filled with good. Thou hidest thy face, they are troubled; thou takest away their breath, they die, and return to their dust. Thou sendest forth thy Spirit, they are created; and thou renewest the face of the earth.

9. The glory of the Lord shall endure forever: the Lord shall rejoice in his works. He looketh on the earth, and it trembleth: he toucheth the hills, and they smoke.

10. O that men would praise the Lord for his goodness, and for his wonderful works to the children of men! And let them sacrifice the sacrifices of thanksgiving, and declare his works with rejoicing.

11. O give thanks unto the Lord; call upon his name; make known his deeds among the people. Sing unto him, sing psalms unto him: talk ye of all his wondrous works. Glory ye in his holy name: let the heart of them rejoice that seek the Lord. Seek the Lord, and his strength; seek his face evermore.

12. Remember his marvelous works that he hath done; his wonders, and the judgments of his mouth. He is the Lord our God; his judgments are in all the earth. I will sing unto the Lord as long as I live: I will sing praise to my God while I have my being.

— *Extracts from the Bible.*

DEFINITIONS. — 2. Found′ed, *built, established.* 3. Hăb-i-tā′-tion, *place of abode.* 5. Rĕf′ūge, *shelter, protection.* Cō′ny, *a kind of rabbit.* 6. Ap-point′ed, *ordained.*

NOTES.—5. *Cedars of Lebanon.* A species of cedar, of great magnificence, formerly abundant in Mt. Lebanon and the Taurus Range in Asia Minor, but now almost entirely destroyed. The wood is durable and fragrant, and was used in the construction of costly buildings, such as the palace of David and Solomon's Temple.

7. *Leviathan.* This name is applied in the Old Testament to some huge water animal. In some cases it appears to mean the crocodile, but in others the whale or a large sea serpent.

LII. MY MOTHER.

1. OFTEN into folly straying,
   O, my mother! how I've grieved her!
Oft I've heard her for me praying,
   Till the gushing tears relieved her;
And she gently rose and smiled,
Whispering, "God will keep my child."

2. She was youthful then, and sprightly,
   Fondly on my father leaning,
Sweet she spoke, her eyes shone brightly,
   And her words were full of meaning;
Now, an autumn leaf decayed;
I, perhaps, have made it fade.

3. But, whatever ills betide thee,
   Mother, in them all I share;
In thy sickness watch beside thee,
   And beside thee kneel in prayer.
Best of mothers! on my breast
Lean thy head, and sink to rest.

LIII. THE HOUR OF PRAYER.

Felicia Dorothea Hemans (*b.* 1794, *d.* 1835) was born in Liverpool, England. Her maiden name was Browne. Her childhood was spent in Wales. Her first volume of poems was published in 1808; her second in 1812. In 1812 she was married to Captain Hemans, but he left her about six years after their marriage, and they never again lived together. She went, with her five sons, to reside with her mother, then living near St. Asaph, in North Wales. Mrs. Hemans then resumed her literary pursuits, and wrote much and well. Her poetry is smooth and graceful, and she excels in description. Many of her poems are exceedingly beautiful.

1. Child, amid the flowers at play,
While the red light fades away;
Mother, with thine earnest eye,
Ever following silently;
Father, by the breeze at eve
Called thy harvest work to leave;
Pray! Ere yet the dark hours be,
Lift the heart, and bend the knee.

2. Traveler, in the stranger's land,
Far from thine own household band;
Mourner, haunted by the tone
Of a voice from this world gone;
Captive, in whose narrow cell
Sunshine hath not leave to dwell;
Sailor, on the darkening sea;
Lift the heart and bend the knee.

3. Warrior, that from battle won,
Breathest now at set of sun;
Woman, o'er the lowly slain
Weeping on his burial plain;
Ye that triumph, ye that sigh,
Kindred by one holy tie,
Heaven's first star alike ye see;
Lift the heart, and bend the knee.

LIV. THE WILL.

Characters.—SWIPES, *a brewer;* CURRIE, *a saddler;* FRANK MILLINGTON; *and* SQUIRE DRAWL.

Swipes. A SOBER occasion, this, brother Currie. Who would have thought the old lady was so near her end?

Currie. Ah! we must all die, brother Swipes; and those who live the longest outlive the most.

Swipes. True, true; but, since we must die and leave our earthly possessions, it is well that the law takes such good care of us. Had the old lady her senses when she departed?

Cur. Perfectly, perfectly. Squire Drawl told me she read every word of the will aloud, and never signed her name better.

Swipes. Had you any hint from the Squire what disposition she made of her property?

Cur. Not a whisper; the Squire is as close as an underground tomb; but one of the witnesses hinted to me that she had cut off her graceless nephew, Frank, without a shilling.

Swipes. Has she, good soul, has she? You know I come in, then, in right of my wife.

Cur. And I in my own right; and this is no doubt the reason why we have been called to hear the reading of the will. Squire Drawl knows how things should be done, though he is as air-tight as one of your beer barrels. But here comes the young reprobate. He must be present, as a matter of course, you know. [*Enter* FRANK MILLINGTON.] Your servant, young gentleman. So your benefactress has left you at last.

Swipes. It is a painful thing to part with old and good friends, Mr. Millington.

Frank. It is so, sir; but I could bear her loss better

had I not so often been ungrateful for her kindness. She was my only friend, and I knew not her value.

Cur. It is too late to repent, Master Millington. You will now have a chance to earn your own bread.

Swipes. Ay, ay, by the sweat of your brow, as better people are obliged to. You would make a fine brewer's boy, if you were not too old.

Cur. Ay, or a saddler's lackey, if held with a tight rein.

Frank. Gentlemen, your remarks imply that my aunt has treated me as I deserved. I am above your insults, and only hope you will bear your fortune as modestly as I shall mine submissively. I shall retire. [*Going: he meets* SQUIRE DRAWL.]

Squire. Stop, stop, young man. We must have your presence. Good morning, gentlemen; you are early on the ground.

Cur. I hope the Squire is well to-day.

Squire. Pretty comfortable, for an invalid.

Swipes. I trust the damp air has not affected your lungs again.

Squire. No, I believe not. But, since the heirs at law are all convened, I shall now proceed to open the last will and testament of your deceased relative, according to law.

Swipes. [*While the* SQUIRE *is breaking the seal.*] It is a trying thing to leave all one's possessions, Squire, in this manner.

Cur. It really makes me feel melancholy when I look around and see everything but the venerable owner of these goods. Well did the Preacher say, "All is vanity."

Squire. Please to be seated, gentlemen. [*He puts on his spectacles and begins to read slowly.*] "*Imprimis;* whereas, my nephew, Francis Millington, by his disobedience and ungrateful conduct, has shown himself unworthy of my bounty, and incapable of managing my large estate, I do hereby give and bequeath all my houses, farms, stocks, bonds, moneys, and property, both personal and real, to my dear cousins, Samuel Swipes, of Malt Street, brewer, and Christopher Currie, of Fly Court, saddler." [*The* SQUIRE *here takes off his spectacles, and begins to wipe them very leisurely.*]

Swipes. Generous creature! kind soul! I always loved her!

Cur. She was good, she was kind;—and, brother Swipes, when we divide, I think I'll take the mansion house.

Swipes. Not so fast, if you please, Mr. Currie. My wife has long had her eye upon that, and must have it.

Cur. There will be two words to that bargain, Mr. Swipes. And, besides, I ought to have the first choice. Did I not lend her a new chaise every time she wished to ride? And who knows what influence—

Swipes. Am I not named first in her will? and did I not furnish her with my best small beer for more than six months? And who knows—

Frank. Gentlemen, I must leave you. [*Going.*]

Squire. [*Putting on his spectacles very deliberately.*] Pray, gentlemen, keep your seats, I have not done yet. Let me see; where was I? Ay, "All my property, both personal and real, to my dear cousins, Samuel Swipes, of Malt Street, brewer,"—

Swipes. Yes!

Squire. "And Christopher Currie, of Fly Court, saddler,"

Cur. Yes!

Squire. "To have and to hold, IN TRUST, for the sole and exclusive benefit of my nephew, Francis Millington, until he shall have attained the age of twenty-one years, by which time I hope he will have so far reformed his evil habits, as that he may safely be intrusted with the large fortune which I hereby bequeath to him."

Swipes. What is all this? You don't mean that we are humbugged? In trust! How does that appear? Where is it?

Squire. There; in two words of as good old English as I ever penned.

Cur. Pretty well, too, Mr. Squire, if we must be sent for to be made a laughingstock of. She shall pay for every ride she has had out of my chaise, I promise you.

Swipes. And for every drop of my beer. Fine times, if two sober, hard-working citizens are to be brought here to be made the sport of a graceless profligate. But we will manage his property for him, Mr. Currie; we will make him feel that trustees are not to be trifled with.

Cur. That we will.

Squire. Not so fast, gentlemen; for the instrument is dated three years ago; and the young gentleman must be already of age, and able to take care of himself. Is it not so, Francis?

Frank. It is, your worship.

Squire. Then, gentlemen, having attended to the breaking of the seal, according to law, you are released from any further trouble about the business.

Definitions. – Dĭs-po-ṣĭ′tion, *disposal.* Grāçe′less, *depraved, corrupt.* Rĕp′ro-bate, *one morally lost.* Lăck′ey, *an attending servant, a footman.* De-çēased′, *dead.* Con-vēned′, *met together, assembled.* Im-prī′mis (*Latin*), *in the first place.* Chāiṣe (*pro.* shāz), *a kind of two-wheeled carriage.* Re-fôrmed′, *returned to a good state.* Prŏf′li-ḡate, *a person openly and shamelessly vicious.* In′strṳ-ment (a term in law), *a writing expressive of some act, contract,* etc.

Notes. — Terms having the same, or nearly the same, meaning, as, "will and testament," "give and bequeath," "to have and to hold," "sole and exclusive," are commonly joined in this way in legal documents.

Personal property usually consists of things temporary and movable, while *real property* includes things fixed and immovable, such as lands and tenements.

LV. THE NOSE AND THE EYES.

William Cowper (*b.* 1731, *d.* 1800) was the son of an English clergyman, and was born in Great Berkhampstead, Hertfordshire, England. He was sent to Westminster School when he was ten years of age, and he remained there, a diligent student, eight years. He then studied law, and was admitted to the bar, but he never practiced his profession. He was appointed to a clerkship in the House of Lords when he was about thirty years old, but he never entered upon the discharge of his duties. He became insane, and was sent to a private asylum. After his recovery, he found a home in the family of the Rev. Mr. Unwin. On the death of this gentleman, he resided with the widow till her death — most of the time at Olney. His first writings were published in 1782. "The Task," some hymns, a number of minor poems, and his translations of Homer, composed his published works. His insanity returned at times, and darkened a pure and gentle life at its close.

1. BETWEEN Nose and Eyes a strange contest arose;
The spectacles set them, unhappily, wrong;
The point in dispute was, as all the world knows,
To which the said spectacles ought to belong.

2. So Tongue was the lawyer, and argued the cause,
With a great deal of skill and a wig full of learning,
While chief baron Ear sat to balance the laws,
So famed for his talent in nicely discerning.

3. "In behalf of the Nose, it will quickly appear,
And your lordship," he said, "will undoubtedly find,
That the Nose has the spectacles always to wear,
Which amounts to possession, time out of mind."

4. Then, holding the spectacles up to the court,
"Your lordship observes, they are made with a straddle
As wide as the ridge of the Nose is; in short,
Designed to sit close to it, just like a saddle.

5. "Again, would your lordship a moment suppose
('T is a case that has happened, and may happen again)
That the visage or countenance had not a Nose,
Pray, who would or who could wear spectacles then?

6. "On the whole it appears, and my argument shows,
With a reasoning the court will never condemn,
That the spectacles plainly were made for the Nose,
And the Nose was as plainly intended for them."

7. Then shifting his side (as a lawyer knows how),
He pleaded again in behalf of the Eyes:
But what were his arguments, few people know,
For the court did not think them equally wise.

8. So his lordship decreed, with a grave, solemn tone,
Decisive and clear, without one *if* or *but*,
That whenever the Nose put his spectacles on,
By daylight or candlelight,—Eyes should be shut.

Definitions.—2. Ar'gūed, *discussed, treated by reasoning*. Dis-çẽrn'ing (*pro.* diz-zẽrn'ing), *marking as different, distinguishing*. 3. Be-hälf', *support, defense*. 8. De-creed', *determined judicially by authority, ordered*.

LVI. AN ICEBERG.

Louis Legrand Noble (*b.* 1813, *d.* 1882) was born in Otsego County, New York. When twelve years of age, he removed with his family to the wilds of Michigan, but after the death of his father he returned to New York to study for the ministry, which he entered in 1840. About this time he published his first productions, two Indian romances in the form of poems, entitled "Pewatem" and "Nimahmin." Mr. Noble lived for a time in North Carolina, and later at Catskill on the Hudson, where he became a warm friend of the artist Cole. After the latter's death he wrote a memorial of him. Other works of this author are "The Hours, and other Poems," and "After Icebergs with a Painter," from which this selection is taken.

1. We have just passed a fragment of some one of the surrounding icebergs that had amused us. It bore the resemblance of a huge polar bear, reposing upon the base of an inverted cone, with a twist of a seashell, and whirling slowly round and round. The ever-attending green

water, with its aërial clearness, enabled us to see its spiral folds and horns as they hung suspended in the deep.

2. The bear, a ten-foot mass in tolerable proportion, seemed to be regularly beset by a pack of hungry little swells. First, one would take him on the haunch, then whip back into the sea over his tail and between his legs. Presently a bolder swell would rise and pitch into his back with a ferocity that threatened instant destruction. It only washed his satin fleece the whiter.

3. While Bruin was turning to look the daring assailant in the face, the rogue had pitched himself back into his cave. No sooner that, than a very bulldog of a billow would attack him in the face. The serenity with which the impertinent assault was borne was complete. It was but a puff of silvery dust, powdering his mane with fresher brightness. Nothing would be left of bull but a little froth of all the foam displayed in the fierce onset. He too would turn and scud into his hiding place.

4. Persistent little waves! After a dash, singly, all around, upon the common enemy, as if by some silent agreement underwater, they would all rush on at once, with their loudest roar and shaggiest foam, and overwhelm poor bear so completely that nothing less might be expected than to behold him broken in four quarters, and floating helplessly asunder. Mistaken spectators! Although, by his momentary rolling and plunging, he was evidently aroused, yet neither Bruin nor his burrow was at all the worse for all the wear and washing.

5. The deep fluting, the wrinkled folds, and cavities, over and through which the green and silvery water rushed back into the sea, rivaled the most exquisite sculpture. And nature not only gives her marbles, with the finest lines, the most perfect lights and shades, she colors them also. She is no monochromist, but polychroic, imparting such touches of dove tints, emerald, and azure as she bestows upon her gems and skies.

6. We are bearing up under the big berg as closely as we dare. To our delight, what we have been wishing and watching for is actually taking place: loud explosions, with heavy falls of ice, followed by the cataract-like roar, and the high, thin seas, wheeling away beautifully crested with sparkling foam. If it is possible, imagine the effect upon the beholder: this precipice of ice, with tremendous cracking, is falling toward us with a majestic and awful motion.

7. Down sinks the long water line into the black deep; down go the porcelain crags and galleries of glassy sculpture — a speechless and awful baptism. Now it pauses, and returns: up rise sculptures and crags streaming with the shining white brine; up comes the great encircling line, followed by things new and strange — crags, niches, balconies, and caves; up, up, it rises, higher and higher still, crossing the very breast of the grand ice, and all bathed with rivulets of gleaming foam. Over goes the summit, ridge, pinnacles, and all, standing off obliquely in the opposite air. Now it pauses in its upward roll: back it comes again, cracking, cracking, cracking, "groaning out harsh thunder" as it comes, and threatening to burst, like a mighty bomb, into millions of glittering fragments. The spectacle is terrific and magnificent. Emotion is irrepressible, and peals of wild hurrah burst forth from all.

Definitions. — 1. Cōne, *a solid body having a circular base, from which it tapers gradually to a point.* 2. Swĕlls, *waves.* 3. Se-rĕn'i-ty, *quietness, calmness.* 5. Ex'qui-site, *exceedingly nice, giving rare satisfaction.* Seŭlp'ture, *carved work.* Mŏn'o-chrō-mist, *one who paints in a single color.* Pŏl-y-chrō'ic, *given to the use of many colors.* 7. Pĭn'na-cles, *high, spirelike points.* Ob-lïque'ly, *slantingly.* Ir-re-prĕss'i-ble, *not to be restrained.*

Note. — Only about one eighth of an iceberg appears above the surface of the water. When one side of it grows heavier than another, through unequal melting and the action of the waves, the whole mass rolls over in the water in the manner so well described in this lesson.

LVII. ABOUT QUAIL.

William Post Hawes (*b.* 1803, *d.* 1842) was born in New York City, and was a graduate of Columbia College. He was a lawyer by profession. His writings consist mainly of essays, contributed to various newspapers and magazines, and show great descriptive power. He was a frequent contributor to the "Spirit of the Times," under the title of "Cypress, Jr.," on various sporting topics. After his death a collection of his writings was published in two volumes, entitled, "Sporting Scenes" and "Sundry Sketches."

1. The quail is peculiarly a domestic bird, and is attached to his birthplace and the home of his forefathers. The various members of the aquatic families educate their children in the cool summer of the far north, and bathe their warm bosoms in July in the iced waters of Hudson Bay; but when Boreas scatters the rushes where they had builded their bedchambers, they desert their fatherland, and fly to disport in the sunny waters of the south.

2. The songsters of the woodland, when their customary crops of insects and berries are cut off in the fall, gather themselves to renew their loves and get married in more genial climes. Presently, the groves so vocal, and the sky so full, shall be silent and barren. The "melancholy days" will soon be here; only thou, dear Bob White, wilt remain.

3. The quail is the bird for me. He is no rover, no emigrant. He stays at home, and is identified with the soil. Where the farmer works, he lives, and loves, and whistles. In budding springtime, and in scorching summer — in bounteous autumn, and in barren winter, his voice is heard from the same bushy hedge fence, and from his customary cedars. Cupidity and cruelty may drive him to the woods, and to seek more quiet seats; but be merciful and kind to him, and he will visit your barnyard, and sing for you upon the boughs of the apple tree by your gateway.

4. When warm May first wooes the young flowers to open and receive her breath, then begin the cares and re-

sponsibilities of wedded life. Away fly the happy pair to seek some grassy tussock, where, safe from the eye of the hawk and the nose of the fox, they may rear their expectant brood in peace.

5. Oats harvest arrives, and the fields are waving with yellow grain. Now be wary, O kind-hearted cradler, and tread not into those pure white eggs ready to burst with life! Soon there is a peeping sound heard, and lo! a proud mother walketh magnificently in the midst of her children, scratching and picking, and teaching them how to swallow. Happy she, if she may be permitted to bring them up to maturity, and uncompelled to renew her joys in another nest.

6. The assiduities of a mother have a beauty and a sacredness about them that command respect and reverence in all animal nature, human or inhuman — what a lie does that word carry — except, perhaps, in monsters, insects, and fish. I never yet heard of the parental tenderness of a trout, eating up his little baby, nor of the filial gratitude of a spider, nipping the life out of his gray-headed father, and usurping his web.

7. But if you would see the purest, the sincerest, the most affecting piety of a parent's love, startle a young family of quails, and watch the conduct of the mother. She will not leave you. No, not she. But she will fall at your feet, uttering a noise which none but a distressed mother can make, and she will run, and flutter, and seem to try to be caught, and cheat your outstretched hand, and affect to be wing-broken and wounded, and yet have just strength to tumble along, until she has drawn you, fatigued, a safe distance from her threatened children and the young hopes of her heart; and then will she mount, whirring with glad strength, and away through the maze of trees you have not seen before, like a close-shot bullet, fly to her skulking infants.

8. Listen now. Do you hear those three half-plaintive notes, quickly and clearly poured out? She is calling the boys and girls together. She sings not now "Bob White!" nor "Ah! Bob White!" That is her husband's love call, or his trumpet blast of defiance. But she calls sweetly and

softly for her lost children. Hear them "Peep! peep! peep!" at the welcome voice of their mother's love! They are coming together. Soon the whole family will meet again.

9. It is a foul sin to disturb them; but retread your devious way, and let her hear your coming footsteps, breaking down the briers, as you renew the danger. She is quiet. Not a word is passed between the fearful fugitives. Now, if you have the heart to do it, lie low, keep still, and imitate the call of the hen quail. O mother! mother! how your heart would die if you could witness the deception! The little ones raise up their trembling heads, and catch comfort and imagined safety from the sound. "Peep! peep!" They come to you, straining their little eyes, and, clustering together and answering, seem to say, "Where is she? Mother! mother! we are here!"

Definitions.—1. A-quăt'ie, *frequenting the water.* 2. Vō'eal, *having a voice.* 3. I-dĕn'ti-fīed, *united.* Cu-pĭd'i-ty, *eager desire to possess something.* 4. Tŭs'sock, *a tuft of grass or twigs.* 5. Crā'dler, *one who uses a cradle, which is an instrument attached to a scythe in cutting grain.* 6. U-ṣûrp'ing, *seizing and holding in possession by force.* 7. Af-fĕet', *to pretend.* 9. Dē'vi-oŭs, *winding.*

Note.—1. *Boreas* is the name which the ancient Greeks gave to the north wind.

LVIII. THE BLUE AND THE GRAY.

1. By the flow of the inland river,
 Whence the fleets of iron have fled,
Where the blades of the grave grass quiver,
 Asleep are the ranks of the dead;—
  Under the sod and the dew,
   Waiting the judgment day;
  Under the one, the Blue;
   Under the other, the Gray.

2. These, in the robings of glory,
   Those, in the gloom of defeat,
All, with the battle blood gory,
   In the dusk of eternity meet;—
      Under the sod and the dew,
         Waiting the judgment day;
      Under the laurel, the Blue;
         Under the willow, the Gray.

3. From the silence of sorrowful hours,
   The desolate mourners go,
Lovingly laden with flowers,
   Alike for the friend and the foe;—
      Under the sod and the dew,
         Waiting the judgment day;
      Under the roses, the Blue;
         Under the lilies, the Gray.

4. So, with an equal splendor,
   The morning sun rays fall,
With a touch, impartially tender,
   On the blossoms blooming for all;—
      Under the sod and the dew,
         Waiting the judgment day;
      Broidered with gold, the Blue;
         Mellowed with gold, the Gray.

5. So, when the summer calleth,
   On forest and field of grain,
With an equal murmur falleth
   The cooling drip of the rain;—
      Under the sod and the dew,
         Waiting the judgment day;
      Wet with the rain, the Blue;
         Wet with the rain, the Gray.

6. Sadly, but not with upbraiding,
The generous deed was done;
In the storm of the years that are fading,
No braver battle was won;—
Under the sod and the dew,
Waiting the judgment day;
Under the blossoms, the Blue;
Under the garlands, the Gray.

7. No more shall the war cry sever,
Or the winding rivers be red;
They banish our anger forever,
When they laurel the graves of our dead;—
Under the sod and the dew,
Waiting the judgment day;
Love and tears, for the Blue;
Tears and love, for the Gray.

—*F. M. Finch.*

NOTE.—The above touching little poem first appeared in the "Atlantic Monthly" in September, 1867. It commemorates the noble action on the part of the women at Columbus, Miss., who in decorating the graves strewed flowers impartially on those of the Confederate and of the Federal soldiers.

LIX. THE MACHINIST'S RETURN.

[Adapted from a letter written by a correspondent of the Washington "Capital."]

1. ON our way from Springfield to Boston, a stout, black-whiskered man sat immediately in front of me, in the drawing-room car, whose maneuvers were a source of constant amusement. He would get up every five minutes, hurry away to the narrow passage leading to the

door of the car, and commence laughing in the most violent manner, continuing that healthful exercise until he observed that some one was watching him, when he would return to his seat.

2. As we neared Boston these demonstrations increased in frequency and violence, but the stranger kept his seat and chuckled to himself. He shifted the position of his two portmanteaus, or placed them on the seat as if he was getting ready to leave. As we were at least twenty-five miles from Boston, such early preparations seemed extremely ridiculous. He became so excited at last that he could not keep his secret. Some one must be made a confidant; and as I happened to be the nearest to him, he selected me.

3. Turning around suddenly, and rocking himself to and fro in his chair, he said, "I have been away from home three years. Have been in Europe. My folks don't expect me for three months yet, but I got through and started. I telegraphed them at the last station — they 've got the dispatch by this time." As he said this he rubbed his hands, and changed the portmanteau on his left to the right, and then the one on the right to the left.

4. "Have you a wife?" said I. "Yes, and three children," was the answer. He then got up and folded his overcoat anew, and hung it over the back of the seat. "You are somewhat nervous just now, are you not?" said I.

5. "Well, I should think so," he replied. "I have n't slept soundly for a week. Do you know," he went on, speaking in a low tone, "I am almost certain this train will run off the track and break my neck before I get to Boston. I have had too much good luck lately for one man. It can't last. It rains so hard, sometimes, that you think it 's never going to stop; then it shines so bright you think it 's always going to shine; and just as you are set-

tled in either belief, you are knocked over by a change, to show you that you know nothing about it."

6. "Well, according to your philosophy," I said, "you will continue to have sunshine because you are expecting a storm." "Perhaps so," he replied; "but it is curious that the only thing which makes me think I shall get through safe is, I fear that I shall not."

7. "I am a machinist," he continued; "I made a discovery; nobody believed in it; I spent all my money in trying to bring it out; I mortgaged my home — everything went. Everybody laughed at me — everybody but my wife. She said she would work her fingers off before I should give it up. I went to England. At first I met with no encouragement whatever, and came very near jumping off London Bridge. I went into a workshop to earn money enough to come home with: there I met the man I wanted. To make a long story short, I 've brought home £50,000 with me, and here I am."

8. "Good!" I exclaimed. "Yes," said he, "and the best of it is, she knows nothing about it. She has been disappointed so often that I concluded I would not write to her about my unexpected good luck. When I got my money, though, I started for home at once."

9. "And now, I suppose, you will make her happy?" "Happy!" he replied; "why, you don't know anything about it! She 's worked night and day since I have been in England, trying to support herself and the children decently. They paid her thirteen cents apiece for making shirts, and that 's the way she has lived half the time. She 'll come down to the depot to meet me in a gingham dress and a shawl a hundred years old, and she 'll think she 's dressed up! Perhaps she won't have any fine dresses in a week or so, eh?"

10. The stranger then strode down the passageway again, and getting in a corner where he seemed to suppose that he was out of sight, went through the strangest pan-

tomime,—laughing, putting his mouth into the drollest shapes, and swinging himself back and forth in the limited space.

11. As the train was going into the depot, I placed myself on the platform of the car in front of the one in which I had been riding, and opposite the stranger, who, with a portmanteau in each hand, was standing on the lowest step, ready to jump to the ground. I looked from his face to the faces of the people before us, but saw no sign of recognition. Suddenly he cried, "There they are!"

12. Then he laughed outright, but in a hysterical way, as he looked over the crowd in front of him. I followed his eye and saw, some distance back, as if crowded out by the well-dressed and elbowing throng, a little woman in a faded dress and a well-worn hat, with a face almost painful in its intense but hopeful expression, glancing rapidly from window to window as the coaches passed by.

13. She had not seen the stranger, but a moment after she caught his eye. In another instant he had jumped to the platform with his two portmanteaus, and, pushing his way through the crowd, he rushed towards the place where she was standing. I think I never saw a face assume so many different expressions in so short a time as did that of the little woman while her husband was on his way to meet her.

14. She was not pretty,—on the contrary, she was very plain-looking; but somehow I felt a big lump rise in my throat as I watched her. She was trying to laugh, but, God bless her, how completely she failed in the attempt! Her mouth got into the position to laugh, but it never moved after that, save to draw down at the corners and quiver, while her eyes blinked so fast that I suspect she only caught occasional glimpses of the broad-shouldered fellow who elbowed his way so rapidly toward her.

15. As he drew close, and dropped the portmanteaus, she turned to one side, and covered her face with her

hands; and thus she was when the strong man gathered her up in his arms as if she were a child, and held her sobbing to his breast.

16. There were enough staring at them, heaven knows; so I turned my eyes away a moment, and then I saw two boys in threadbare roundabouts standing near, wiping their eyes on their sleeves, and bursting into tears anew at every fresh demonstration on the part of their mother. When I looked at the stranger again he had his hat drawn over his eyes; but his wife was looking up at him, and it seemed as if the pent-up tears of those weary months of waiting were streaming through her eyelids.

Definitions. — 1. Ma-neṳ′vers̹, *movements.* 2. Dĕm-on-strā′-tions̹, *expression of the feelings by outward signs.* Port-măn′teau (*pro.* port-măn′to), *a traveling bag, usually made of leather.* Cŏn-fi-dănt′, *one to whom secrets are intrusted.* 3. Dis-pătch′, *a message.* 6. Phi-lŏs′o-phy, *reasoning.* 7. Ma-ç̱hïn′ist, *a constructor of machines and engines.* Môrt′ḡaġed (*pro.* môr′ḡajd), *given as security for debt.* 9. Gĭng′ham, *a kind of cotton cloth which is dyed before it is woven.* 10. Păn′to-mīme, *acting without speaking, dumb show.* 12. Hys-tĕr′ic-al, *convulsive, fitful.*

LX. MAKE WAY FOR LIBERTY.

James Montgomery (*b.* 1771, *d.* 1854) was born in Irvine, Ayrshire, Scotland. His father, a Moravian preacher, sent him to a Moravian school at Fulneck, Yorkshire, England, to be educated. In 1794 he started "The Sheffield Iris," a weekly paper, which he edited, with marked ability, till 1825. He was fined and imprisoned twice for publishing articles decided to be seditious. His principal poetical works are "The World before the Flood," "Greenland," "The West Indies," "The Wanderer in Switzerland," "The Pelican Island," and "Original Hymns, for Public, Private, and Social Devotion." Mr. Montgomery's style is generally too diffuse; but its smoothness and the evident sincerity of his emotions have made many of his hymns and minor poems very popular. A pension of £300 a year was granted to him in 1833.

1. "Make way for Liberty!" he cried;
Made way for Liberty, and died!

2. In arms the Austrian phalanx stood,
A living wall, a human wood!
A wall, where every conscious stone
Seemed to its kindred thousands grown;
A rampart all assaults to bear,
Till time to dust their frames should wear
A wood like that enchanted grove,
In which, with fiends, Rinaldo strove,
Where every silent tree possessed
A spirit prisoned in its breast,
Which the first stroke of coming strife
Would startle into hideous life:
So dense, so still, the Austrians stood,
A living wall, a human wood!

3. Impregnable their front appears,
All horrent with projected spears,
Whose polished points before them shine,
From flank to flank, one brilliant line,
Bright as the breakers' splendors run
Along the billows to the sun.

4. Opposed to these, a hovering band,
Contending for their native land;
Peasants, whose new-found strength had broke
From manly necks the ignoble yoke,
And forged their fetters into swords,
On equal terms to fight their lords;
And what insurgent rage had gained,
In many a mortal fray maintained:
Marshaled once more at Freedom's call,
They came to conquer or to fall,
Where he who conquered, he who fell.
Was deemed a dead or living Tell!

5. And now the work of life and death
Hung on the passing of a breath;
The fire of conflict burned within;
The battle trembled to begin;
Yet, while the Austrians held their ground,
Point for attack was nowhere found;
Where'er the impatient Switzers gazed,
The unbroken line of lances blazed;
That line 't were suicide to meet,
And perish at their tyrants' feet;
How could they rest within their graves,
And leave their homes the homes of slaves?
Would they not feel their children tread
With clanking chains above their head?

6. It must not be: this day, this hour,
Annihilates the oppressor's power
All Switzerland is in the field,
She will not fly, she can not yield;
Few were the numbers she could boast,
But every freeman was a host,
And felt as though himself were he
On whose sole arm hung victory.

7. It did depend on *one*, indeed:
Behold him! Arnold Winkelried!
There sounds not to the trump of fame
The echo of a nobler name.
Unmarked he stood amid the throng,
In rumination deep and long,
Till you might see with sudden grace,
The very thought come o'er his face;
And by the motion of his form,
Anticipate the bursting storm;

And by the uplifting of his brow,
Tell where the bolt would strike, and how.
But 't was no sooner thought than done;
The field was in a moment won.

8. "Make way for Liberty!" he cried:
Then ran, with arms extended wide,
As if his dearest friend to clasp;
Ten spears he swept within his grasp:
"Make way for Liberty!" he cried,
Their keen points met from side to side;
He bowed among them like a tree,
And thus made way for Liberty.

9. Swift to the breach his comrades fly;
"Make way for Liberty!" they cry,
And through the Austrian phalanx dart,
As rushed the spears through Arnold's heart;
While instantaneous as his fall,
Rout, ruin, panic, scattered all.
An earthquake could not overthrow
A city with a surer blow.

10. Thus Switzerland again was free,
Thus Death made way for Liberty!

DEFINITIONS. — 2. Phā'lanx, *a body of troops formed in close array.* Cŏn'sciŏus, *sensible, knowing.* Kĭn'dred, *those of like nature, relatives.* Răm'pärt, *that which defends from assault, a bulwark.* 3. Im-prĕg'na-ble, *that can not be moved or shaken.* Hŏr'rent, *standing out like bristles.* 4. In-sûr'ġent, *rising in opposition to authority.* 6. An-nī'hi-lātes, *destroys.* 7. Ru-mi-nā'tion, *the act of musing, meditation.* 9. Brēach, *a gap or opening made by breaking.*

NOTES.—The incident related in this poem is one of actual occurrence, and took place at the battle of Sempach, fought in 1386 A.D., between only 1,300 Swiss and a large army of Austrians. The latter had obtained possession of a narrow pass in the mountains, from which it seemed impossible to dislodge them until Arnold von Winkelried made a breach in their line, as narrated.

Rinaldo is a knight in Tasso's "Jerusalem Delivered" (Canto XVIII, 17–40), who enters an enchanted wood, and, by cutting down a tree in spite of the nymphs and phantoms that endeavor in every way to stop him, breaks the spell; the Christian army are thus enabled to enter the grove and obtain timber for their engines of war.

LXI. THE ENGLISH SKYLARK.

Elihu Burritt (*b.* 1810, *d.* 1879), "the learned blacksmith," was born in New Britain, Conn. His father was a shoemaker. Having received only a limited amount of instruction at the district school, he was apprenticed to a blacksmith about 1827. During his apprenticeship he labored hard at self-instruction. He worked at his trade many years, from ten to twelve hours each day, but managed, in the meantime, to acquire a knowledge of many ancient and modern languages. He made translations from several of these, which were published in the "American Eclectic Review." In 1844 he commenced the publication of "The Christian Citizen." His leading literary works are "Sparks from the Anvil," "A Voice from the Forge," "Peace Papers," and "Walks to John o' Groat's House." From the last of these the following selection is abridged.

1. TAKE it in all, no bird in either hemisphere equals the English lark in heart or voice, for both unite to make it the sweetest, the happiest, the welcomest singer that was ever winged, like the high angels of God's love. It is the living ecstasy of joy when it mounts up into its "glorious privacy of light."

2. On the earth it is timid, silent, and bashful, as if not at home, and not sure of its right to be there at all. It is rather homely withal, having nothing in feather, fea-

ture, or form to attract notice. It is seemingly made to be heard, not seen, reversing the old axiom addressed to children when getting noisy.

3. Its mission is music, and it floods a thousand acres of the blue sky with it several times a day. Out of that palpitating speck of living joy there wells forth a sea of twittering ecstasy upon the morning and evening air. It does not ascend by gyrations, like the eagle and birds of prey. It mounts up like a human aspiration.

4. It seems to spread its wings and to be lifted straight upwards out of sight by the afflatus of its own happy heart. To pour out this in undulating rivulets of rhapsody is apparently the only motive of its ascension. This it is that has made it so loved of all generations.

5. It is the singing angel of man's nearest heaven, whose vital breath is music. Its sweet warbling is only the metrical palpitation of its life of joy. It goes up over the rooftrees of the rural hamlet on the wings of its song, as if to train the human soul to trial flights heavenward.

6. Never did the Creator put a voice of such volume into so small a living thing. It is a marvel — almost a miracle. In a still hour you can hear it at nearly a mile's distance. When its form is lost in the hazy lace work of the sun's rays above, it pours down upon you all the thrilling semitones of its song as distinctly as if it were warbling to you in your window.

Definitions. — 1. Ec'sta-sy, *overmastering joy, rapture.* 2. Ax'i-om, *a self-evident truth.* 3. Păl'pi-tāt-ing, *throbbing, fluttering.* Wĕlls̹, *pours, flows.* Gy-rā'tions̹, *circular or spiral motions.* 4. Af-flā'tus, *breath, inspiration.* Un'du-lā-ting, *rising and falling like waves.* Rhăp'so-dy, *that which is uttered in a disconnected way under strong excitement.* Gĕn-er-ā'tion, *the mass of beings living at one period.* 5. Mĕt'ric-al, *arranged in measures, as poetry and music.* Ro͞of'tree, *the beam in the angle of a roof, hence the roof itself.* Hăm'let, *a little cluster of houses.*

LXII. HOW SLEEP THE BRAVE.

William Collins (*b.* 1721, *d.* 1759) was born at Chichester, England. He was educated at Winchester and Oxford. About 1745, he went to London as a literary adventurer, and there won the esteem of Dr. Johnson. His "Odes" were published in 1746, but were not popular. He was subsequently relieved from pecuniary embarrassment by a legacy of £2,000 from a maternal uncle; but he soon became partially insane, and was for some time confined in an asylum for lunatics. He afterwards retired to Chichester, where he was cared for by his sister until his death.

1. How sleep the brave who sink to rest
By all their country's wishes blessed!
When Spring, with dewy fingers cold,
Returns to deck their hallowed mold,
She there shall dress a sweeter sod
Than Fancy's feet have ever trod.

2. By fairy hands their knell is rung;
By forms unseen their dirge is sung;
There Honor comes a pilgrim gray,
To bless the turf that wraps their clay;
And Freedom shall awhile repair
To dwell a weeping hermit there!

LXIII. THE RAINBOW.

John Keble (*b.* 1792, *d.* 1866) was born near Fairfax, Gloucestershire, England. He graduated at Oxford with remarkably high honors, and afterwards was appointed to the professorship of poetry in that university. Since his death, Keble College, at Oxford, has been erected to his memory. In 1835, he became vicar of Hursley and rector of Otterbourne, and held these livings until his death. His most famous work is "The Christian Year," a collection of sacred poems.

1. A FRAGMENT of a rainbow bright
Through the moist air I see,
All dark and damp on yonder height,
All bright and clear to me.

2. An hour ago the storm was here,
   The gleam was far behind;
So will our joys and grief appear,
   When earth has ceased to blind.

3. Grief will be joy if on its edge
   Fall soft that holiest ray,
Joy will be grief if no faint pledge
   Be there of heavenly day.

LXIV. SUPPOSED SPEECH OF JOHN ADAMS.

Daniel Webster (*b.* 1782, *d.* 1852) was born in Salisbury, N.H. He spent a few months of his boyhood at Phillips Academy, Exeter, but fitted for college under Rev. Samuel Wood, of Boscawen, N.H. He graduated from Dartmouth College in 1801. He taught school several terms, during and after his college course. In 1805, he was admitted to the bar in Boston, and practiced law in New Hampshire for the succeeding eleven years. In 1812, he was elected to the United States House of Representatives. In 1816, he removed to Boston, and in 1827 was elected to the United States Senate, which position he held for twelve years. In 1841, he was appointed Secretary of State. He returned to the Senate in 1845. In 1850, he was reappointed Secretary of State, and continued in office until his death. He died at his residence, in Marshfield, Mass. Mr. Webster's fame rests chiefly on his state papers and speeches. As a speaker he was dignified and stately, using clear, pure English. During all his life he took great interest in agriculture, and was very fond of outdoor sports.

1. Sink or swim, live or die, survive or perish, I give my hand and my heart to this vote. It is true, indeed, that, in the beginning, we aimed not at independence. But

"There 's a divinity that shapes our ends."

The injustice of England has driven us to arms; and, blinded to her own interest, she has obstinately persisted, till independence is now within our grasp. We have but to reach forth to it, and it is ours. Why then should we defer the declaration? Is any man so weak as now to hope for a reconciliation with England, which shall leave either safety to the country and its liberties, or security to his own life and his own honor! Are not you, sir, who sit in that chair, is not he, our venerable colleague, near you, are you not both already the proscribed and predestined objects of punishment and of vengeance? Cut off from all hope of royal clemency, what are you, what can you be, while the power of England remains, but *outlaws?*

2. If we postpone independence, do we mean to carry on, or to give up, the war? Do we mean to submit, and consent that we shall be ground to powder, and our country and its rights trodden down in the dust? I *know* we do not mean to submit. We NEVER *shall submit!* Do we intend to violate that most solemn obligation ever entered into by men, that plighting, before God, of our sacred honor to Washington, when, putting him forth to incur the dangers of war, as well as the political hazards of the times, we promised to adhere to him in every extremity with our fortunes and our lives? I know there is not a man here, who would not rather see a general conflagration sweep over the land, or an earthquake sink it, than one jot or tittle of that plighted faith fall to the ground. For myself, having twelve months ago, in this place, moved you that George Washington be appointed commander of the forces raised, or to be raised, for the defense of American liberty; may my right hand forget her cunning, and my tongue cleave to the roof of my mouth, if I hesitate or waver in the support I give him.

3. The war, then, must go on. We must fight it through. And if the war must go on, why put off the Declaration of Independence? That measure will strengthen us. It will give us character abroad. Nations will then treat with us, which they never can do while we acknowledge ourselves subjects in arms against our sovereign. Nay, I maintain that England herself will sooner treat for peace with us

on the footing of independence, than consent, by repealing her acts, to acknowledge that her whole conduct toward us has been a course of injustice and oppression. Her pride will be less wounded by submitting to that course of things, which now predestinates our independence, than by yielding the points in controversy to her rebellious subjects. The former, she would regard as the result of fortune; the latter, she would feel as her own deep disgrace. Why, then, do we not change this from a civil to a national war? And since we must fight it through, why not put ourselves in a state to enjoy all the benefits of victory, if we gain the victory.

4. If we fail, it can be no worse for us. But we shall not fail. The cause will raise up armies; the cause will create navies. The people — the people, if we are true to them, will carry us, and will carry themselves, gloriously through this struggle. I care not how fickle other people have been found. I know the people of these colonies; and I know that resistance to British aggression is deep and settled in their hearts, and can not be eradicated. Sir, the Declaration of Independence will inspire the people with increased courage. Instead of a long and bloody war for the restoration of privileges, for redress of grievances, for chartered immunities, held under a British king, set before them the glorious object of entire independence, and it will breathe into them anew the spirit of life.

5. Read this declaration at the head of the army; every sword will be drawn, and the solemn vow uttered to maintain it, or perish on the bed of honor. Publish it from the pulpit; religion will approve it, and the love of religious liberty will cling around it, resolved to stand with it or fall with it. Send it to the public halls; proclaim it there; let *them* see it who saw their brothers and their sons fall on the field of Bunker Hill and in the streets of Lexington and Concord, and the very walls will cry out in its support.

6. Sir, I know the uncertainty of human affairs, but I see — I see clearly through this day's business. You and I, indeed, may rue it. We may not live to see the time this declaration shall be made good. We may die; die colonists; die slaves; die, it may be, ignominiously and on the scaffold. Be it so: be it so. If it be the pleasure of Heaven that my country shall require the poor offering of my life, the victim shall be ready at the appointed hour of sacrifice, come when that hour may. But while I do live, let me have a country, or at least the *hope* of a country, and that a FREE *country.*

7. But whatever may be our fate, be assured — be assured that this Declaration will stand. It may cost treasure, and it may cost blood; but it will stand, and it will richly compensate for both. Through the thick gloom of the present I see the brightness of the future as the sun in heaven. We shall make this a glorious, an immortal day. When we are in our graves, our children will honor it. They will celebrate it with thanksgiving, with festivity, with bonfires, and illuminations. On its annual return they will shed tears, — copious, gushing tears; not of subjection and slavery, not of agony and distress, but of exultation, of gratitude, and of joy.

8. Sir, before God I believe the hour is come. My judgment approves the measure, and my whole heart is in it. All that I have, and all that I am, and all that I hope in this life, I am now ready here to stake upon it; and I leave off as I began, that, live or die, survive or perish, I am for the Declaration. It is my living sentiment, and, by the blessing of God, it shall by my dying sentiment; independence *now,* and INDEPENDENCE FOREVER.

DEFINITIONS. — 1. Rĕc-on-çĭl-i-ā′tion, *renewal of friendship.* Cŏl′lēaḡue (*pro.* kŏl′lēḡ), *an associate in some civil office.* Pro-scrībed′, *doomed to destruction, put out of the protection of the law.* Pre-dĕs′tĭned, *decreed beforehand.* Clĕm′en-çy, *mercy, indulgence.*

2. Tĭt′tle, *a small particle, a jot.* 3. Cŏn′tro-vẽr-sy, *dispute, debate.* 4. E-răd′i-eāt-ed, *rooted out.* Re-drĕss′, *deliverance from wrong, injury, or oppression.* Chär′tered, *secured by an instrument in writing from a king or other proper authority.* Im-mū′ni-ty, *freedom from any duty, tax, imposition, etc.* 7. Cŏm′pen-sāte, *make amends for.*

NOTES.—Mr. Webster, in a speech upon the life and character of John Adams, imagines some one opposed to the Declaration of Independence to have stated his fears and objections before Congress while deliberating on that subject. He then supposes Mr. Adams to have replied in the language above.

1. The quotation is from "Hamlet," *Act* V, *Scene* 2.

You, sir, who sit in that chair. This was addressed to John Hancock, president of the Continental Congress. *Our venerable colleague* refers to Samuel Adams. After the battles of Concord and Lexington, Governor Gage offered pardon to all the rebels who would lay down their arms, excepting Samuel Adams and John Hancock.

LXV. THE RISING.

Thomas Buchanan Read (*b.* 1822, *d.* 1872) was born in Chester County, Pennsylvania. In 1839 he entered a sculptor's studio in Cincinnati, where he gained reputation as a portrait painter. He afterwards went to New York, Boston, and Philadelphia, and, in 1850, to Italy. He divided his time between Cincinnati, Philadelphia, and Rome, in the later years of his life. Some of his poems are marked by vigor and strength, while others are distinguished by smoothness and delicacy. The following selection is abridged from "The Wagoner of the Alleghanies."

1. OUT of the North the wild news came,
Far flashing on its wings of flame,
Swift as the boreal light which flies
At midnight through the startled skies.

2. And there was tumult in the air,
The fife's shrill note, the drum's loud beat,
And through the wide land everywhere
The answering tread of hurrying feet,

While the first oath of Freedom's gun
Came on the blast from Lexington.
And Concord, roused, no longer tame,
Forgot her old baptismal name,
Made bare her patriot arm of power,
And swelled the discord of the hour.

3. The yeoman and the yoeman's son,
With knitted brows and sturdy dint,
Renewed the polish of each gun,
Reoiled the lock, reset the flint;
And oft the maid and matron there,
While kneeling in the firelight glare,
Long poured, with half-suspended breath,
The lead into the molds of death.

4. The hands by Heaven made silken soft
To soothe the brow of love or pain,
Alas! are dulled and soiled too oft
By some unhallowed earthly stain;
But under the celestial bound
No nobler picture can be found
Than woman, brave in word and deed,
Thus serving in her nation's need:
Her love is with her country now,
Her hand is on its aching brow.

5. Within its shade of elm and oak
The church of Berkley Manor stood:
There Sunday found the rural folk,
And some esteemed of gentle blood.
In vain their feet with loitering tread
Passed 'mid the graves where rank is naught:
All could not read the lesson taught
In that republic of the dead.

6. The pastor rose: the prayer was strong;
The psalm was warrior David's song;
The text, a few short words of might,—
"The Lord of hosts shall arm the right!"

7. He spoke of wrongs too long endured,
Of sacred rights to be secured;
Then from his patriot tongue of flame
The startling words for Freedom came.
The stirring sentences he spake
Compelled the heart to glow or quake,
And, rising on his theme's broad wing,
  And grasping in his nervous hand
  The imaginary battle brand,
In face of death he dared to fling
Defiance to a tyrant king.

8. Even as he spoke, his frame, renewed
In eloquence of attitude,
Rose, as it seemed, a shoulder higher;
Then swept his kindling glance of fire
From startled pew to breathless choir;
When suddenly his mantle wide
His hands impatient flung aside,
And, lo! he met their wondering eyes
Complete in all a warrior's guise.

9. A moment there was awful pause,—
  When Berkley cried, "Cease, traitor! cease!
  God's temple is the house of peace!"
The other shouted, "Nay, not so,
When God is with our righteous cause:
  His holiest places then are ours,
  His temples are our forts and towers
That frown upon the tyrant foe:
In this the dawn of Freedom's day
There is a time to fight and pray!"

10. And now before the open door—
The warrior priest had ordered so—
The enlisting trumpet's sudden soar
Rang through the chapel, o'er and o'ėr,
Its long reverberating blow,
So loud and clear, it seemed the ear
Of dusty death must wake and hear.
And there the startling drum and fife
Fired the living with fiercer life;
While overhead with wild increase,
Forgetting its ancient toll of peace,
The great bell swung as ne'er before;
It seemed as it would never cease;
And every word its ardor flung
From off its jubilant iron tongue
Was, "WAR! WAR! WAR!"

11. "Who dares"—this was the patriot's cry,
As striding from the desk he came—
"Come out with me, in Freedom's name,
For her to live, for her to die?"
A hundred hands flung up reply,
A hundred voices answered "*I!*"

DEFINITIONS.—1. Bo′re-al, *northern*. 3. Yeō′man, *a freeholder, a man freeborn*. Dĭnt, *stroke*. 5. Măn′or, *a tract of land occupied by tenants*. Gĕn′tle (*pro.* jĕn′tl), *well born, of good family*. 7. Thēme, *a subject on which a person speaks or writes*. 8. Guīṣe, *external appearance in manner or dress*. 10. Sōar, *a towering flight*.

NOTES.—2. *Forgot her . . . name*. The reference is to the meaning of the word "concord,"—*harmony, union*.

4. *Celestial bound; i.e.*, the sky, heaven.

6. *The pastor*. This was John Peter Gabriel Muhlenberg, who was at this time a minister at Woodstock, in Virginia. He was a leading spirit among those opposed to Great Britain, and in 1775 he was elected colonel of a Virginia regiment. The above

poem describes his farewell sermon. At its close he threw off his ministerial gown, and appeared in full regimental dress. Almost every man in the congregation enlisted under him at the church door. Muhlenberg became a well-known general in the Revolution, and after the war served his country in Congress and in various official positions.

LXVI. CONTROL YOUR TEMPER.

John Todd, D.D. (*b.* 1800, *d.* 1873), was born in Rutland, Vt. In 1842 he was settled as a pastor of a Congregational Church, in Pittsfield, Mass. In 1834, he published "Lectures to Children"; in 1835, "The Student's Manual," a valuable and popular work, which has been translated into several European languages; in 1836, "The Sabbath-School Teacher"; and in 1841, "The Lost Sister of Wyoming." He was one of the founders of the Mount Holyoke Female Seminary.

1. No one has a temper naturally so good, that it does not need attention and cultivation, and no one has a temper so bad, but that, by proper culture, it may become pleasant. One of the best disciplined tempers ever seen, was that of a gentleman who was naturally quick, irritable, rash, and violent; but, by having the care of the sick, and especially of deranged people, he so completely mastered himself that he was never known to be thrown off his guard.

2. The difference in the happiness which is received or bestowed by the man who governs his temper, and that by the man who does not, is immense. There is no misery so constant, so distressing, and so intolerable to others, as that of having a disposition which is your master, and which is continually fretting itself. There are corners enough, at every turn in life, against which we may run, and at which we may break out in impatience, if we choose.

3. Look at Roger Sherman, who rose from a humble occupation to a seat in the first Congress of the United States, and whose judgment was received with great defer-

ence by that body of distinguished men. He made himself master of his temper, and cultivated it as a great business in life. There are one or two instances which show this part of his character in a light that is beautiful.

4. One day, after having received his highest honors, he was sitting and reading in his parlor. A roguish student, in a room close by, held a looking-glass in such a position as to pour the reflected rays of the sun directly in Mr. Sherman's face. He moved his chair, and the thing was repeated. A third time the chair was moved, but the looking-glass still reflected the sun in his eyes. He laid aside his book, went to the window, and many witnesses of the impudence expected to hear the ungentlemanly student severely reprimanded. He raised the window gently, and then—shut the window blind!

5. I can not forbear adducing another instance of the power he had acquired over himself. He was naturally possessed of strong passions; but over these he at length obtained an extraordinary control. He became habitually calm, sedate, and self-possessed. Mr. Sherman was one of those men who are not ashamed to maintain the forms of religion in their families. One morning he called them all together, as usual, to lead them in prayer to God; the "old family Bible" was brought out, and laid on the table.

6. Mr. Sherman took his seat, and placed beside him one of his children, a child of his old age; the rest of the family were seated around the room; several of these were now grown up. Besides these, some of the tutors of the college were boarders in the family, and were present at the time alluded to. His aged and superannuated mother occupied a corner of the room, opposite the place where the distinguished judge sat.

7. At length, he opened the Bible, and began to read. The child who was seated beside him made some little disturbance, upon which Mr. Sherman paused and told it to be still. Again he proceeded; but again he paused to

reprimand the little offender, whose playful disposition would scarcely permit it to be still. And this time he gently tapped its ear. The blow, if blow it might be called, caught the attention of his aged mother, who now, with some effort, rose from the seat, and tottered across the room. At length she reached the chair of Mr. Sherman, and, in a moment, most unexpectedly to him, she gave him a blow on the ear with all the force she could summon. "There," said she, "you strike your child, and I will strike mine."

8. For a moment, the blood was seen mounting to the face of Mr. Sherman; but it was only for a moment, when all was calm and mild as usual. He paused; he raised his spectacles; he cast his eye upon his mother; again it fell upon the book from which he had been reading. Not a word escaped him; but again he calmly pursued the service, and soon after sought in prayer an ability to set an example before his household which would be worthy of their imitation. Such a victory was worth more than the proudest one ever achieved on the field of battle.

Definitions.—1. Con-trōl′, *subdue, restrain, govern.* Cŭl′ture, *cultivation, improvement by effort.* Dĭs′çi-plĭned, *brought under control, trained* 2. In-tŏl′er-a-ble, *not capable of being borne.* 3. Dĕf′er-ençe, *regard, respect.* 4. Rĕp′ri-mănd-ed, *reproved for a fault.* 6. Sū-per-ăn′nu-ā-ted, *impaired by old age and infirmity.* 8. A-chiēved′, *gained.*

Note.—*Roger Sherman* (*b.* 1721, *d.* 1793) was born at Newton Massachusetts, and until twenty-two years of age was a shoemaker. He then removed to New Milford, Connecticut, and was soon afterward appointed surveyor of lands for the county. In 1754, he was admitted to the bar. At various times he was elected a judge; sent to the Legislature, to the Colonial Assembly, and to the United States Congress; made a member of the governor's council of safety; and, in 1776, a member of the committee appointed to draft the Declaration of Independence, of which he was one of the signers.

LXVII. WILLIAM TELL.

James Sheridan Knowles (*b.* 1784, *d.* 1862), a dramatist and actor, was born in Cork, Ireland. In 1792 his father removed to London with his family. At the age of fourteen, Sheridan wrote an opera called "The Chevalier de Grillon." In 1798 he removed to Dublin, and soon after began his career as an actor and author. In 1835 he visited America. In 1839 an annual pension of £200 was granted him by the British government. Several years before his death he left the stage and became a Baptist minister. The best known of his plays are "Caius Gracchus," "Virginius," "Leo, the Gypsy," "The Hunchback," and "William Tell," from the last of which the following two lessons are abridged.

SCENE 1. — *A Chamber in the Castle. Enter Gesler, Officers, and Sarnem, with Tell in chains and guarded.*

Sar. DOWN, slave! Behold the governor.
Down! down! and beg for mercy.
Ges. (*Seated.*) Does he hear?
Sar. He does, but braves thy power.
Officer. Why don't you smite him for that look?
Ges. Can I believe
My eyes? He smiles! Nay, grasps
His chains as he would make a weapon of them
To lay the smiter dead. (*To Tell.*)
Why speakest thou not?
Tell. For wonder.
Ges. Wonder?
Tell. Yes, that thou shouldst seem a man.
Ges. What should I seem?
Tell. A monster.
Ges. Ha! Beware! Think on thy chains.
Tell. Though they were doubled, and did weigh me down
Prostrate to the earth, methinks I could rise up
Erect, with nothing but the honest pride
Of telling thee, usurper, to thy teeth,
Thou art a monster! Think upon my chains?
How came they on me?

Ges. Darest thou question me?
Tell. Darest thou not answer?
Ges. Do I hear?
Tell. Thou dost.
Ges. Beware my vengeance!
Tell. Can it more than kill?
Ges. Enough; it can do that.
Tell. No; not enough:
It can not take away the grace of life;
Its comeliness of look that virtue gives;
Its port erect with consciousness of truth;
Its rich attire of honorable deeds;
Its fair report that's rife on good men's tongues;
It can not lay its hands on these, no more
Than it can pluck the brightness from the sun,
Or with polluted finger tarnish it.
Ges. But it can make thee writhe.
Tell. It may.
Ges. And groan.
Tell. It may; and I may cry
Go on, though it should make me groan again.
Ges. Whence comest thou?
Tell. From the mountains. Wouldst thou learn
What news from thence?
Ges. Canst tell me any?
Tell. Ay: they watch no more the avalanche.
Ges. Why so?
Tell. Because they look for thee. The hurricane
Comes unawares upon them; from its bed
The torrent breaks, and finds them in its track.
Ges. What do they then?
Tell. Thank heaven it is not thou!
Thou hast perverted nature in them.
There's not a blessing heaven vouchsafes them, but
The thought of thee—doth wither to a curse.
Ges. That's right! I'd have them like their hills,

That never smile, though wanton summer tempt
Them e'er so much.

Tell. But they do sometimes smile.

Ges. Ay! when is that?

Tell. When they do talk of vengeance.

Ges. Vengeance? Dare they talk of that?

Tell. Ay, and expect it too.

Ges. From whence?

Tell. From heaven!

Ges. From heaven?

Tell. And their true hands
Are lifted up to it on every hill
For justice on thee.

Ges. Where's thy abode?

Tell. I told thee, on the mountains.

Ges. Art married?

Tell. Yes.

Ges. And hast a family?

Tell. A son.

Ges. A son? Sarnem!

Sar. My lord, the boy — (*Gesler signs to Sarnem to keep silence, and, whispering, sends him off.*)

Tell. The boy? What boy?
Is 't mine? and have they netted my young fledgeling?
Now heaven support me, if they have! He'll own me,
And share his father's ruin! But a look
Would put him on his guard — yet how to give it!
Now heart, thy nerve; forget thou 'rt flesh, be rock.
They come, they come!
That step — that step — that little step, so light
Upon the ground, how heavy does it fall
Upon my heart! I feel my child! (*Enter Sarnem with Albert, whose eyes are riveted on Tell's bow, which Sarnem carries.*)
'T is he! We can but perish.

Alb. (*Aside.*) Yes; I was right. It is my father's bow!
For there's my father! I'll not own him though!

Sar. See!

Alb. What?

Sar. Look there!

Alb. I do, what would you have me see?

Sar. Thy father.

Alb. Who? That—that my father?

Tell. My boy! my boy! my own brave boy!
He's safe! (*Aside.*)

Sar. (*Aside to Gesler.*) They're like each other.

Ges. Yet I see no sign
Of recognition to betray the link
Unites a father and his child.

Sar. My lord,
I am sure it is his father. Look at them.
That boy did spring from him; or never cast
Came from the mold it fitted! It may be
A preconcerted thing 'gainst such a chance,
That they survey each other coldly thus.

Ges. We shall try. Lead forth the caitiff.

Sar. To a dungeon?

Ges. No; into the court.

Sar. The court, my lord?

Ges. And send
To tell the headsman to make ready. Quick!
The slave shall die! You marked the boy?

Sar. I did. He started; 't is his father.

Ges. We shall see. Away with him!

Tell. Stop! Stop!

Ges. What would you?

Tell. Time,—
A little time to call my thoughts together!

Ges. Thou shalt not have a minute.

Tell. Some one, then, to speak with.

Ges. Hence with him!

Tell. A moment! Stop!
Let me speak to the boy.
Ges. Is he thy son?
Tell. And if
He were, art thou so lost to nature, as
To send me forth to die before his face?
Ges. Well! speak with him.
Now, Sarnem, mark them well.
Tell. Thou dost not know me, boy; and well for thee
Thou dost not. I'm the father of a son
About thy age. Thou,
I see, wast born, like him, upon the hills:
If thou shouldst 'scape thy present thraldom, he
May chance to cross thee; if he should, I pray thee
Relate to him what has been passing here,
And say I laid my hand upon thy head,
And said to thee, if he were here, as thou art,
Thus would I bless him. Mayst thou live, my boy,
To see thy country free, or die for her,
As I do! (*Albert weeps.*)
Sar. Mark! he weeps.
Tell. Were he my son,
He would not shed a tear! He would remember
The cliff where he was bred, and learned to scan
A thousand fathoms' depth of nether air;
Where he was trained to hear the thunder talk,
And meet the lightning, eye to eye; where last
We spoke together, when I told him death
Bestowed the brightest gem that graces life,
Embraced for virtue's sake. He shed a tear!
Now were he by, I'd talk to him, and his cheek
Should never blanch, nor moisture dim his eye—
I'd talk to him—
Sar. He falters!
Tell. 'T is too much!
And yet it must be done! I'd talk to him—

Ges. Of what?

Tell. The mother, tyrant, thou dost make
A widow of! I'd talk to him of her.
I'd bid him tell her, next to liberty,
Her name was the last word my lips pronounced.
And I would charge him never to forget
To love and cherish her, as he would have
His father's dying blessing rest upon him!

Sar. You see, as he doth prompt, the other acts.

Tell. So well he bears it, he doth vanquish me.
My boy! my boy! Oh, for the hills, the hills,
To see him bound along their tops again,
With liberty.

Sar. Was there not all the father in that look?

Ges. Yet 't is 'gainst nature.

Sar. Not if he believes
To own the son would be to make him share
The father's death.

Ges. I did not think of that! 'T is well
The boy is not thy son. I've destined him
To die along with thee.

Tell. To die? For what?

Ges. For having braved my power, as thou hast. Lead them forth.

Tell. He's but a child.

Ges. Away with them!

Tell. Perhaps an only child.

Ges. No matter.

Tell. He may have a mother.

Ges. So the viper hath;
And yet, who spares it for the mother's sake?

Tell. I talk to stone! I talk to it as though
'T were flesh; and know 't is none. I'll talk to it
No more. Come, my boy;
I taught thee how to live, I'll show thee how to die.

Ges. He is thy child?

Tell. He is my child. (*Weeps.*)

Ges. I've wrung a tear from him! Thy name?

Tell. My name?
It matters not to keep it from thee now;
My name is Tell.

Ges. Tell? William Tell?

Tell. The same.

Ges. What! he, so famed 'bove all his countrymen,
For guiding o'er the stormy lake the boat?
And such a master of his bow, 't is said
His arrows never miss! Indeed! I'll take
Exquisite vengeance! Mark! I'll spare thy life;
Thy boy's too; both of you are free; on one
Condition.

Tell. Name it.

Ges. I would see you make
A trial of your skill with that same bow
You shoot so well with.

Tell. Name the trial you
Would have me make.

Ges. You look upon your boy
As though instinctively you guessed it.

Tell. Look upon my boy? What mean you? Look upon
My boy as though I guessed it? Guessed the trial
You'd have me make? Guessed it
Instinctively? You do not mean — no — no,
You would not have me make a trial of
My skill upon my child! Impossible!
I do not guess your meaning.

Ges. I would see
Thee hit an apple at the distance of
A hundred paces.

Tell. Is my boy to hold it?

Ges. No.

Tell. No? I'll send the arrow through the core!

Ges. It is to rest upon his head.

Tell. Great heaven, you hear him!
Ges. Thou dost hear the choice I give:
Such trial of the skill thou art master of,
Or death to both of you, not otherwise
To be escaped.
Tell. O, monster!
Ges. Wilt thou do it?
Alb. He will! he will!
Tell. Ferocious monster! Make
A father murder his own child!
Ges. Take off his chains if he consent.
Tell. With his own hand!
Ges. Does he consent?
Alb. He does. (*Gesler signs to his officers, who proceed to take off Tell's chains; Tell unconscious what they do.*)
Tell. With his own hand!
Murder his child with his own hand? This hand?
The hand I've led him, when an infant, by?
'T is beyond horror! 'T is most horrible!
Amazement! (*His chains fall off.*) What 's that you 've done to me?
Villains! put on my chains again. My hands
Are free from blood, and have no gust for it,
That they should drink my child's! Here! here! I'll
Not murder my boy for Gesler.
Alb. Father! Father!
You will not hit me, father!
Tell. Hit thee? Send
The arrow through thy brain? Or, missing that,
Shoot out an eye? Or, if thine eye escape,
Mangle the cheek I've seen thy mother's lips
Cover with kisses? Hit thee? Hit a hair
Of thee, and cleave thy mother's heart?
Ges. Dost thou consent?
Tell. Give me my bow and quiver.
Ges. For what?

Tell. To shoot my boy!
Alb. No, father, no!
To save me! You'll be sure to hit the apple.
Will you not save me, father?
Tell. Lead me forth;
I'll make the trial!
Alb. Thank you!
Tell. Thank me? Do
You know for what? I will not make the trial.
To take him to his mother in my arms!
And lay him down a corse before her!
Ges. Then he dies this moment, and you certainly
Do murder him whose life you have a chance
To save, and will not use it.
Tell. Well, I'll do it; I'll make the trial.
Alb. Father!
Tell. Speak not to me:
Let me not hear thy voice: thou must be dumb,
And so should all things be. Earth should be dumb;
And heaven — unless its thunders muttered at
The deed, and sent a bolt to stop! Give me
My bow and quiver!
Ges. When all's ready.
Tell. Ready! —
I must be calm with such a mark to hit!
Don't touch me, child! — Don't speak to me! — Lead on!

DEFINITIONS. — Cȯme′li-ness, *that which is becoming or graceful.* Pōrt, *manner of movement or walk.* At-tīre′, *dress, clothes.* Tär′-nish, *to soil, to sully.* Av′a-lănçhe, *a vast body of snow, earth, and ice, sliding down from a mountain.* Vouch-sāfes′, *yields, condescends, gives.* Wạn′ton, *luxuriant.* Nĕt′ted, *caught in a net.* Flĕdġe′ling, *a young bird.* Rĕe-oḡ-nĭ′tion, *acknowledgment of acquaintance.* Pre-con-çẽrt′ed, *planned beforehand.* Cāi′tiff (*pro.* kā′tif), *a mean villain.* Thrạl′dȯm, *bondage, slavery.* Seăn, *to examine closely.* Nĕth′er, *lower, lying beneath.* Blȧnch, *to turn white.* Gŭst, *taste, relish.*

NOTE.—*William Tell* is a legendary hero of Switzerland. The events of this drama are represented as occurring in 1307 A.D., when Austria held Switzerland under her control. Gesler, also a purely mythical personage, is one of the Austrian bailiffs. The legend relates that Gesler had his cap placed on a pole in the market place, and all the Swiss were required to salute it in passing in recognition of his authority. Tell refusing to do this was arrested, and condemned to death. This and the following lesson narrate how the sentence was changed, and the result.

LXVIII. WILLIAM TELL.

(Concluded.)

SCENE 2.—*Enter slowly, people in evident distress—Officers, Sarnem, Gesler, Tell, Albert, and soldiers—one bearing Tell's bow and quiver—another with a basket of apples.*

Ges. That is your ground. Now shall they measure thence
A hundred paces. Take the distance.
Tell. Is the line a true one?
Ges. True or not, what is't to thee?
Tell. What is't to me? A little thing.
A very little thing; a yard or two
Is nothing here or there—were it a wolf
I shot at! Never mind.
Ges. Be thankful, slave,
Our grace accords thee life on any terms.
Tell. I will be thankful, Gesler! Villain, stop!
You measure to the sun.
Ges. And what of that?
What matter whether to or from the sun?
Tell. I'd have it at my back. The sun should shine
Upon the mark, and not on him that shoots.

I can not see to shoot against the sun:
I will not shoot against the sun!

Ges. Give him his way! Thou hast cause to bless my mercy.

Tell. I shall remember it. I'd like to see
The apple I'm to shoot at.

Ges. Stay! show me the basket! there!

Tell. You've picked the smallest one.

Ges. I know I have.

Tell. Oh, do you? But you see
The color of it is dark: I'd have it light,
To see it better.

Ges. Take it as it is;
Thy skill will be the greater if thou hitt'st it.

Tell. True! true! I did not think of that; I wonder
I did not think of that. Give me some chance
To save my boy!—
I will not murder him,
If I can help it—for the honor of
The form thou wearest, if all the heart is gone.
(*Throws away the apple with all his force.*)

Ges. Well: choose thyself.

Tell. Have I a friend among the lookers-on?

Verner. (*Rushing forward.*) Here, Tell.

Tell. I thank thee, Verner!
He is a friend runs out into a storm
To shake a hand with us. I must be brief.
When once the bow is bent, we can not take
The shot too soon. Verner, whatever be
The issue of this hour, the common cause
Must not stand still. Let not to-morrow's sun
Set on the tyrant's banner! Verner! Verner!
The boy! the boy! Thinkest thou he hath the courage
To stand it?

Ver. Yes.

Tell. Does he tremble?
Ver. No.
Tell. Art sure?
Ver. I am.
Tell. How looks he?
Ver. Clear and smilingly.
If you doubt it, look yourself.
Tell. No, no, my friend:
To hear it is enough.
Ver. He bears himself so much above his years—
Tell. I know! I know!
Ver. With constancy so modest—
Tell. I was sure he would—
Ver. And looks with such relying love
And reverence upon you—
Tell. Man! Man! Man!
No more! Already I'm too much the father
To act the man! Verner, no more, my friend!
I would be flint—flint—flint. Don't make me feel
I'm not—do not mind me! Take the boy
And set him, Verner, with his back to me.
Set him upon his knees, and place this apple
Upon his head, so that the stem may front me.
Thus, Verner; charge him to keep steady; tell him
I'll hit the apple! Verner, do all this
More briefly than I tell it thee.
Ver. Come, Albert! (*Leading him out.*)
Alb. May I not speak with him before I go?
Ver. No.
Alb. I would only kiss his hand.
Ver. You must not.
Alb. I must; I can not go from him without.
Ver. It is his will you should.
Alb. His will, is it?
I am content, then; come.
Tell. My boy! (*Holding out his arms to him.*)

Alb. My father! (*Rushing into Tell's arms.*)

Tell. If thou canst bear it, should not I? Go now,
My son; and keep in mind that I can shoot;
Go, boy; be thou but steady, I will hit
The apple. Go! God bless thee; go. My bow!
(*The bow is handed to him.*)
Thou wilt not fail thy master, wilt thou? Thou
Hast never failed him yet, old servant. No,
I'm sure of thee. I know thy honesty,
Thou art stanch, stanch. Let me see my quiver.

Ges. Give him a single arrow.

Tell. Do you shoot?

Soldier. I do.

Tell. Is it so you pick an arrow, friend?
The point, you see, is bent; the feather, jagged.
That's all the use 't is fit for.. (*Breaks it.*)

Ges. Let him have another.

Tell. Why, 't is better than the first,
But yet not good enough for such an aim
As I'm to take. 'T is heavy in the shaft;
I'll not shoot with it! (*Throws it away.*) Let me see my quiver.
Bring it! 'T is not one arrow in a dozen
I'd take to shoot with at a dove, much less
A dove like that.

Ges. It matters not.
Show him the quiver.

Tell. See if the boy is ready.
(*Tell here hides an arrow under his vest.*)

Ver. He is.

Tell. I'm ready too! Keep silent, for
Heaven's sake, and do not stir; and let me have
Your prayers, your prayers, and be my witnesses
That if his life's in peril from my hand,
'T is only for the chance of saving it. (*To the people.*)

Ges. Go on.

Tell. I will.
O friends, for mercy's sake keep motionless and silent. (*Tell shoots. A shout of exultation bursts from the crowd. Tell's head drops on his bosom; he with difficulty supports himself on his bow.*)

Ver. (*Rushing in with Albert.*) The boy is safe, no hair of him is touched.

Alb. Father, I'm safe. Your Albert's safe, dear father. Speak to me! Speak to me!

Ver. He can not, boy!

Alb. You grant him life?

Ges. I do.

Alb. And we are free?

Ges. You are. (*Crossing angrily behind.*)

Alb. Open his vest,
And give him air. (*Albert opens his father's vest, and the arrow drops. Tell starts, fixes his eyes on Albert and clasps him to his breast.*)

Tell. My boy! My boy!

Ges. For what
Hid you that arrow in your breast? Speak, slave!

Tell. To kill thee, tyrant, had I slain my boy!

Definitions.—Ac-côrds′, *grants, concedes.* Is′sue (*pro.* ĭsh′u), *event, consequence.* Stȧnch, *sound, strong.* Jăg′ged, *notched, uneven.* Shȧft, *the stem of an arrow upon which the feather and head are inserted.* Quĭv′er, *a case for arrows.*

Note.—The legend further relates that on the discovery of the concealed arrow Tell was again put in chains. Gesler then embarked for another place, taking Tell with him. A storm overtook them, and Tell was released to steer the boat. In passing a certain point of land, now known as "Tell's Rock" or "Leap," Tell leaped ashore and escaped: then going to a point where he knew the boat must land, he lay concealed until it arrived, when he shot Gesler through the heart.

LXIX. THE CRAZY ENGINEER.

1. My train left Dantzic in the morning generally about eight o'clock; but once a week we had to wait for the arrival of the steamer from Stockholm. It was the morning of the steamer's arrival that I came down from the hotel, and found that my engineer had been so seriously injured that he could not perform his work. I went immediately to the engine house to procure another engineer, for I supposed there were three or four in reserve there, but I was disappointed.

2. I heard the puffing of the steamer, and the passengers would be on hand in fifteen minutes. I ran to the guards and asked them if they knew where there was an engineer, but they did not. I then went to the firemen and asked them if any one of them felt competent to run the engine to Bromberg. No one dared to attempt it. The distance was nearly one hundred miles. What was to be done?

3. The steamer stopped at the wharf, and those who were going on by rail came flocking to the station. They had eaten breakfast on board the boat, and were all ready for a fresh start. The train was in readiness in the long station house, and the engine was steaming and puffing away impatiently in the distant firing house.

4. It was past nine o'clock. "Come, why don't we start?" growled an old, fat Swede, who had been watching me narrowly for the last fifteen minutes. And upon this there was a general chorus of anxious inquiry, which soon settled to downright murmuring. At this juncture some one touched me on the elbow. I turned, and saw a stranger by my side. I thought that he was going to remonstrate with me for my backwardness. In fact, I began to have strong temptations to pull off my uniform, for every anxious eye was fixed upon the glaring badges which marked me as the chief officer of the train.

5. However, this stranger was a middle-aged man, tall

and stout, with a face of great energy and intelligence. His eye was black and brilliant,—so brilliant that I could not gaze steadily into it, though I tried; and his lips, which were very thin, seemed more like polished marble than human flesh. His dress was black throughout, and not only set with exact nicety, but was scrupulously clean and neat.

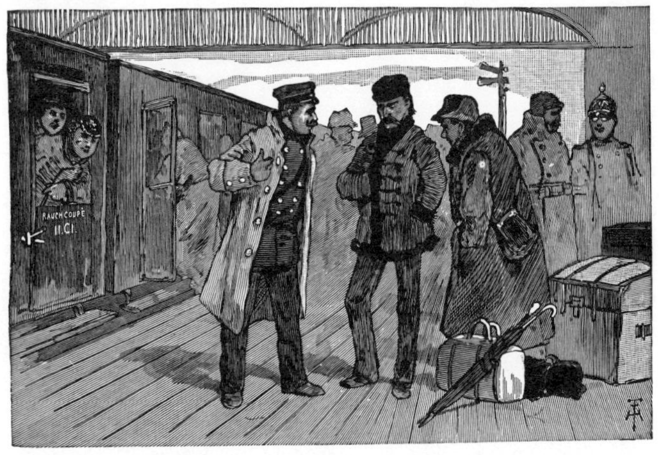

6. "You want an engineer, I understand," he said in a low, cautious tone, at the same time gazing quietly about him, as though he wanted no one to hear what he said.

"I do," I replied. "My train is all ready, and we have no engineer within twenty miles of this place."

"Well, sir, I am going to Bromberg; I must go, and I will run the engine for you."

"Ha!" I uttered, "are you an engineer?"

"I am, sir—one of the oldest in the country—and am now on my way to make arrangements for a great improvement I have invented for the application of steam to a locomotive. My name is Martin Kroller. If you wish, I will run as far as Bromberg; and I will show you running that is running."

7. Was I not fortunate? I determined to accept the man's offer at once, and so I told him. He received my answer with a nod and a smile. I went with him to the house, where we found the engine in charge of the fireman, and all ready for a start. Kroller got upon the platform, and I followed him. I had never seen a man betray such a peculiar aptness amid machinery as he did. He let on the steam in an instant, but yet with care and judgment, and he backed up to the baggage carriage with the most exact nicety.

8. I had seen enough to assure me that he was thoroughly acquainted with the business, and I felt composed once more. I gave my engine up to the new man, and then hastened away to the office. Word was passed for all the passengers to take their seats, and soon afterward I waved my hand to the engineer. There was a puff, a groaning of the heavy axletrees, a trembling of the building, and the train was in motion. I leaped upon the platform of the guard carriage, and in a few minutes more the station house was far behind us.

9. In less than an hour we reached Dirschau, where we took up the passengers that had come on the Königsberg railway. Here I went forward and asked Kroller how he liked the engine. He replied that he liked it very much.

"But," he added, with a strange sparkling of the eye, "wait until I get my improvement, and then you will see traveling. Why, I could run an engine of my construction to the moon in four and twenty hours?"

10. I smiled at what I thought his enthusiasm, and then went back to my station. As soon as the Königsberg passengers were all on board, and their baggage carriage attached, we started on again. Soon after, I went into the guard carriage and sat down. An early train from Königsberg had been through two hours before, and was awaiting us at Little Oscue, where we took on board the Western mail.

11. "How we go," uttered one of the guards, some fifteen minutes after we had left Dirschau.

"The new engineer is trying the speed," I replied, not yet having any fear. But ere long I began to apprehend he was running a little too fast. The carriages began to sway to and fro, and I could hear exclamations of fright from the passengers.

"Good heavens!" cried one of the guards, coming in at that moment, "what is that fellow doing? Look, sir, and see how we are going."

12. I looked at the window, and found that we were dashing along at a speed never before traveled on that road. Posts, fences, rocks, and trees flew by in one undistinguished mass, and the carriages now swayed fearfully. I started to my feet, and met a passenger on the platform. He was one of the chief owners of our road, and was just on his way to Berlin. He was pale and excited.

13. "Sir," he gasped, "is Martin Kroller on the engine?"

"Yes," I told him.

"What! didn't you know him?"

"Know?" I repeated, somewhat puzzled; "what do you mean? He told me his name was Kroller, and that he was an engineer. We had no one to run the engine, and—"

"You took *him!*" interrupted the man. "Good heavens, sir, he is as crazy as a man can be! He turned his brain over a new plan for applying steam power. I saw him at the station, but did not fully recognize him, as I was in a hurry. Just now one of your passengers told me that your engineers were all gone this morning, and that you found one that was a stranger to you. Then I knew the man whom I had seen was Martin Kroller. He had escaped from the hospital at Stettin. You must get him off somehow."

14. The whole fearful truth was now open to me. The speed of the train was increasing every moment, and I knew that a few more miles per hour would launch us all into destruction. I called to the guard, and then made my

way forward as quickly as possible. I reached the back platform of the tender, and there stood Kroller upon the engine board, his hat and coat off, his long black hair floating wildly in the wind, his shirt unbuttoned at the front, his sleeves rolled up, with a pistol in his teeth, and thus glaring upon the fireman, who lay motionless upon the fuel. The furnace was stuffed till the very latch of the door was red-hot, and the whole engine was quivering and swaying as though it would shiver to pieces.

15. "Kroller! Kroller!" I cried, at the top of my voice.

The crazy engineer started, and caught the pistol in his hand. Oh, how those great black eyes glared, and how ghastly and frightful the face looked!

"Ha! ha! ha!" he yelled demoniacally, glaring upon me like a roused lion.

"They said that I could not make it! But see! see! See my new power! See my new engine! I made it, and they are jealous of me! I made it, and when it was done, they stole it from me. But I have found it! For years I have been wandering in search of my great engine, and they said it was not made. But I have found it! I knew it this morning when I saw it at Dantzic, and I was determined to have it. And I've got it! Ho! ho! ho! we're on the way to the moon, I say! We'll be in the moon in four and twenty hours. Down, down, villain! If you move, I'll shoot you."

This was spoken to the poor fireman, who at that moment attempted to rise, and the frightened man sank back again.

16. "Here's Little Oscue just before us," cried out one of the guard. But even as he spoke, the buildings were at hand. A sickening sensation settled upon my heart, for I supposed that we were now gone. The houses flew by like lightning. I knew if the officers here had turned the switch as usual, we should be hurled into eternity in one fearful crash. I saw a flash,—it was another engine,—I closed my eyes; but still we thundered on! The officers had seen

our speed, and knowing that we would not be able to stop, in that distance, they had changed the switch, so that we went forward.

17. But there was sure death ahead, if we did not stop. Only fifteen miles from us was the town of Schwetz, on the Vistula; and at the rate we were going we should be there in a few minutes, for each minute carried us over a mile. The shrieks of the passengers now rose above the crash of the rails, and more terrific than all else arose the demoniac yells of the mad engineer.

"Merciful heavens!" gasped the guardsman, "there's not a moment to lose; Schwetz is close. But hold," he added; "let's shoot him."

18. At that moment a tall, stout German student came over the platform where we stood, and saw that the madman had his heavy pistol aimed at us. He grasped a huge stick of wood, and, with a steadiness of nerve which I could not have commanded, he hurled it with such force and precision that he knocked the pistol from the maniac's hand. I saw the movement, and on the instant that the pistol fell, I sprang forward, and the German followed me. I grasped the man by the arm; but I should have been nothing in his mad power, had I been alone. He would have hurled me from the platform, had not the student at that moment struck him upon the head with a stick of wood, which he caught as he came over the tender.

19. Kroller settled down like a dead man, and on the next instant I shut off the steam and opened the valve. As the free steam shrieked and howled in its escape, the speed began to decrease, and in a few minutes more the danger was passed. As I settled back, entirely overcome by the wild emotions that had raged within me, we began to turn the river; and before I was fairly recovered, the fireman had stopped the train in the station house at Schwetz.

20. Martin Kroller, still insensible, was taken from the

platform; and, as we carried him to the guard room, one of the guard recognized him, and told us that he had been there about two weeks before.

"He came," said the guard, "and swore that an engine which stood near by was his. He said it was one he had made to go to the moon in, and that it had been stolen from him. We sent for more help to arrest him, and he fled."

"Well," I replied, with a shudder, "I wish he had approached me in the same way; but he was more cautious at Dantzic."

At Schwartz we found an engineer to run the engine to Bromberg; and having taken out the western mail for the next northern mail to carry along, we saw that Kroller would be properly attended to, and then started on.

21. The rest of the trip we ran in safety, though I could see the passengers were not wholly at ease, and would not be until they were entirely clear of the railway. Martin Kroller remained insensible from the effects of the blow nearly two weeks; and when he recovered from that, he was sound again; his insanity was all gone. I saw him about three weeks afterward, but he had no recollection of me. He remembered nothing of the past year, not even his mad freak on my engine. But I remembered it, and I remember it still; and the people need never fear that I shall be imposed upon again by a crazy engineer.

Definitions.—2. Cŏm′pe-tent, *fit, qualified*. 4. Jŭn͟e′ture, *point of time, crisis*. Re-mŏn′strāte, *to present strong reasons against any course of proceedings*. 7. Apt′ness, *fitness, suitableness*. 8. Com-pōṣed′, *calm*. 11. Ap-pre-hĕnd′, *to entertain suspicion or fear of*. 14. Tĕn′der, *a car attached to a locomotive to supply it with fuel and water*. 18. Pre-çĭ′ṣion (*pro*. pre-sĭzh′un), *accuracy, exactness*.

Note.—This incident is said to have taken place on the railway following the valley of the Vistula River, in Prussia, from Dantzic to Bromberg. The cities mentioned are all in Prussia, excepting Stockholm, which is the capital of Sweden.

LXX. THE HERITAGE.

James Russell Lowell (*b.* 1819, *d.* 1891) was born in Cambridge, Mass., and was graduated from Harvard College. He entered the profession of law; but, in 1843, turned aside to publish "The Pioneer, a Literary and Critical Magazine." In 1855 he was appointed professor of Belles-lettres in Harvard College. From 1877 to 1885 he was U.S. Minister, first to Spain, afterwards to Great Britain. Lowell's powers as a writer were very versatile, and his poems range from the most dreamy and imaginative to the most trenchant and witty. Among his most noted poetical works are "The Biglow Papers," "A Fable for Critics," "The Vision of Sir Launfal," "The Cathedral," and "The Legend of Brittany;" while "Conversations on some of the Old Poets," "Among my Books," and "My Study Windows," place him in the front rank as an essayist.

1. The rich man's son inherits lands,
   And piles of brick, and stone, and gold,
And he inherits soft white hands,
   And tender flesh that fears the cold,
   Nor dares to wear a garment old;
A heritage, it seems to me,
One scarce would wish to hold in fee.

2. The rich man's son inherits cares;
   The bank may break, the factory burn,
A breath may burst his bubble shares,
   And soft white hands could hardly earn
   A living that would serve his turn;
A heritage, it seems to me,
One scarce would wish to hold in fee.

3. The rich man's son inherits wants,
   His stomach craves for dainty fare;
With sated heart, he hears the pants
   Of toiling hinds with brown arms bare,
   And wearies in his easy-chair;
A heritage, it seems to me,
One scarce would wish to hold in fee.

4. What doth the poor man's son inherit?
Stout muscles and a sinewy heart,
A hardy frame, a hardier spirit;
King of two hands, he does his part
In every useful toil and art;
A heritage, it seems to me,
A king might wish to hold in fee.

5. What doth the poor man's son inherit?
Wishes o'erjoyed with humble things,
A rank adjudged by toil-won merit,
Content that from employment springs,
A heart that in his labor sings;
A heritage, it seems to me,
A king might wish to hold in fee.

6. What doth the poor man's son inherit?
A patience learned of being poor,
Courage, if sorrow come, to bear it,
A fellow-feeling that is sure
To make the outcast bless his door;
A heritage, it seems to me,
A king might wish to hold in fee.

7. O rich man's son! there is a toil
That with all others level stands:
Large charity doth never soil,
But only whiten soft, white hands,—
This is the best crop from thy lands;
A heritage, it seems to me,
Worth being rich to hold in fee.

8. O poor man's son! scorn not thy state;
There is worse weariness than thine
In merely being rich and great:

Toil only gives the soul to shine,
And makes rest fragrant and benign;
A heritage, it seems to me,
Worth being poor to hold in fee.

9. Both, heirs to some six feet of sod,
Are equal in the earth at last;
Both, children of the same dear God,
Prove title to your heirship vast
By record of a well-filled past;
A heritage, it seems to me,
Well worth a life to hold in fee.

Definitions. — 1. Hĕr′it-aġe, *that which is inherited, or taken by descent, from an ancestor*. 3. Săt′ed, *surfeited, glutted*. Hinds, *peasants, countrymen*. 5. Ad-jŭdġed′, *decided, determined*. 8. Be-nign′ (*pro.* be-nīn′), *having healthful qualities, wholesome*.

Notes. — 1. *To hold in fee*, means to have as an inheritance.
9. *Prove title.* That is, to prove the right of ownership.

LXXI. NO EXCELLENCE WITHOUT LABOR.

William Wirt (*b.* 1772, *d.* 1834) was born in Bladensburg, Md. He was admitted to the bar in 1799, and afterwards practiced law, with eminent success, at Richmond and Norfolk, Va. He was one of the counsel for the prosecution in the trial of Aaron Burr for treason. From 1817 to 1829 he was attorney-general for the United States. In 1803 he published the "Letters of a British Spy," a work which attracted much attention, and in 1817 a "Life of Patrick Henry."

1. The education, moral and intellectual, of every individual, must be chiefly his own work. Rely upon it that the ancients were right; both in morals and intellect we give the final shape to our characters, and thus become, emphatically, the architects of our own fortune. How else

could it happen that young men, who have had precisely the same opportunities, should be continually presenting us with such different results, and rushing to such opposite destinies?

2. Difference of talent will not solve it, because that difference is very often in favor of the disappointed candidate. You will see issuing from the walls of the same college, nay, sometimes from the bosom of the same family, two young men, of whom one will be admitted to be a genius of high order, the other scarcely above the point of mediocrity; yet you will see the genius sinking and perishing in poverty, obscurity, and wretchedness; while, on the other hand, you will observe the mediocre plodding his slow but sure way up the hill of life, gaining steadfast footing at every step, and mounting, at length, to eminence and distinction, an ornament to his family, a blessing to his country.

3. Now, whose work is this? Manifestly their own. They are the architects of their respective fortunes. The best seminary of learning that can open its portals to you can do no more than to afford you the opportunity of instruction; but it must depend, at last, on yourselves, whether you will be instructed or not, or to what point you will push your instruction.

4. And of this be assured, I speak from observation a certain truth: THERE IS NO EXCELLENCE WITHOUT GREAT LABOR. It is the fiat of fate, from which no power of genius can absolve you.

5. Genius, unexerted, is like the poor moth that flutters around a candle till it scorches itself to death. If genius be desirable at all, it is only of that great and magnanimous kind, which, like the condor of South America, pitches from the summit of Chimborazo, above the clouds, and sustains itself at pleasure in that empyreal region with an energy rather invigorated than weakened by the effort.

6. It is this capacity for high and long-continued exertion, this vigorous power of profound and searching investigation, this careering and wide-spreading comprehension of mind, and these long reaches of thought, that

"Pluck bright honor from the pale-faced moon,
Or dive into the bottom of the deep,
And pluck up drowned honor by the locks;"

this is the prowess, and these the hardy achievements, which are to enroll your names among the great men of the earth.

DEFINITIONS.—1. Mŏr'al, *relating to duty or obligation.* Ar'-chi-tĕets, *builders, makers.* Dĕs'ti-ny, *ultimate fate, appointed condition.* 2. Căn'di-date, *one who seeks after some honor or office.* Gēn'ius (*pro.* jēn'yus), *a man of superior intellectual powers.* Mē-di-ŏe'ri-ty, *a middle state or degree of talents.* Mē'di-ō-ere (*pro.* mē'di-ō-kr), *a man of moderate talents.* 3. Re-spĕe'tĭve, *particular, own.* 4. Ab-sŏlve', *set free, release from.* Fī'at, *a decree.* 5. Cŏn'-dor, *a large bird of the vulture family.* Em-pŷr'e-al, *relating to the highest and purest region of the heavens.* 6. Ca-reer'ing, *moving rapidly.* Prow'ess (*pro.* prou'es), *bravery, boldness.*

NOTES.—5. *Chimborazo* (*pro.* chim-bo-rä'zo), is an extinct volcano in Ecuador, whose height is 20,517 feet above the sea.

6. The quotation is from Shakespeare's "King Henry IV," *Part* 1, *Act* I, *Scene* 3.

LXXII. THE OLD HOUSE CLOCK.

1. OH! the old, old clock of the household stock,
Was the brightest thing, and neatest;
Its hands, though old, had a touch of gold,
And its chimes rang still the sweetest;

'T was a monitor, too, though its words were few,
  Yet they lived, though nations altered;
And its voice, still strong, warned old and young,
  When the voice of friendship faltered:
"Tick! tick!" it said, "quick, quick, to bed:
  For ten I've given warning;
Up! up! and go, or else you know,
  You'll never rise soon in the morning!"

2. A friendly voice was that old, old clock,
  As it stood in the corner smiling,
And blessed the time with merry chime,
  The wintry hours beguiling;
But a cross old voice was that tiresome clock,
  As it called at daybreak boldly;
When the dawn looked gray o'er the misty way,
  And the early air looked coldly:
"Tick! tick!" it said, "quick out of bed:
  For five I've given warning;
You'll never have health, you'll never have wealth.
  Unless you're up soon in the morning!"

3. Still hourly the sound goes round and round,
  With a tone that ceases never:
While tears are shed for bright days fled,
  And the old friends lost forever!
Its heart beats on, though hearts are gone
  That beat like ours, though stronger;
Its hands still move, though hands we love
  Are clasped on earth no longer!
"Tick! tick!" it said, "to the churchyard bed,
  The grave hath given warning;
Up! up! and rise, and look at the skies,
  And prepare for a heavenly morning!"

LXXIII. THE EXAMINATION

Daniel Pierce Thompson (*b.* 1793, *d.* 1868) was born at Charlestown, Mass., but soon removed with his father to Vermont, where he lived until twenty years of age, on a farm. His means of schooling were most limited, but he was very ambitious and seized every opportunity. By his own efforts he earned enough money to carry him through Middlebury College, where he graduated in 1820. He then went to Virginia as private tutor, and while there was entered at the bar. He shortly returned to Vermont, and opened a law office in Montpelier. In time he was elected a judge, and later secretary of state. From his college days Mr. Thompson was a writer for the various magazines. Among his novels may be mentioned "Locke Amsden, the Schoolmaster," "May Martin, or the Money Diggers," "The Green Mountain Boys," and "The Rangers, or the Tory's Daughter."

1. "HAVE you any questions to ask me in the other branches, sir?" asked Locke.

"Not many," replied Bunker. "There is reading, writing, grammar, etc., which I know nothing about; and as to them, I must, of course, take you by guess, which will not be much of a guess, after all, if I find you have thought well on all other matters. Do you understand philosophy?"

2. "To what branch of philosophy do you allude, sir?"

"To the only branch there is."

"But you are aware that philosophy is divided into different kinds; as, natural, moral, and intellectual."

"Nonsense! philosophy is philosophy, and means the study of the reasons and causes of the things which we see, whether it be applied to a crazy man's dreams, or the roasting of potatoes. Have you attended to it?"

"Yes, to a considerable extent, sir."

3. "I will put a question or two, then, if you please. What is the reason of the fact, for it is a fact, that the damp breath of a person blown on a good knife and on a bad one, will soonest disappear from the well-tempered blade?"

"It may be owing to the difference in the polish of the two blades, perhaps," replied Locke.

4. "Ah! that is an answer that don't go deeper than the surface," rejoined Bunker, humorously. "As good a thinker as you evidently are, you have not thought on this subject, I suspect. It took me a week, in all, I presume, of hard thinking, and making experiments at a blacksmith's shop, to discover the reason of this. It is not the polish; for take two blades of equal polish, and the breath will disappear from one as much quicker than it does from the other, as the blade is better. It is because the material of the blade is more compact or less porous in one case than in the other.

5. "In the first place, I ascertained that the steel was made more compact by being hammered and tempered, and that the better it was tempered the more compact it would become; the size of the pores being made, of course, less in the same proportion. Well, then, I saw the reason I was in search of, at once. For we know a wet sponge is longer in drying than a wet piece of green wood, because the pores of the first are bigger. A seasoned or shrunk piece of wood dries quicker than a green one, for the same reason.

6. "Or you might bore a piece of wood with large gimlet holes, and another with small ones, fill them both with water, and let them stand till the water evaporated, and the difference of time it would take to do this would make the case still more plain. So with the blades: the vapor lingers longest on the worst wrought and tempered one, because the pores, being larger, take in more of the wet particles, and require more time in drying."

7. "Your theory is at least a very ingenious one," observed Locke, "and I am reminded by it of another of the natural phenomena, of the true explanation of which I have not been able to satisfy myself. It is this: what makes the earth freeze harder and deeper under a trodden

path than the untrodden earth around it? All that I have asked, say it is because the trodden earth is more compact. But is that reason a sufficient one?"

8. "No," said Bunker, "but I will tell you what the reason is, for I thought that out long ago. You know that, in the freezing months, much of the warmth we get is given out by the earth, from which, at intervals, if not constantly, to some extent, ascend the warm vapors to mingle with and moderate the cold atmosphere above.

9. "Now these ascending streams of warm air would be almost wholly obstructed by the compactness of a trodden path, and they would naturally divide at some distance below it, and pass up through the loose earth on each side, leaving the ground along the line of the path, to a great depth beneath it, a cold, dead mass, through which the frost would continue to penetrate, unchecked by the internal heat, which, in its unobstructed ascent on each side, would be continually checking or overcoming the frost in its action on the earth around.

10. "That, sir, is the true philosophy of the case, you may depend upon it. But we will now drop the discussion of these matters; for I am abundantly satisfied that you have not only knowledge enough, but that you can think for yourself. And now, sir, all I wish to know further about you is, whether you can teach others to think, which is half the battle with a teacher. But as I have had an eye on this point, while attending to the others, probably one experiment, which I will ask you to make on one of the boys here, will be all I shall want."

"Proceed, sir," said the other.

11. "Ay, sir," rejoined Bunker, turning to the open fire-place, in which the burning wood was sending up a column of smoke, "there, you see that smoke rising, don't you? Well, you and I know the reason why smoke goes upward, but my youngest boy does not, I think. Now take your own way, and see if you can make him understand it."

12. Locke, after a moment's reflection, and a glance round the room for something to serve for apparatus, took from a shelf, where he had espied a number of articles, the smallest of a set of cast-iron cart boxes, as are usually termed the round hollow tubes in which the axletree of a carriage turns. Then selecting a tin cup that would just take in the box, and turning into the cup as much water as he judged, with the box, would fill it, he presented them separately to the boy, and said,

"There, my lad, tell me which of these is the heavier."

13. "Why, the cart box, to be sure," replied the boy, taking the cup, half-filled with water, in one hand, and the hollow iron in the other.

"Then you think this iron is heavier than as much water as would fill the place of it, do you?" resumed Locke.

"Why, yes, as heavy again, and more too—I know it is," promptly said the boy.

14. "Well, sir, now mark what I do," proceeded the former, dropping into the cup the iron box, through the hollow of which the water instantly rose to the brim of the vessel.

"There, you saw that water rise to the top of the cup, did you?"

"Yes, I did."

"Very well, what caused it to do so?"

15. "Why, I know well enough, if I could only think: why, it is because the iron is the heavier, and as it comes all around the water so it can't get away sideways, it is forced up."

"That is right; and now I want you to tell what makes that smoke rise up the chimney."

16. "Why,—I guess," replied the boy, hesitating, "I guess,—I guess I don't know."

"Did you ever get up in a chair to look on some high shelf, so that your head was brought near the ceiling of a heated room, in winter? and did you notice any difference between the air up there and the air near the floor?"

17. "Yes, I remember I have, and found the air up there as warm as mustard; and when I got down, and bent my head near the floor to pick up something, I found it as cold as could be."

"That is ever the case; but I wish you to tell me how the cold air always happens to settle down to the lower part of the room, while the warm air, somehow, at the same time, gets above."

18. "Why, why, heavy things settle down, and the cold air—yes, yes, that's it, I am sure—the cold air is heavier, and so settles down, and crowds up the warm air."

"Very good. You then understand that cold air is heavier than the heated air, as that iron is heavier than the water; so now we will go back to the main question—what makes the smoke go upwards?"

19. "Oh! I see now as plain as day; the cold air settles down all round, like the iron box, and drives up the hot air as fast as the fire heats it, in the middle, like the water; and so the hot air carries the smoke along up with it, just as feathers and things in a whirlwind. Well! I have found out what makes smoke go up—is n't it curious?"

20. "Done like a philosopher!" cried Bunker. "The thing is settled. I will grant that you are a teacher among a thousand. You can not only think yourself, but can teach others to think; so you may call the position yours as quick as you please."

Definitions.—2. In-tel-lĕc′tu-al, *treating of the mind.* 3. Tĕm′-pered, *brought to a proper degree of hardness.* 4. Com-păct′, *closely and firmly united, solid, dense.* 4. Pōr′oŭs, *full of pores or minute openings.* 6. E-văp′o-rāt-ed, *passed off in vapor.* 7. In-ġēn′ioŭs (*pro.* in-jēn′yŭs), *well formed, skillful.* 7. Phe-nŏm′e-nŏn, *whatever is presented to the eye.* 8. In′ter-vals, *spaces of time.* 12. Ap-pa-rā′tus, *utensils for performing experiments.*

NOTE.—*Locke Amsden* is represented as a bright young student in search of a position as teacher of a district school in Vermont. *Mr. Bunker*, the "Examining Committee," is a queer, shrewd old farmer, who can neither read nor write, but by careful observation has picked up a large amount of valuable information. The story opens in the midst of the examination.

LXXIV. THE ISLE OF LONG AGO.

Benjamin Franklin Taylor (*b.* 1819, *d.* 1887) was born at Lowville, N.Y. He graduated at Madison University, of which his father was president. In 1845 he published "Attractions of Language." For many years he was literary editor of the "Chicago Journal." Mr. Taylor wrote considerably for the magazines, was the author of many well-known favorite pieces both in prose and verse, and achieved success as a lecturer.

1. OH, a wonderful stream is the river of Time,
   As it runs through the realm of tears,
With a faultless rhythm and a musical rhyme,
And a boundless sweep and a surge sublime,
   As it blends with the ocean of Years.

2. How the winters are drifting, like flakes of snow,
   And the summers, like buds between;
And the year in the sheaf—so they come and they go,
On the river's breast, with its ebb and flow,
   As it glides in the shadow and sheen.

3. There's a magical isle up the river of Time,
   Where the softest of airs are playing;
There's a cloudless sky and a tropical clime,
And a song as sweet as a vesper chime,
   And the Junes with the roses are staying.

4. And the name of that isle is the Long Ago,
   And we bury our treasures there;
There are brows of beauty and bosoms of snow—
There are heaps of dust—but we love them so!—
   There are trinkets and tresses of hair;

5. There are fragments of song that nobody sings,
   And a part of an infant's prayer,
There's a lute unswept, and a harp without strings;
There are broken vows and pieces of rings,
   And the garments that she used to wear.

6. There are hands that are waved, when the fairy shore
   By the mirage is lifted in air;
And we sometimes hear, through the turbulent roar,
Sweet voices we heard in the days gone before,
   When the wind down the river is fair.

7. Oh, remembered for aye be the blessed Isle,
   All the day of our life till night—
When the evening comes with its beautiful smile,
And our eyes are closing to slumber awhile,
   May that "Greenwood" of Soul be in sight!

DEFINITIONS.—1. Rĕalm, *region, country.* Rhy̆thm, *the harmonious flow of vocal sounds.* Rhȳme, *a word answering in sound to another word.* Sûrġe, *a great, rolling swell of water.* 3. Vĕs′per, *pertaining to the evening service in the Roman Catholic Church.* 6. Mi-räġe′ (*pro.* me-räzh′), *an optical illusion causing objects at a distance to seem as though suspended in the air.* 7. Aye (*pro.* ā), *always, ever.*

NOTES.—5. *A lute unswept;* that is, unplayed.

7. *Greenwood* is a noted and very beautiful cemetery at the southern extremity of Brooklyn, N.Y. The expression means, then, the resting place of the soul.

LXXV. THE BOSTON MASSACRE.

George Bancroft (*b.* 1800, *d.* 1891) was born at Worcester, Mass. He was an ambitious student, and graduated at Harvard College before he was eighteen years of age. He then traveled in Europe, spending some time at the German universities. On his return, in 1822, he was appointed tutor in Greek at Harvard. His writings at this time were a small volume of original poems, some translations from Schiller and Goethe, and a few striking essays. Mr. Bancroft has held numerous high political offices. In 1838 he was appointed collector of the port at Boston; in 1845 he was made secretary of the navy; in 1849 he was sent as United States Minister to Great Britain; and in 1867 he was sent in the same capacity to Prussia. The work which has given Mr. Bancroft his great literary reputation is his "History of the United States, from the Discovery of the American Continent." The first volume appeared in 1834. Philosophical in reasoning, interesting, terse in style, and founded on careful research, under the most favorable advantages, the work stands alone in its sphere.

1. THE evening of the fifth came on. The young moon was shining brightly in a cloudless winter sky, and its light was increased by a new-fallen snow. Parties of soldiers were driving about the streets, making a parade of valor, challenging resistance, and striking the inhabitants indiscriminately with sticks or sheathed cutlasses.

2. A band, which poured out from Murray's barracks, in Brattle Street, armed with clubs, cutlasses, and bayonets, provoked resistance, and a fray ensued. Ensign Maul, at the gate of the barrack yard, cried to the soldiers: "Turn out, and I will stand by you; kill them; stick them; knock them down; run your bayonets through them." One soldier after another leveled a firelock, and threatened to "make a lane" through the crowd.

3. Just before nine, as an officer crossed King Street, now State Street, a barber's lad cried after him: "There goes a mean fellow who hath not paid my father for dressing his hair;" on which, the sentinel stationed at the westerly end of the customhouse, on the corner of King Street and Exchange Lane, left his post, and with his musket gave the boy a stroke on the head, that made him stagger and cry for pain.

4. The street soon became clear, and nobody troubled the sentry, when a party of soldiers issued violently from the main guard, their arms glittering in the moonlight, and passed on, hallooing: "Where are they? where are they? Let them come."

5. Presently twelve or fifteen more, uttering the same cries, rushed from the south into King Street, and so by the way of Cornhill towards Murray's barracks. "Pray, soldiers, spare my life," cried a boy of twelve, whom they met. "No, no, I'll kill you all," answered one of them, and knocked him down with his cutlass. They abused and insulted several persons at their doors and others in the street; "running about like madmen in a fury," crying, "Fire!" which seemed their watchword, and, "Where are they? Knock them down." Their outrageous behavior occasioned the ringing of the bell at the head of King Street.

6. The citizens, whom the alarm set in motion, came out with canes and clubs; and, partly by the interference of well-disposed officers, partly by the courage of Crispus Attucks, a mulatto, and some others, the fray at the barracks was soon over. Of the citizens, the prudent shouted, "Home! home!" others, it is said, cried out, "Huzza for the main guard! there is the nest;" but the main guard was not molested the whole evening.

7 A body of soldiers came up Royal Exchange Lane, crying, "Where are the cowards?" and, brandishing their arms, passed through King Street. From ten to twenty boys came after them, asking, "Where are they? where are they?" "There is the soldier who knocked me down," said the barber's boy; and they began pushing one another towards the sentinel. He loaded and primed his musket. "The lobster is going to fire," cried a boy. Waving his piece about, the sentinel pulled the trigger.

8. "If you fire you must die for it," said Henry Knox, who was passing by. "I don't care," replied the sentry,

"if they touch me, I'll fire." "Fire!" shouted the boys, for they were persuaded he could not do it without leave from a civil officer; and a young fellow spoke out, "We will knock him down for snapping," while they whistled through their fingers and huzzaed. "Stand off!" said the sentry, and shouted aloud, "Turn out, main guard!" "They are killing the sentinel," reported a servant from the customhouse, running to the main guard. "Turn out! why don't you turn out?" cried Preston, who was captain of the day, to the guard.

9. A party of six, two of whom, Kilroi and Montgomery, had been worsted at the ropewalk, formed, with a corporal in front and Preston following. With bayonets fixed, they "rushed through the people" upon the trot, cursing them, and pushing them as they went along. They found about ten persons round the sentry, while about fifty or sixty came down with them. "For God's sake," said Knox, holding Preston by the coat, "take your men back again; if they fire, your life must answer for the consequences." "I know what I am about," said he hastily, and much agitated.

10. None pressed on them or provoked them till they began loading, when a party of about twelve in number, with sticks in their hands, moved from the middle of the street where they had been standing, gave three cheers, and passed along the front of the soldiers, whose muskets some of them struck as they went by. "You are cowardly rascals," they said, "for bringing arms against naked men." "Lay aside your guns, and we are ready for you." "Are the soldiers loaded?" inquired Palmes of Preston. "Yes," he answered, "with powder and ball." "Are they going to fire upon the inhabitants?" asked Theodore Bliss. "They can not, without my orders," replied Preston; while "the town-born" called out, "Come on, you rascals, you bloody backs, you lobster scoundrels, fire, if you dare. We know you dare not."

11. Just then, Montgomery received a blow from a stick which had hit his musket; and the word "fire!" being given by Preston, he stepped a little to one side, and shot Attucks, who at the time was quietly leaning on a long stick. "Don't fire!" said Langford, the watchman, to Kilroi, looking him full in the face; but yet he did so, and Samuel Gray, who was standing next Langford, fell lifeless. The rest fired slowly and in succession on the people, who were dispersing. Three persons were killed, among them Attucks, the mulatto; eight were wounded, two of them mortally. Of all the eleven, not more than one had any share in the disturbance.

12. So infuriated were the soldiers that, when the men returned to take up the dead, they prepared to fire again, but were checked by Preston, while the Twenty-ninth Regiment appeared under arms in King Street. "This is our time," cried the soldiers of the Fourteenth; and dogs were never seen more greedy for their prey.

13. The bells rung in all the churches; the town drums beat. "To arms! to arms!" was the cry. "Our hearts," said Warren, "beat to arms, almost resolved by one stroke to avenge the death of our slaughtered brethren;" but they stood self-possessed, demanding justice according to the law. "Did you not know that you should not have fired without the order of a civil magistrate?" asked Hutchinson, on meeting Preston. "I did it," answered Preston, "to save my men."

14. The people would not be pacified or retire till the regiment was confined to the guardroom and the barracks; and Hutchinson himself gave assurances that instant inquiries should be made by the county magistrates. One hundred persons remained to keep watch on the examination, which lasted till three hours after midnight. A warrant was issued against Preston, who surrendered himself to the sheriff; and the soldiers of his party were delivered up and committed to prison.

Definitions. — 1. In-dis-crĭm′i-nate-ly, *without distinction.* 2. En-sūed′, *followed, resulted from.* En′sīgn (*pro.* ĕn′sīn), *an officer of low rank.* Fīre′lŏck, *an old-style musket, with a flintlock.* 7. Brăn′-dish-ing, *waving, flourishing.* 13. Sĕlf′-pos-sessed, *undisturbed, calm in mind, manner, etc.* 14. Păç′i-fīed, *calmed, quieted.* W̤ar′rant, *a writ authorizing an officer to seize an offender.*

Notes. — This massacre took place Monday, March 5, 1770.

5. *Cornhill* is the name of a street in Boston.

7. *Lobster* was the epithet applied to a British soldier by the Americans on account of his red coat.

8. *Henry Knox* (*b.* 1750, *d.* 1806) was then a bookseller in Boston. He afterwards became one of the American generals.

9. *Ropewalk.* The active trouble resulting in the massacre arose from a soldier's being thrashed the Friday before at Gray's ropewalk, where he had challenged one of the workmen to fight; other soldiers joined in the affray from time to time, but were always worsted.

13. *Warren.* This was Joseph Warren (*b.* 1741, *d.* 1775), the American patriot, killed shortly after at Bunker Hill.

Thomas Hutchinson was at this time lieutenant governor of Massachusetts. Although born in Boston, he sided with the British government in the troubles before the Revolution, and sailed for England in 1774.

LXXVI. DEATH OF THE BEAUTIFUL.

Eliza Lee Follen (*b.* 1787, *d.* 1859) was born in Boston, Mass. Her maiden name was Cabott. In 1828, she married Charles Follen, Professor of the German language and its literature in Harvard University. Her principal works are "Sketches of Married Life," "The Skeptic," "Twilight Stories," and "Little Songs." For several years Mrs. Follen was editor of the "Children's Friend."

1. The young, the lovely, pass away,
Ne'er to be seen again;
Earth's fairest flowers too soon decay,
Its blasted trees remain.

2. Full oft, we see the brightest thing
   That lifts its head on high,
Smile in the light, then droop its wing,
   And fade away and die.

3. And kindly is the lesson given;
   Then dry the falling tear:
They came to raise our hearts to Heaven;
   They go to call us there.

LXXVII. SNOW FALLING.

John James Piatt (*b.* 1835, ——) was born in Dearborn County, Ind., and is of French descent. He began to write verses at the age of fourteen, and has been connected editorially with several papers. Several editions of his poems have been issued from time to time, each edition usually containing some additional poems. Of these volumes we may mention: "Poems in Sunshine and Firelight," "Western Windows," "The Lost Farm," and "Poems of House and Home."

1. The wonderful snow is falling
   Over river and woodland and wold;
The trees bear spectral blossom
   In the moonshine blurr'd and cold.

2. There 's a beautiful garden in Heaven;
   And these are the banished flowers,
Falling and driven and drifted
   Into this dark world of ours.

Definitions. — 1. Wōld, *a plain or open country, a country without wood whether hilly or not.* Spĕc'tral, *ghostly.* 2. Băn'ished, *condemned to exile, driven away.*

LXXVIII. SQUEERS'S METHOD.

Charles Dickens (*b.* 1812, *d.* 1870). This celebrated novelist was born in Portsmouth, England. He began his active life as a lawyer's apprentice, in London; but soon became a reporter, and followed this occupation from 1831 to 1836. His first book was entitled "Sketches of London Society, by Boz." In 1837 he published the "Pickwick Papers," a work which established his reputation as a writer. His other works followed with great rapidity, and his last, "Edwin Drood," was unfinished when he died. He visited America in 1842 and in 1867. He is buried in Westminster Abbey. Mr. Dickens excelled in humor and pathos, and was particularly successful in delineating the joys and griefs of childhood. His writings have a tendency to prompt to deeds of kindness and benevolence. The following extract is taken from "Nicholas Nickleby," one of the best of his novels.

1. "Come," said Squeers, "let's go to the schoolroom; and lend me a hand with my school coat, will you?"

Nicholas assisted his master to put on an old fustian shooting jacket, which he took down from a peg in the passage; and Squeers, arming himself with his cane, led the way across a yard to a door in the rear of the house.

"There," said the schoolmaster, as they stepped in together; "this is our shop, Nickleby."

2. It was such a crowded scene, and there were so many objects to attract attention, that at first Nicholas stared about him, really without seeing anything at all. By degrees, however, the place resolved itself into a bare and dirty room with a couple of windows, whereof a tenth part might be of glass, the remainder being stopped up with old copy books and paper.

3. There were a couple of long, old, rickety desks, cut and notched, and inked and damaged in every possible way; two or three forms, a detached desk for Squeers, and another for his assistant. The ceiling was supported like that of a barn, by crossbeams and rafters, and the walls were so stained and discolored that it was impossible to tell whether they had ever been touched by paint or whitewash.

4. Pale and haggard faces, lank and bony figures, children with the countenances of old men, deformities with irons upon their limbs, boys of stunted growth, and others whose long, meager legs would hardly bear their stooping bodies, all crowded on the view together. There were little faces which should have been handsome, darkened with the scowl of sullen, dogged suffering; there was childhood with the light of its eye quenched, its beauty gone, and its helplessness alone remaining.

5. And yet this scene, painful as it was, had its grotesque features, which, in a less interested observer than Nicholas, might have provoked a smile. Mrs. Squeers stood at one of the desks, presiding over an immense basin of brimstone and treacle, of which delicious compound she administered a large installment to each boy in succession, using for the purpose a common wooden spoon, which might have been originally manufactured for some gigantic top, and which widened every young gentleman's mouth considerably, they being all obliged, under heavy corporeal penalties, to take in the whole bowl at a gasp.

6. "Now," said Squeers, giving the desk a great rap with his cane, which made half the little boys nearly jump out of their boots, "is that physicking over?"

"Just over," said Mrs. Squeers, choking the last boy in her hurry, and tapping the crown of his head with the wooden spoon to restore him. "Here, you Smike: take away now. Look sharp!"

7. Smike shuffled out with the basin, and Mrs. Squeers hurried out after him into a species of washhouse, where there was a small fire, and a large kettle, together with a number of little wooden bowls which were arranged upon a board. Into these bowls Mrs. Squeers, assisted by the hungry servant, poured a brown composition which looked like diluted pincushions without the covers, and was called porridge. A minute wedge of brown bread was inserted in each bowl, and when they had eaten their porridge by

means of the bread, the boys ate the bread itself, and had finished their breakfast, whereupon Mr. Squeers went away to his own.

8. After some half-hour's delay Mr. Squeers reappeared, and the boys took their places and their books, of which latter commodity the average might be about one to eight

learners. A few minutes having elapsed, during which Mr. Squeers looked very profound, as if he had a perfect apprehension of what was inside all the books, and could say every word of their contents by heart, if he only chose to take the trouble, that gentleman called up the first class.

9. Obedient to this summons there ranged themselves in front of the schoolmaster's desk, half a dozen scarecrows, out at knees and elbows, one of whom placed a torn and filthy book beneath his learned eye.

"This is the first class in English spelling and philosophy, Nickleby," said Squeers, beckoning Nicholas to stand beside him. "We 'll get up a Latin one, and hand that over to you. Now, then, where 's the first boy?"

10. "Please, sir, he 's cleaning the back parlor window," said the temporary head of the philosophical class.

"So he is, to be sure," rejoined Squeers. "We go upon the practical mode of teaching, Nickleby; the regular education system. C-l-e-a-n, clean, verb active, to make bright, to scour. W-i-n, win, d-e-r, der, winder, a casement. When the boy knows this out of book, he goes and does it. It 's just the same principle as the use of the globes. Where 's the second boy?"

11. "Please, sir, he is weeding the garden," replied a small voice.

"To be sure," said Squeers, by no means disconcerted, "so he is. B-o-t, bot, t-i-n, tin, n-e-y, ney, bottinney, noun substantive, a knowledge of plants. When he has learned that bottinney means a knowledge of plants, he goes and knows 'em. That 's our system, Nickleby: what do you think of it?"

"It 's a very useful one, at any rate," answered Nicholas, significantly.

12. "I believe you," rejoined Squeers, not remarking the emphasis of his usher. "Third boy, what 's a horse?"

"A beast, sir," replied the boy.

"So it is," said Squeers. "Ain't it, Nickleby?"

"I believe there is no doubt of that, sir," answered Nicholas.

"Of course there is n't," said Squeers. "A horse is a quadruped, and quadruped 's Latin for beast, as everybody that 's gone through the grammar knows, or else where 's the use of having grammars at all?"

"Where, indeed!" said Nicholas, abstractedly.

13. "As you 're perfect in that," resumed Squeers, turning to the boy, "go and look after *my* horse, and rub him down well, or I 'll rub you down. The rest of the class go and draw water up till somebody tells you to leave off, for it 's washing day to-morrow, and they want the coppers filled."

Definitions.—1. Fŭs′tian, *a kind of cotton stuff, including corduroy, velveteen, etc.* 2. Re-ṣŏlved′, *made clear, disentangled.* 4. De-fôrm′i-tieṣ, *misshapen persons.* Stŭnt′ed, *checked in growth.* Mēa′g̅er, *thin, lean.* 5. Gro-tĕsque′ (*pro.* g̅ro-tĕsk′), *fanciful, absurd.* Ad-mĭn′is-tered, *gave, dispensed.* In-stạll′ment (literally, *part of a debt*), *part, portion.* Cor-pō′re-al, *bodily.* 6. Phy̆ṣ′ic-ing, *doctoring, treating with medicine.* 7. Dĭ-lūt′ed, *weakened by the addition of water.* 8. Com-mŏd′i-ty, *article, wares.* Pro-found′, *intellectually deep, wise.* Ap-pre-hĕn′sion, *comprehension, knowledge.* 10. Tĕm′po-ra-ry, *for the time being.* 11. Dĭs-con-çẽrt′ed, *confused, abashed.* Sĭg̅-nĭf′i-cant-ly, *with meaning.* 12. Ab-străct′-ed-ly, *in an absent-minded way.*

Notes.—1. *Mr. Squeers* is represented as an ignorant, brutal teacher, many of whom were to be found in Yorkshire, England, at the time of this story.

Nicholas Nickleby is a well-educated, refined young man, who has just obtained the position of assistant teacher, not knowing Squeers's true character.

6. *Smike* is a poor scholar, disowned by his parents, and made almost idiotic by harsh treatment.

The novel from which this story is abridged, aided greatly in a much-needed reform in the Yorkshire schools; and the character of Squeers was so true to life, that numerous suits were threatened against Mr. Dickens by those who thought themselves caricatured.

LXXIX. THE GIFT OF EMPTY HANDS.

Mrs. S. M. B. Piatt (*b.* 1835,——) was born near Lexington, Ky. While still a young girl she began to write poetry, which was well received. In 1861 she was married to the poet John James Piatt. Mrs. Piatt's poetry is marked by tender pathos, thoughtfulness, and musical flow of rhythm. The following selection is from "That New World."

1. They were two princes doomed to death;
Each loved his beauty and his breath:
"Leave us our life and we will bring
Fair gifts unto our lord, the king."

2. They went together. In the dew
A charméd bird before them flew.
Through sun and thorn one followed it;
Upon the other's arm it lit.

3. A rose, whose faintest flush was worth
All buds that ever blew on earth,
One climbed the rocks to reach; ah, well,
Into the other's breast it fell.

4. Weird jewels, such as fairies wear,
When moons go out, to light their hair,
One tried to touch on ghostly ground;
Gems of quick fire the other found.

5. One with the dragon fought to gain
The enchanted fruit, and fought in vain;
The other breathed the garden's air
And gathered precious apples there.

6. Backward to the imperial gate
One took his fortune, one his fate:
One showed sweet gifts from sweetest lands,
The other, torn and empty hands.

7. At bird, and rose, and gem, and fruit,
The king was sad, the king was mute;
At last he slowly said: "My son,
True treasure is not lightly won.

8. "Your brother's hands, wherein you see
Only these scars, show more to me
Than if a kingdom's price I found
In place of each forgotten wound."

DEFINITIONS.—1. Dōōmed, *destined, condemned.* 2. Chärmed, *bewitched, enchanted.* 3. Blew, *blossomed, bloomed.* 4. Wēird, *tainted with witchcraft, supernatural.* Quĭck, *alive, living.* 6. Im-pē′ri-al, *royal.* 7 Mūte, *silent.*

LXXX. CAPTURING THE WILD HORSE.

1. WE left the buffalo camp about eight o'clock, and had a toilsome and harassing march of two hours, over ridges of hills covered with a ragged forest of scrub oaks, and broken by deep gullies.

2. About ten o'clock in the morning we came to where this line of rugged hills swept down into a valley, through which flowed the north fork of Red River. A beautiful meadow, about half a mile wide, enameled with yellow, autumnal flowers, stretched for two or three miles along the foot of the hills, bordered on the opposite side by the river, whose banks were fringed with cottonwood trees, the bright foliage of which refreshed and delighted the eye, after being wearied by the contemplation of monotonous wastes of brown forest.

3. The meadow was finely diversified by groves and clumps of trees, so happily dispersed that they seemed as

if set out by the hand of art. As we cast our eyes over this fresh and delightful valley, we beheld a troop of wild horses quietly grazing on a green lawn, about a mile distant, to our right, while to our left, at nearly the same distance, were several buffaloes; some feeding, others reposing, and ruminating among the high, rich herbage, under the shade of a clump of cottonwood trees. The whole had the appearance of a broad, beautiful tract of pasture land, on the highly ornamented estate of some gentleman farmer, with his cattle grazing about the lawns and meadows.

4. A council of war was now held, and it was determined to profit by the present favorable opportunity, and try our hand at the grand hunting maneuver which is called "ringing the wild horse." This requires a large party of horsemen, well mounted. They extend themselves in each direction, at a certain distance apart, and gradually form a ring of two or three miles in circumference, so as to surround the game. This must be done with extreme care, for the wild horse is the most readily alarmed inhabitant of the prairie, and can scent a hunter a great distance, if to windward.

5. The ring being formed, two or three ride toward the horses, which start off in an opposite direction. Whenever they approach the bounds of the ring, however, a huntsman presents himself, and turns them from their course. In this way they are checked, and driven back at every point, and kept galloping round and round this magic circle, until, being completely tired down, it is easy for hunters to ride up beside them and throw the lariat over their heads. The prime horses of the most speed, courage, and bottom, however, are apt to break through and escape, so that, in general, it is the second-rate horses that are taken.

6. Preparations were now made for a hunt of this kind. The pack horses were now taken into the woods and firmly

tied to trees, lest in a rush of the wild horses they should break away. Twenty-five men were then sent under the command of a lieutenant to steal along the edge of the valley within the strip of wood that skirted the hills. They were to station themselves about fifty yards apart, within the edge of the woods, and not advance or show themselves until the horses dashed in that direction. Twenty-five men were sent across the valley to steal in like manner along the river bank that bordered the opposite side, and to station themselves among the trees.

7. A third party of about the same number was to form a line, stretching across the lower part of the valley, so as to connect the two wings. Beatte and our other half-breed, Antoine, together with the ever-officious Tonish, were to make a circuit through the woods so as to get to the upper part of the valley, in the rear of the horses, and drive them forward into the kind of sack that we had formed, while the two wings should join behind them and make a complete circle.

8. The flanking parties were quietly extending themselves out of sight, on each side of the valley, and the residue were stretching themselves like the links of a chain across it, when the wild horses gave signs that they scented an enemy; snuffing the air, snorting, and looking about. At length they pranced off slowly toward the river, and disappeared behind a green bank.

9. Here, had the regulations of the chase been observed, they would have been quietly checked and turned back by the advance of a hunter from among the trees. Unluckily, however, we had our wildfire, Jack-o'-lantern little Frenchman to deal with. Instead of keeping quietly up the right side of the valley, to get above the horses, the moment he saw them move toward the river he broke out of the covert of woods and dashed furiously across the plain in pursuit of them. This put an end to all system. The half-breeds, and half a score of rangers, joined in the chase.

10. Away they all went over the green bank. In a moment or two the wild horses reappeared, and came thundering down the valley, with Frenchman, half-breeds, and rangers galloping and bellowing behind them. It was in vain that the line drawn across the valley attempted to check and turn back the fugitives; they were too hotly pressed by their pursuers: in their panic they dashed through the line, and clattered down the plain.

11. The whole troop joined in the headlong chase, some of the rangers without hats or caps, their hair flying about their ears, and others with handkerchiefs tied round their heads. The buffaloes, which had been calmly ruminating among the herbage, heaved up their huge forms, gazed for a moment at the tempest that came scouring down the meadow, then turned and took to heavy, rolling flight. They were soon overtaken; the promiscuous throng were pressed together by the contracting sides of the valley, and away they went, pellmell, hurry-skurry, wild buffalo, wild horse, wild huntsman, with clang and clatter, and whoop and halloo, that made the forests ring.

12. At length the buffaloes turned into a green brake, on the river bank, while the horses dashed up a narrow defile of the hills, with their pursuers close to their heels. Beatte passed several of them, having fixed his eye upon a fine Pawnee horse that had his ears slit and saddle marks upon his back. He pressed him gallantly, but lost him in the woods.

13. Among the wild horses was a fine black mare, which in scrambling up the defile tripped and fell. A young ranger sprang from his horse and seized her by the mane and muzzle. Another ranger dismounted and came to his assistance. The mare struggled fiercely, kicking and biting, and striking with her fore feet, but a noose was slipped over her head, and her struggles were in vain.

14. It was some time, however, before she gave over rearing and plunging, and lashing out with her feet on

every side. The two rangers then led her along the valley, by two strong lariats, which enabled them to keep at a sufficient distance on each side to be out of the reach of her hoofs, and whenever she struck out in one direction she was jerked in the other. In this way her spirit was gradually subdued.

15. As to Tonish, who had marred the whole scene by his precipitancy, he had been more successful than he deserved, having managed to catch a beautiful cream-colored colt about seven months old, that had not strength to keep up with its companions. The mercurial little Frenchman was beside himself with exultation. It was amusing to see him with his prize. The colt would rear and kick, and struggle to get free, when Tonish would take him about the neck, wrestle with him, jump on his back, and cut as many antics as a monkey with a kitten.

16. Nothing surprised me more, however, than to witness how soon these poor animals, thus taken from the unbounded freedom of the prairie, yielded to the dominion of man. In the course of two or three days the mare and colt went with the led horses and became quite docile.

— *Washington Irving.*

Definitions. — 1. Gŭl'lieş, *hollows in the earth worn by water.* Dĭ-vẽr'si-fīed, *distinguished by numerous aspects, varied.* 3. Ru̥'mi-nāt-ing, *chewing over what has been slightly chewed before.* Hẽrb'aġe (*pro.* ẽrb'aj), *pasture, grass.* 4. Prāi'rie, *an extensive, level tract without trees, but covered with tall grass.* Wĭnd'ward, *the point from which the wind blows.* 5. Lăr'i-at, *a long cord or thong of leather, with a noose, for catching wild horses.* Bŏt'tom, *power of endurance.* 8. Flăn̲k'ing, *overlooking or commanding on the side.* 9. Jăck-o'-lăn'tern, *a light seen in low, moist grounds, which disappears when approached.* 9. Cȯv'ert, *a covering place, a shelter.* 10. Păn'ie, *sudden fright* (usually, *causeless fright*). 11. Pro-mĭs'eu-oŭs, *mingled, confused.* 15. Märred, *interrupted, spoiled.* Mer-eū'ri-al, *sprightly, full of fire.*

LXXXI. SOWING AND REAPING.

Adelaide Anne Procter (*b.* 1825, *d.* 1864) was the daughter of Bryan Waller Procter (better known as "Barry Cornwall"), a celebrated English poet, living in London. Miss Procter's first volume, "Legends and Lyrics," appeared in 1858, and met with great success; it was republished in this country. A second series, under the same name, was published in 1860; and in 1862 both series were republished with additional poems, and an introduction by Charles Dickens. In 1861 Miss Procter edited "Victoria Regia," a collection of poetical pieces, to which she contributed; and in 1862 "A Chaplet of Verses," composed of her own poems, was published. Besides these volumes, she contributed largely to various magazines and periodicals.

1. Sow with a generous hand;
   Pause not for toil and pain;
Weary not through the heat of summer,
   Weary not through the cold spring rain;
But wait till the autumn comes
   For the sheaves of golden grain.

2. Scatter the seed, and fear not,
   A table will be spread;
What matter if you are too weary
   To eat your hard-earned bread;
Sow, while the earth is broken,
   For the hungry must be fed.

3. Sow;—while the seeds are lying
   In the warm earth's bosom deep,
And your warm tears fall upon it—
   They will stir in their quiet sleep,
And the green blades rise the quicker,
   Perchance, for the tears you weep.

4. Then sow;—for the hours are fleeting,
   And the seed must fall to-day;

And care not what hand shall reap it,
  Or if you shall have passed away
Before the waving cornfields
  Shall gladden the sunny day.

5. Sow; — and look onward, upward,
  Where the starry light appears, —
Where, in spite of the coward's doubting,
  Or your own heart's trembling fears,
You shall reap in joy the harvest
  You have sown to-day in tears.

LXXXII. TAKING COMFORT.

1. For the last few days, the fine weather has led me away from books and papers, and the close air of dwellings, into the open fields, and under the soft, warm sunshine, and the softer light of a full moon. The loveliest season of the whole year — that transient but delightful interval between the storms of the "wild equinox, with all their wet," and the dark, short, dismal days which precede the rigor of winter — is now with us. The sun rises through a soft and hazy atmosphere; the light mist clouds melt gradually before him; and his noontide light rests warm and clear on still woods, tranquil waters, and grasses green with the late autumnal rains.

2. One fine morning, not long ago, I strolled down the Merrimac, on the Tewksbury shore. I know of no walk in the vicinity of Lowell so inviting as that along the margin of the river, for nearly a mile from the village of Belvidere. The path winds, green and flower-skirted, among beeches and oaks, through whose boughs you catch glimpses

of waters sparkling and dashing below. Rocks, huge and picturesque, jut out into the stream, affording beautiful views of the river and the distant city.

3. Half fatigued with my walk, I threw myself down upon a rocky slope of the bank, where the panorama of earth, sky, and water lay clear and distinct about me. Far above, silent and dim as a picture, was the city, with its huge mill masonry, confused chimney tops, and church spires; near it rose the height of Belvidere, with its deserted burial place and neglected gravestones sharply defined on its bleak, bare summit against the sky; before me the river went dashing down its rugged channel, sending up its everlasting murmur; above me the birch tree hung its tassels; and the last wild flowers of autumn profusely fringed the rocky rim of the water.

4. Right opposite, the Dracut woods stretched upwards from the shore, beautiful with the hues of frost, glowing with tints richer and deeper than those which Claude or Poussin mingled, as if the rainbows of a summer shower had fallen among them. At a little distance to the right, a group of cattle stood mid-leg deep in the river; and a troop of children, bright-eyed and mirthful, were casting pebbles at them from a projecting shelf of rock. Over all a warm but softened sunshine melted down from a slumberous autumnal sky.

5. My reverie was disagreeably broken. A low, grunting sound, half bestial, half human, attracted my attention. I was not alone. Close beside me, half hidden by a tuft of bushes, lay a human being, stretched out at full length, with his face literally rooted into the gravel. A little boy, five or six years of age, clean and healthful, with his fair brown locks and blue eyes, stood on the bank above, gazing down upon him with an expression of childhood's simple and unaffected pity.

6. "What ails you?" asked the boy at length. "What makes you lie there?"

The prostrate groveler struggled halfway up, exhibiting the bloated and filthy countenance of a drunkard. He made two or three efforts to get upon his feet, lost his balance, and tumbled forward upon his face.

"What are you doing there?" inquired the boy.

"I 'm taking comfort," he muttered, with his mouth in the dirt.

7. Taking his comfort! There he lay, — squalid and loathsome under the bright heaven, — an imbruted man. The holy harmonies of Nature, the sounds of gushing waters, the rustle of the leaves above him, the wild flowers, the frost bloom of the woods, — what were they to him? Insensible, deaf, and blind, in the stupor of a living death, he lay there, literally realizing that most bitterly significant eastern malediction, "*May you eat dirt.*"

— *Whittier.*

Definitions. — 1. Trăn′sient (*pro.* trăn′shent), *of short duration.* E′qui-nŏx, *the time of year when the days and nights are of equal length, i.e., about September 23d or March 21st.* Rĭg′or, *severity.* 2. Pĭe-tur-ĕsque′ (*pro.* pĭk-tur-ĕsk′), *fitted to form a pleasing picture.* 3. Păn-o-rä′mȧ, *a complete or entire view in every direction.* 5. Rĕv′er-ie, *an irregular train of thoughts occurring in meditation.* Bĕs′tial (*pro.* bĕs′chal), *brutish.* Lĭt′er-al-ly, *according to the first and natural meaning of words.* 6. Prŏs′trate, *lying at length.* Grŏv′el-er, *a base wretch.* Blōat′ed, *puffed out.* 7. Im-bru̥t′ed, *reduced to brutality.* Här′mo-ny, *the fitness of parts to each other in any combination of things.* Rē′al-īz-ing, *making one's own in experience.* Măl-e-dĭe′tion, *a curse.*

Notes. — The localities named in this selection are in the vicinity of Haverhill, Mass., where the old Whittier homestead is situated.

4. *Claude Lorrain* (*b.* 1600, *d.* 1682), whose proper name was Claude Gelée, was a celebrated landscape painter, born in Champagne, Vosges, France.

Nicolas Poussin (*b.* 1594, *d.* 1665) was a French painter, who became one of the most remarkable artists of his age. His fame chiefly arises from his historical and mythological paintings.

LXXXIII. CALLING THE ROLL.

1. "Corporal Green!" the orderly cried;
"Here!" was the answer, loud and clear,
From the lips of a soldier standing near;
And "here!" was the word the next replied.
"Cyrus Drew!" and a silence fell;
This time no answer followed the call;
Only his rear man saw him fall,
Killed or wounded he could not tell.

2. There they stood in the fading light,
These men of battle, with grave, dark looks,
As plain to be read as open books,
While slowly gathered the shades of night.
The fern on the slope was splashed with blood,
And down in the corn, where the poppies grew,
Were redder stains than the poppies knew;
And crimson-dyed was the river's flood.

3. For the foe had crossed from the other side
That day, in the face of a murderous fire
That swept them down in its terrible ire;
And their lifeblood went to color the tide.
"Herbert Cline!" At the call there came
Two stalwart soldiers into the line,
Bearing between them Herbert Cline,
Wounded and bleeding, to answer his name.

4. "Ezra Kerr!" and a voice said "here!"
"Hiram Kerr!" but no man replied:
They were brothers, these two; the sad wind sighed,
And a shudder crept through the cornfield near.

"Ephraim Deane!"—then a soldier spoke:
"Deane carried our regiment's colors," he said,
"When our ensign was shot; I left him dead,
Just after the enemy wavered and broke.

5. "Close to the roadside his body lies;
I paused a moment and gave him to drink;
He murmured his mother's name, I think;
And death came with it and closed his eyes."
'T was a victory—yes; but it cost us dear;
For that company's roll, when called at night,
Of a hundred men who went into the fight,
Numbered but twenty that answered "here!"

—*Shepherd.*

LXXXIV. TURTLE SOUP.

Charles Frederick Briggs (*b.* 1804, *d.* 1877) was born on the island of Nantucket. When quite young, however, he became a resident of New York City. In 1845, in conjunction with Edgar A. Poe, he began the publication of the "Broadway Journal;" he was also connected with the "New York Times," and the "Evening Mirror;" also as editor from 1853 to 1856 with "Putnam's Magazine." Mr. Briggs wrote a few novels, some poetry, and numerous little humorous tales and sketches. The following selection is from "Working a Passage; or, Life on a Liner," one of his best stories.

1. AMONG the luxuries which the captain had provided for himself and passengers was a fine green turtle, which was not likely to suffer from exposure to salt water, so it was reserved until all the pigs, and sheep, and poultry had been eaten. A few days before we arrived, it was determined to kill the turtle and have a feast the next day.

2. Our cabin gentlemen had been long enough deprived of fresh meats to make them cast lickerish glances towards their hard-skinned friend, and there was a great smacking of lips the day before he was killed. As I walked aft

occasionally, I heard them congratulating themselves on their prospective turtle soup and forcemeat balls; and one of them, to heighten the luxury of the feast, ate nothing but a dry biscuit for the twenty-four hours preceding, that he might be prepared to devour his full share of the unctuous compound.

3. It was to be a gala day with them; and though it was not champagne day, that falling on Saturday and this on Friday, they agreed to have champagne a day in advance, that nothing should be wanting to give a finish to

their turtle. It happened to be a rougher day than usual when the turtle was cooked, but they had become too well used to the motion of the ship to mind that.

4. It happened to be my turn at the wheel the hour before dinner, and I had the tantalizing misery of hearing them laughing and talking about their turtle, while I was hungry from want of dry bread and salt meat. I had resolutely kept my thoughts from the cabin during all the passage but once, and now I found my ideas clustering round a tureen of turtle in spite of all my philosophy.

5. Confound them, if they had gone out of my hearing with their exulting smacks, I should not have envied their soup, but their hungry glee so excited my imagination that I could see nothing through the glazing of the binnacle but a white plate with a slice of lemon on the rim, a loaf of delicate bread, a silver spoon, a napkin, two or three wine glasses of different hues and shapes, and a water goblet clustering round it, and a stream of black, thick, and fragrant turtle pouring into the plate.

6. By and by it was four bells: they dined at three. And all the gentlemen, with the captain at their head, darted below into the cabin, where their mirth increased when they caught sight of the soup plates. "Hurry with the soup, steward," roared the captain. "Coming, sir," replied the steward. In a few moments the cook opened the door of his galley, and out came the delicious steam of the turtle.

7. Then came the steward with a large covered tureen in his hand, towards the cabin gangway. I forgot the ship for a moment in looking at this precious cargo, the wheel slipped from my hands, the ship broached to with a sudden jerk; the steward had got only one foot upon the stairs, when this unexpected motion threw him off his balance, and down he went by the run, the tureen slipped from his hands, and part of its contents flew into the lee scuppers, and the balance followed him in his fall.

8. I laughed outright. I enjoyed the turtle a thousand times more than I should have done if I had eaten the whole of it. But I was forced to restrain my mirth, for the next moment the steward ran upon deck, followed by the captain, in a furious rage, threatening if he caught him to throw him overboard. Not a spoonful of the soup had been left in the coppers, for the steward had taken it all away at once to keep it warm. In about an hour afterwards the passengers came upon deck, looking more sober than I had seen them since we left Liverpool. They had dined upon cold ham.

Definitions.—1. Re-ṣẽrved', *kept back, retained.* 2. Lĭck'er-ish, *eager or greedy to swallow.* Aft, *toward the stern of a vessel.* Pro-spĕe'tĭve, *relating to the future.* Fōrçe'mēat, *meat chopped fine and highly seasoned.* Un̲e'tu-oŭs, *fat.* 5. Glāz'ing, *glass or glass-like substance.* Bĭn'na-ele, *a box containing the compass of a ship.* 6. Găl'ley, *the kitchen of a ship.* 7. Tu-reen', *a large deep vessel for holding soup.* Găng'wāy, *a passageway.* Lee, *pertaining to the side opposite that against which the wind blows.* Seŭp'perṣ, *channels cut through the side of a ship for carrying off water from the deck.* 8. Cŏp'perṣ, *large copper boilers.*

Note.—6. *Four bells; i.e.*, two o'clock.

LXXXV. THE BEST KIND OF REVENGE.

1. Some years ago a warehouseman in Manchester, England, published a scurrilous pamphlet, in which he endeavored to hold up the house of Grant Brothers to ridicule. William Grant remarked upon the occurrence that the man would live to repent of what he had done; and this was conveyed by some talebearer to the libeler, who said, "Oh, I suppose he thinks I shall some time or other be in his debt; but I will take good care of that." It happens,

however, that a man in business can not always choose who shall be his creditors. The pamphleteer became a bankrupt, and the brothers held an acceptance of his which had been indorsed to them by the drawer, who had also become a bankrupt.

2. The wantonly libeled men had thus become creditors of the libeler! They now had it in their power to make him repent of his audacity. He could not obtain his certificate without their signature, and without it he could not enter into business again. He had obtained the number of signatures required by the bankrupt law except one. It seemed folly to hope that the firm of "the brothers" would supply the deficiency. What! they who had cruelly been made the laughingstock of the public, forget the wrong and favor the wrongdoer? He despaired. But the claims of a wife and children forced him at last to make the application. Humbled by misery, he presented himself at the countinghouse of the wronged.

3. Mr. William Grant was there alone, and his first words to the delinquent were, "Shut the door, sir!" sternly uttered. The door was shut, and the libeler stood trembling before the libeled. He told his tale and produced his certificate, which was instantly clutched by the injured merchant. "You wrote a pamphlet against us once!" exclaimed Mr. Grant. The suppliant expected to see his parchment thrown into the fire. But this was not its destination. Mr. Grant took a pen, and writing something upon the document, handed it back to the bankrupt. He, poor wretch, expected to see "rogue, scoundrel, libeler," inscribed; but there was, in fair round characters, the signature of the firm.

4. "We make it a rule," said Mr. Grant, "never to refuse signing the certificate of an honest tradesman, and we have never heard that you were anything else." The tears started into the poor man's eyes. "Ah," said Mr. Grant, "my saying was true! I said you would live to

repent writing that pamphlet. I did not mean it as a threat. I only meant that some day you would know us better, and be sorry you had tried to injure us. I see you repent of it now." "I do, I do!" said the grateful man; "I bitterly repent it." "Well, well, my dear fellow, you know us now. How do you get on? What are you going to do?" The poor man stated he had friends who could assist him when his certificate was obtained. "But how are you off in the meantime?"

5. And the answer was, that, having given up every farthing to his creditors, he had been compelled to stint his family of even common necessaries, that he might be enabled to pay the cost of his certificate. "My dear fellow, this will not do; your family must not suffer. Be kind enough to take this ten-pound note to your wife from me. There, there, my dear fellow! Nay, do not cry; it will all be well with you yet. Keep up your spirits, set to work like a man, and you will raise your head among us yet." The overpowered man endeavored in vain to express his thanks; the swelling in his throat forbade words. He put his handkerchief to his face and went out of the door, crying like a child.

Definitions. — 1. Wâre′house-man (English usage), *one who keeps a wholesale store for woolen goods.* Seŭr′ril-oŭs, *low, mean.* Lī′bel-er, *one who defames another maliciously by a writing, etc* 2. Au-dăç′i-ty, *bold impudence.* Sĭg′na-ture, *the name of a person written with his own hand, the name of a firm signed officially.* De-fĭ′cien-çy, *want.* 3. De-lĭn̲′quent, *an offender.* Pärch′ment, *sheep or goat skin prepared for writing upon.* 5. Stĭnt, *to limit.*

Note. — 1. *Acceptance.* When a person upon whom a draft has been made, writes his name across the face of it, the draft then becomes "an acceptance." The person who makes the draft is called "the drawer;" the person to whom the money is ordered paid writes his name on the back of the draft and is called "an indorser." Paper of this kind frequently passes from hand to hand, so that there are several indorsers.

LXXXVI. THE SOLDIER OF THE RHINE.

Caroline Elizabeth Sarah Norton (*b.* 1808, *d.* 1877) was the granddaughter of Richard Brinsley Sheridan. She wrote verses and plays at a very early age. "The Sorrows of Rosalie," published in 1829, was written before she was seventeen years old. In 1827, she was married to the Hon. George Chapple Norton. The marriage was an unhappy one, and they were divorced in 1836. Her principal works are "The Undying One," "The Dream, and Other Poems," "The Child of the Islands," "Stuart of Dunleith, a Romance," and "English Laws for English Women of the 19th Century." She contributed extensively to the magazines and other periodicals.

1. A Soldier of the Legion lay dying in Algiers,
There was lack of woman's nursing, there was dearth of woman's tears;
But a comrade stood beside him, while his lifeblood ebbed away,
And bent, with pitying glances, to hear what he might say.
The dying soldier faltered, as he took that comrade's hand,
And he said: "I nevermore shall see my own, my native land;
Take a message and a token to some distant friends of mine,
For I was born at Bingen,—at Bingen on the Rhine.

2. "Tell my brothers and companions, when they meet and crowd around
To hear my mournful story in the pleasant vineyard ground,
That we fought the battle bravely, and when the day was done,
Full many a corse lay ghastly pale beneath the setting sun;
And, 'mid the dead and dying, were some grown old in wars,—
The death wound on their gallant breasts, the last of many scars;
But some were young, and suddenly beheld life's morn decline,—
And one had come from Bingen,—fair Bingen on the Rhine.

3. "Tell my mother that her other sons shall comfort her old age,
For I was aye a truant bird, that thought his home a cage.
For my father was a soldier, and, even when a child,
My heart leaped forth to hear him tell of struggles fierce and wild;

And when he died, and left us to divide his scanty hoard,
I let them take whate'er they would, but kept my father's sword;
And with boyish love I hung it where the bright light used to shine,
On the cottage wall at Bingen,—calm Bingen on the Rhine.

4. "Tell my sister not to weep for me, and sob with drooping head,
When the troops come marching home again, with glad and gallant tread,
But to look upon them proudly, with a calm and steadfast eye,
For her brother was a soldier, too, and not afraid to die;
And if a comrade seek her love, I ask her in my name
To listen to him kindly, without regret or shame,
And to hang the old sword in its place (my father's sword and mine),
For the honor of old Bingen,—dear Bingen on the Rhine.

5. "There 's another,—not a sister; in the happy days gone by,
You 'd have known her by the merriment that sparkled in her eye;
Too innocent for coquetry,—too fond for idle scorning,—
O friend! I fear the lightest heart makes sometimes heaviest mourning!
Tell her the last night of my life—(for, ere the moon be risen,
My body will be out of pain, my soul be out of prison),
I dreamed I stood with her, and saw the yellow sunlight shine
On the vine-clad hills of Bingen,—fair Bingen on the Rhine.

6. "I saw the blue Rhine sweep along: I heard, or seemed to hear,
The German songs we used to sing, in chorus sweet and clear;
And down the pleasant river, and up the slanting hill,
The echoing chorus sounded, through the evening calm and still;
And her glad blue eyes were on me, as we passed, with friendly talk,
Down many a path beloved of yore, and well-remembered walk;

And her little hand lay lightly, confidingly in mine, —
But we'll meet no more at Bingen, — loved Bingen on the Rhine."

7. His trembling voice grew faint and hoarse; his grasp was childish weak,
His eyes put on a dying look, — he sighed and ceased to speak.
His comrade bent to lift him, but the spark of life had fled, —
The soldier of the Legion in a foreign land was dead!
And the soft moon rose up slowly, and calmly she looked down
On the red sand of the battlefield, with bloody corses strewn;
Yes, calmly on that dreadful scene, her pale light seemed to shine,
As it shone on distant Bingen, — fair Bingen on the Rhine.

DEFINITIONS. — 1. Lē'ġion (*pro.* lē'jun), *division of an army.* Dẽarth (*pro.* dẽrth), *scarcity.* Ebbed, *flowed out.* 2. Côrse, *a dead body.* 4. Stĕad'fȧst, *firm, resolute.* 5. Co-quĕt'ry, *trifling in love.* 6. Chō'rus, *music in which all join.* Yōre, *old times.*

NOTE. — 1. *Bingen* is pronounced Bĭng'en, not Bin̲'ġen, nor Bĭn'jen.

LXXXVII. THE WINGED WORSHIPERS.

Charles Sprague (*b.* 1791, *d.* 1875) was born in Boston, Mass. He engaged in mercantile business when quite young, leaving school for that purpose. In 1825, he was elected cashier of the Globe Bank of Boston, which position he held until 1864. Mr. Sprague has not been a prolific writer; but his poems, though few in number, are deservedly classed among the best productions of American poets. His chief poem is entitled "Curiosity."

1. GAY, guiltless pair,
What seek ye from the fields of heaven?
Ye have no need of prayer,
Ye have no sins to be forgiven.

2. Why perch ye here,
Where mortals to their Maker bend?
Can your pure spirits fear
The God ye never could offend?

3. Ye never knew
The crimes for which we come to weep;
Penance is not for you,
Blessed wanderers of the upper deep.

4. To you 'tis given
To wake sweet Nature's untaught lays;
Beneath the arch of heaven
To chirp away a life of praise.

5. Then spread each wing,
Far, far above, o'er lakes and lands,
And join the choirs that sing
In yon blue dome not reared with hands.

6. Or, if ye stay
To note the consecrated hour,
Teach me the airy way,
And let me try your envied power.

7. Above the crowd,
On upward wings could I but fly,
I'd bathe in yon bright cloud,
And seek the stars that gem the sky.

8. 'T were Heaven indeed,
Through fields of trackless light to soar,
On Nature's charms to feed,
And Nature's own great God adore.

DEFINITIONS. — 2. Pĕrch, *to light or settle on anything.* 3. Pĕn′ançe, *suffering for sin.* 4. Lāys, *songs.* 5. Choir (*pro.* kwīr), *a collection of singers.* Dōme, *an arched structure above a roof; hence, figuratively, the heavens.* 6. Cŏn′se-crāt-ed, *set apart for the service of God.* 8. Trăck′less, *having no path.*

NOTE. — This little poem was addressed to two swallows that flew into church during service.

LXXXVIII. THE PEEVISH WIFE.

Maria Edgeworth (*b.* 1767, *d.* 1849) was born near Reading, Berkshire, England. In 1782 her father removed with his family to Edgeworthtown, Ireland, to reside on his estate. She lived here during the remainder of her life, with the exception of occasional short visits to England, Scotland, and France. She was educated principally by her father, and they were colaborers in literary productions, among which were "Essays on Practical Education," and the "Parent's Assistant." Her novels and tales were written without assistance, and her fame as a writer rests on them. The best known of these are "Castle Rackrent," "Moral Tales," "Tales of Fashionable Life," "Frank," "The Modern Griselda," and "Helen." Miss Edgeworth excels in the truthful delineation of character, and her works are full of practical good sense and genuine humor.

Mrs. Bolingbroke. I WISH I knew what was the matter with me this morning. Why do you keep the newspaper all to yourself, my dear?

Mr. Bolingbroke. Here it is for you, my dear; I have finished it.

Mrs. B. I humbly thank you for giving it to me when you have done with it. I hate stale news. Is there anything in the paper? for I can not be at the trouble of hunting it.

Mr. B. Yes, my dear; there are the marriages of two of our friends.

Mrs. B. Who? Who?

Mr. B. Your friend, the widow Nettleby, to her cousin John Nettleby.

Mrs. B. Mrs. Nettleby? Dear! But why did you tell me?

Mr. B. Because you asked me, my dear.

Mrs. B. Oh, but it is a hundred times pleasanter to read the paragraph one's self. One loses all the pleasure of the surprise by being told. Well, whose was the other marriage?

Mr. B. Oh, my dear, I will not tell you; I will leave you the pleasure of the surprise.

Mrs. B. But you see I can not find it. How provoking you are, my dear! Do pray tell me.

Mr. B. Our friend Mr. Granby.

Mrs. B. Mr. Granby? Dear! Why did you not make me guess? I should have guessed him directly. But why do you call him our friend? I am sure he is no friend of mine, nor ever was. I took an aversion to him, as you remember, the very first day I saw him. I am sure he is no friend of mine.

Mr. B. I am sorry for it, my dear; but I hope you will go and see Mrs. Granby.

Mrs. B. Not I, indeed, my dear. Who was she?

Mr. B. Miss Cooke.

Mrs. B. Cooke? But there are so many Cookes. Can't you distinguish her any way? Has she no Christian name?

Mr. B. Emma, I think. Yes, Emma.

Mrs. B. Emma Cooke? No; it can not be my friend Emma Cooke; for I am sure she was cut out for an old maid.

Mr. B. This lady seems to me to be cut out for a good wife.

Mrs. B. Maybe so. I am sure I'll never go to see her. Pray, my dear, how came you to see so much of her?

Mr. B. I have seen very little of her, my dear. I only saw her two or three times before she was married.

Mrs. B. Then, my dear, how could you decide that she was cut out for a good wife? I am sure you could not judge of her by seeing her only two or three times, and before she was married.

Mr. B. Indeed, my love, that is a very just observation.

Mrs. B. I understand that compliment perfectly, and thank you for it, my dear. I must own I can bear anything better than irony.

Mr. B. Irony? my dear, I was perfectly in earnest.

Mrs. B. Yes, yes; in earnest; so I perceive; I may naturally be dull of apprehension, but my feelings are quick enough; I comprehend too well. Yes, it is impossible to judge of a woman before marriage, or to guess what sort of a wife she will make. I presume you speak from experience; you have been disappointed yourself, and repent your choice.

Mr. B. My dear, what did I say that was like this? Upon my word, I meant no such thing. I really was not thinking of you in the least.

Mrs. B. No, you never think of me now. I can easily believe that you were not thinking of me in the least.

Mr. B. But I said that only to prove to you that I could not be thinking ill of you, my dear.

Mrs. B. But I would rather that you thought ill of me than that you should not think of me at all.

Mr. B. Well, my dear, I will even think ill of you if that will please you.

Mrs. B. Do you laugh at me? When it comes to this I am wretched indeed. Never man laughed at the woman he loved. As long as you had the slightest remains of love for me you could not make me an object of derision; ridicule and love are incompatible, absolutely incompatible. Well, I have done my best, my very best, to make you happy, but in vain. I see I am not cut out to be a good wife. Happy, happy Mrs. Granby!

Mr. B. Happy, I hope sincerely, that she will be with my friend; but my happiness must depend on you, my love; so, for my sake, if not for your own, be composed, and do not torment yourself with such fancies.

Mrs. B. I do wonder whether this Mrs. Granby is really that Miss Emma Cooke. I 'll go and see her directly; see her I must.

Mr. B. I am heartily glad of it, my dear; for I am sure a visit to his wife will give my friend Granby real pleasure.

Mrs. B. I promise you, my dear, I do not go to give him pleasure, or you either, but to satisfy my own curiosity.

Definitions.—I'ron-y, *language intended to convey a meaning contrary to its literal signification.* De-rĭ'sion, *the act of laughing at in contempt.* In-com-păt'i-ble, *that can not exist together.*

LXXXIX. THE RAINY DAY.

1. The day is cold, and dark, and dreary;
It rains, and the wind is never weary;
The vine still clings to the moldering wall,
But at every gust the dead leaves fall.
And the day is dark and dreary.

2. My life is cold, and dark, and dreary;
It rains, and the wind is never weary;
My thoughts still cling to the moldering Past,
But the hopes of youth fall thick in the blast,
And the days are dark and dreary.

3. Be still, sad heart! and cease repining;
Behind the clouds is the sun still shining;
Thy fate is the common fate of all,
Into each life some rain must fall,
Some days must be dark and dreary.

— Longfellow.

XC. BREAK, BREAK, BREAK.

Alfred Tennyson (*b.* 1809, *d.* 1892) was born in Somersby, Lincolnshire, England. He graduated at Trinity College, Cambridge. His first volume of poems was published in 1830, but it made little impression and was severely criticised. On the publication of his third series in 1842, his poetic genius began to receive general recognition. Mr. Tennyson was made poet laureate in 1850, and was regarded as the foremost living poet of England. For several years his residence was on the Isle of Wight. In 1884, he was raised to the peerage.

1. Break, break, break,
On thy cold gray stones, O sea!
And I would that my tongue could utter
The thoughts that arise in me.

2. Oh, well for the fisherman's boy,
That he shouts with his sister at play!
Oh, well for the sailor lad,
That he sings in his boat on the bay!

3. And the stately ships go on
To their haven under the hill;
But oh for the touch of a vanished hand,
And the sound of a voice that is still!

4. Break, break, break,
At the foot of thy crags, O sea!
But the tender grace of a day that is dead
Will never come back to me.

XCI. TRANSPORTATION AND PLANTING OF SEEDS.

Henry David Thoreau (*b.* 1817, *d.* 1862). This eccentric American author and naturalist was born at Concord, Mass. He graduated at Harvard University in 1837. He was a good English and classical scholar, and was well acquainted with the literature of the East. His father was a maker of lead pencils, and he followed the business for a time, but afterwards supported himself mainly by teaching, lecturing, land surveying, and carpentering. In 1845 he built himself a small wooden house near Concord, on the shore of Walden Pond, where he lived about two years. He was intimate with Hawthorne, Emerson, and other literary celebrities. His principal works are "Walden, or Life in the Woods," "A Week on Concord and Merrimac Rivers," "Excursions," "Maine Woods," "Cape Cod," "A Yankee in Canada," and "Letters to Various Persons." In descriptive power Mr. Thoreau has few, if any, superiors.

1. In all the pines a very thin membrane, in appearance much like an insect's wing, grows over and around the seed, and independent of it, while the latter is being developed within its base. In other words, a beautiful thin sack is woven around the seed, with a handle to it such as the wind can take hold of, and it is then committed to the wind, expressly that it may transport the seed and extend the range of the species; and this it does as effectually as when seeds are sent by mail, in a different kind of sack, from the patent office.

2. There is, then, no necessity for supposing that the pines have sprung up from nothing, and I am aware that I am not at all peculiar in asserting that they come from seeds, though the mode of their propagation by Nature has been but little attended to. They are very extensively raised from the seed in Europe, and are beginning to be here.

3. When you cut down an oak wood, a pine wood will not at once spring up there unless there are, or have been quite recently, seed-bearing pines near enough for the seeds to be blown from them. But, adjacent to a forest of pines, if you prevent other crops from growing there, you will

surely have an extension of your pine forest, provided the soil is suitable.

4. As I walk amid hickories, even in August, I hear the sound of green pignuts falling from time to time, cut off by the chickaree over my head. In the fall I notice on the ground, either within or in the neighborhood of oak woods, on all sides of the town, stout oak twigs three or four inches long, bearing half a dozen empty acorn cups, which twigs have been gnawed off by squirrels, on both sides of the nuts, in order to make them more portable. The jays scream and the red squirrels scold while you are clubbing and shaking the chestnut trees, for they are there on the same errand, and two of a trade never agree.

5. I frequently see a red or a gray squirrel cast down a green chestnut burr, as I am going through the woods, and I used to think, sometimes, that they were cast at me. In fact, they are so busy about it, in the midst of the chestnut season, that you can not stand long in the woods without hearing one fall.

6. A sportsman told me that he had, the day before — that was in the middle of October — seen a green chestnut burr dropped on our great river meadow, fifty rods from the nearest wood, and much farther from the nearest chestnut tree, and he could not tell how it came there. Occasionally, when chestnutting in midwinter, I find thirty or forty nuts in a pile, left in its gallery just under the leaves, by the common wood mouse.

7. But especially, in the winter, the extent to which this transportation and planting of nuts is carried on, is made apparent by the snow. In almost every wood you will see where the red or gray squirrels have pawed down through the snow in a hundred places, sometimes two feet deep, and almost always directly to a nut or a pine cone, — as directly as if they had started from it and bored upward, — which you and I could not have done. It would be difficult for us to find one before the snow falls. Commonly,

no doubt, they had deposited them there in the fall. You wonder if they remember the localities cr discover them by the scent.

8. The red squirrel commonly has its winter abode in the earth under a thicket of evergreens, frequently under a small clump of evergreens in the midst of a deciduous wood. If there are any nut trees, which still retain their nuts, standing at a distance without the wood, their paths often lead directly to and from them. We, therefore, need not suppose an oak standing here and there in the wood in order to seed it, but if a few stand within twenty or thirty rods of it, it is sufficient.

9. I think that I may venture to say that every white-pine cone that falls to the earth naturally in this town, before opening and losing its seeds, and almost every pitch-pine one that falls at all, is cut off by a squirrel; and they begin to pluck them long before they are ripe, so that when the crop of white-pine cones is a small one, as it commonly is, they cut off thus almost everyone of these before it fairly ripens.

10. I think, moreover, that their design, if I may so speak, in cutting them off green, is partly to prevent their opening and losing their seeds, for these are the ones for which they dig through the snow, and the only white-pine cones which contain anything then. I have counted in one heap the cores of two hundred and thirty-nine pitch-pine cones which had been cut off and stripped by the red squirrel the previous winter.

11. The nuts thus left on the surface, or buried just beneath it, are placed in the most favorable circumstances for germinating. I have sometimes wondered how those which merely fell on the surface of the earth got planted; but, by the end of December, I find the chestnut of the same year partially mixed with the mold, as it were, under the decaying and moldy leaves, where there is all the moisture and manure they want, for the nuts fall fast. In a

plentiful year a large proportion of the nuts are thus covered loosely an inch deep, and are, of course, somewhat concealed from squirrels.

12. One winter, when the crop had been abundant, I got, with the aid of a rake, many quarts of these nuts as late as the tenth of January; and though some bought at the store the same day were more than half of them moldy, I did not find a single moldy one among those which I picked from under the wet and moldy leaves, where they had been snowed on once or twice. Nature knew how to pack them best. They were still plump and tender. Apparently they do not heat there, though wet. In the spring they are all sprouting.

13. Occasionally, when threading the woods in the fall, you will hear a sound as if some one had broken a twig, and, looking up, see a jay pecking at an acorn, or you will see a flock of them at once about it, in the top of an oak, and hear them break it off. They then fly to a suitable limb, and placing the acorn under one foot, hammer away at it busily, making a sound like a woodpecker's tapping, looking round from time to time to see if any foe is approaching, and soon reach the meat, and nibble at it, holding up their heads to swallow while they hold the remainder very firmly with their claws. Nevertheless, it often drops to the ground before the bird has done with it.

14. I can confirm what William Barton wrote to Wilson, the ornithologist, that "The jay is one of the most useful agents in the economy of nature for disseminating forest trees and other nuciferous and hard-seeded vegetables on which they feed. In performing this necessary duty they drop abundance of seed in their flight over fields, hedges, and by fences, where they alight to deposit them in the post holes, etc. It is remarkable what numbers of young trees rise up in fields and pastures after a wet winter and spring. These birds alone are capable in a few years' time to replant all the cleared lands."

15. I have noticed that squirrels also frequently drop nuts in open land, which will still further account for the oaks and walnuts which spring up in pastures; for, depend on it, every new tree comes from a seed. When I examine the little oaks, one or two years old, in such places, I invariably find the empty acorn from which they sprung.

Definitions. — 1. Mĕm'brāne, *a thin, soft tissue of interwoven fibers.* 2. Prŏp-a-ḡā'tion, *the continuance of a kind by successive production.* 4. Pōrt'a-ble, *capable of being carried.* 7. Trăns-por-tā'tion, *the act of conveying from one place to another.* 8. De-çĭd'u-oŭs, *said of trees whose leaves fall in autumn.* 11. Gẽr'mi-nāt-ing, *sprouting, beginning to grow.* 14. Or-ni-thŏl'o-ḡĭst, *one skilled in the science which treats of birds.* E-eŏn'o-my, *orderly system.* Dis-sĕm'i-nāt-ing, *scattering for growth and propagation.* Nu-çĭf'er-oŭs, *bearing nuts.*

XCII. SPRING AGAIN.

Celia Thaxter (*b.* 1836, *d.* 1894), whose maiden name was Laighton, was born in Portsmouth, N.H. Much of her early life was passed on White Island, one of a group of small islands, called the Isles of Shoals, about ten miles from the shore, where she lived in the lighthouse cottage. In 1867–68, she published, in the "Atlantic Monthly," a number of papers on these islands, which were afterwards bound in a separate volume. Mrs. Thaxter was a contributor to several periodicals, and in strength and beauty of style has few equals among American writers. The following selection is from a volume of her poems entitled "Drift Weed."

1. I stood on the height in the stillness
   And the planet's outline scanned,
And half was drawn with the line of sea
   And half with the far blue land.

2. With wings that caught the sunshine
   In the crystal deeps of the sky,
Like shapes of dreams, the gleaming gulls
   Went slowly floating by.

3. Below me the boats in the harbor
   Lay still, with their white sails furled;
Sighing away into silence,
   The breeze died off the world.

4. On the weather-worn, ancient ledges
   Peaceful the calm light slept;
And the chilly shadows, lengthening,
   Slow to the eastward crept.

5. The snow still lay in the hollows,
   And where the salt waves met
The iron rock, all ghastly white
   The thick ice glimmered yet.

6. But the smile of the sun was kinder,
   The touch of the air was sweet;
The pulse of the cruel ocean seemed
   Like a human heart to beat.

7. Frost-locked, storm-beaten, and lonely,
   In the midst of the wintry main,
Our bleak rock yet the tidings heard:
   "There shall be spring again!"

8. Worth all the waiting and watching,
   The woe that the winter wrought,
Was the passion of gratitude that shook
   My soul at the blissful thought!

9. Soft rain and flowers and sunshine,
   Sweet winds and brooding skies,
Quick-flitting birds to fill the air
   With clear delicious cries;

10. And the warm sea's mellow murmur
Resounding day and night;
A thousand shapes and tints and tones
Of manifold delight,

11. Nearer and ever nearer
Drawing with every day!
But a little longer to wait and watch
'Neath skies so cold and gray;

12. And hushed is the roar of the bitter north
Before the might of the spring,
And up the frozen slope of the world
Climbs summer, triumphing.

XCIII. RELIGION THE ONLY BASIS OF SOCIETY.

William Ellery Channing (*b.* 1780, *d.* 1842), an eminent divine and orator, was born at Newport, R.I. He graduated from Harvard with the highest honors in 1798, and, in 1803, he was made pastor of the Federal Street Church, Boston, with which he maintained his connection until his death. Towards the close of his life, being much enfeebled, he withdrew almost entirely from his pastoral duties, and devoted himself to literature. Dr. Channing's writings are published in six volumes, and are mainly devoted to theology.

1. Religion is a social concern; for it operates powerfully on society, contributing in various ways to its stability and prosperity. Religion is not merely a private affair; the community is deeply interested in its diffusion; for it is the best support of the virtues and principles, on which the social order rests. Pure and undefiled religion is to do good; and it follows, very plainly, that if God be the Author and Friend of society, then, the recognition of him must enforce all social duty, and enlightened piety must give its whole strength to public order.

2. Few men suspect, perhaps no man comprehends, the extent of the support given by religion to every virtue. No man, perhaps, is aware how much our moral and social sentiments are fed from this fountain; how powerless conscience would become without the belief of a God; how palsied would be human benevolence, were there not the sense of a higher benevolence to quicken and sustain it; how suddenly the whole social fabric would quake, and with what a fearful crash it would sink into hopeless ruin, were the ideas of a Supreme Being, of accountableness and of a future life to be utterly erased from every mind.

3. And, let men thoroughly believe that they are the work and sport of chance; that no superior intelligence concerns itself with human affairs; that all their improvements perish forever at death; that the weak have no guardian, and the injured no avenger; that there is no recompense for sacrifices to uprightness and the public good; that an oath is unheard in heaven; that secret crimes have no witness but the perpetrator; that human existence has no purpose, and human virtue no unfailing friend; that this brief life is everything to us, and death is total, everlasting extinction; once let them *thoroughly* abandon religion, and who can conceive or describe the extent of the desolation which would follow?

4. We hope, perhaps, that human laws and natural sympathy would hold society together. As reasonably might we believe that were the sun quenched in the heavens, *our* torches would illuminate, and *our* fires quicken and fertilize the creation. What is there in human nature to awaken respect and tenderness, if man is the unprotected insect of a day? And what is he more, if atheism be true?

5. Erase all thought and fear of God from a community, and selfishness and sensuality would absorb the whole man. Appetite, knowing no restraint, and suffering, having no solace or hope, would trample in scorn on the restraints

of human laws. Virtue, duty, principle, would be mocked and spurned as unmeaning sounds. A sordid self-interest would supplant every feeling; and man would become, in fact, what the theory in atheism declares him to be,—*a companion for brutes.*

DEFINITIONS.—1. Com-mū'ni-ty, *society at large, the public.* Dĭf-fū'ṣion, *extension, spread.* En-līght'ened, *elevated by knowledge and religion.* 2. Făb'ric, *any system composed of connected parts.* E-rāsed', *blotted out.* 3. Pĕr'pe-trā-tor, *one who commits a crime.* Ex-tĭnc'tion, *a putting an end to.* 4. Fĕr'ti-līze, *to make fruitful.* A'the-ĭṣm, *disbelief in God.* Sĕn-sụ-ăl'i-ty, *indulgence in animal pleasure.*

XCIV. ROCK ME TO SLEEP.

Elizabeth Akers Allen (*b.* 1832, ——) was born at Strong, Maine, and passed her childhood amidst the picturesque scenery of that neighborhood. She lost her mother when very young, but inherited her grace and delicacy of thought. Shortly after her mother's death, her father removed to Farmington, Maine, a town noted for its literary people. Mrs. Allen's early pieces appeared over the pseudonym of "Florence Percy." Her first verses appeared when she was twelve years old; and her first volume, entitled "Forest Buds from the Woods of Maine," was published in 1856. For some years she was assistant editor of the "Portland Transcript." The following selection was claimed by five different persons, who attempted to steal the honor of its composition.

1. BACKWARD, turn backward, O Time, in your flight,
Make me a child again, just for to-night!
Mother, come back from the echoless shore,
Take me again to your heart as of yore;
Kiss from my forehead the furrows of care,
Smooth the few silver threads out of my hair;
Over my slumbers your loving watch keep;—
Rock me to sleep, mother,—rock me to sleep!

2. Backward, flow backward, O tide of the years!
I am so weary of toil and of tears;
Toil without recompense, tears all in vain;
Take them, and give me my childhood again!
I have grown weary of dust and decay,—
Weary of flinging my soul wealth away;
Weary of sowing for others to reap;—
Rock me to sleep, mother,—rock me to sleep!

3. Tired of the hollow, the base, the untrue,
Mother, O mother, my heart calls for you!
Many a summer the grass has grown green,
Blossomed and faded, our faces between:
Yet with strong yearning and passionate pain,
Long I to-night for your presence again.
Come from the silence so long and so deep;—
Rock me to sleep, mother,—rock me to sleep!

4. Over my heart in the days that are flown,
No love like mother love ever has shone;
No other worship abides and endures,
Faithful, unselfish, and patient like yours:
None like a mother can charm away pain
From the sick soul, and the world-weary brain.
Slumber's soft calms o'er my heavy lids creep;—
Rock me to sleep, mother,—rock me to sleep!

5. Come, let your brown hair, just lighted with gold,
Fall on your shoulders again, as of old;
Let it drop over my forehead to-night,
Shading my faint eyes away from the light;
For with its sunny-edged shadows once more,
Haply will throng the sweet visions of yore;
Lovingly, softly, its bright billows sweep;—
Rock me to sleep, mother,—rock me to sleep!

6. Mother, dear mother, the years have been long
Since I last listened your lullaby song;
Sing, then, and unto my soul it shall seem
Womanhood's years have been only a dream;
Clasped to your heart in a loving embrace,
With your light lashes just sweeping my face,
Never hereafter to wake or to weep;—
Rock me to sleep, mother,—rock me to sleep!

XCV. MAN AND THE INFERIOR ANIMALS.

1. THE chief difference between man and the other animals consists in this, that the former has reason, whereas the latter have only instinct; but, in order to understand what we mean by the terms reason and instinct, it will be necessary to mention three things in which the difference very distinctly appears.

2. Let us first, to bring the parties as nearly on a level as possible, consider man in a savage state, wholly occupied, like the beasts of the field, in providing for the wants of his animal nature; and here the first distinction that appears between them is the use of implements. When the savage provides himself with a hut or a wigwam for shelter, or that he may store up his provisions, he does no more than is done by the rabbit, the beaver, the bee, and birds of every species.

3. But the man can not make any progress in this work without tools; he must provide himself with an ax even before he can cut down a tree for its timber; whereas these animals form their burrows, their cells, or their nests, with no other tools than those with which nature has provided them. In cultivating the ground, also, man can do nothing without a spade or a plow; nor can he reap what he has sown till he has shaped an implement with which to

cut down his harvest. But the inferior animals provide for themselves and their young without any of these things.

4. Now for the second distinction. Man, in all his operations, makes mistakes; animals make none. Did you ever hear of such a thing as a bird sitting on a twig lamenting over her half-finished nest and puzzling her little head to know how to complete it? Or did you ever see the cells of a beehive in clumsy, irregular shapes, or observe anything like a discussion in the little community, as if there were a difference of opinion among the architects?

5. The lower animals are even better physicians than we are; for when they are ill, they will, many of them, seek out some particular herb, which they do not use as food, and which possesses a medicinal quality exactly suited to the complaint; whereas, the whole college of physicians will dispute for a century about the virtues of a single drug.

6. Man undertakes nothing in which he is not more or less puzzled; and must try numberless experiments before he can bring his undertakings to anything like perfection; even the simplest operations of domestic life are not well performed without some experience; and the term of man's life is half wasted before he has done with his mistakes and begins to profit by his lessons.

7. The third distinction is that animals make no improvements; while the knowledge, and skill, and the success of man are perpetually on the increase. Animals, in all their operations, follow the first impulse of nature or that instinct which God has implanted in them. In all they do undertake, therefore, their works are more perfect and regular than those of man.

8. But man, having been endowed with the faculty of thinking or reasoning about what he does, is enabled by patience and industry to correct the mistakes into which he at first falls, and to go on constantly improving. A bird's

nest is, indeed, a perfect structure; yet the nest of a swallow of the nineteenth century is not at all more commodious or elegant than those that were built amid the rafters of Noah's ark. But if we compare the wigwam of the savage with the temples and palaces of ancient Greece and Rome, we then shall see to what man's mistakes, rectified and improved upon, conduct him.

9. "When the vast sun shall veil his golden light
Deep in the gloom of everlasting night;
When wild, destructive flames shall wrap the skies,
When ruin triumphs, and when nature dies;
Man shall alone the wreck of worlds survive;
'Mid falling spheres, immortal man shall live."

—*Jane Taylor.*

DEFINITIONS.—2. Dis-tĭn̲e'tion, *a point of difference.* Im'ple-ments, *utensils, tools.* Wĭg̅'wa̤m, *an Indian hut.* 3. Bŭr'rowş, *holes in the earth where animals lodge.* 4. Dis-eŭs'sion, *the act of arguing a point, debate.* 5. Me-dĭç'i-nal, *healing.* 8. En-dowed', *furnished with any gift, quality, etc.* Făe'ul-ty, *ability to act or perform.* Rĕe'ti-fīed, *corrected.*

XCVI. THE BLIND MEN AND THE ELEPHANT.

John Godfrey Saxe (*b.* 1816, *d.* 1887), an American humorist, lawyer, and journalist, was born at Highgate, Vt. He graduated at Middlebury College in 1839; was admitted to the bar in 1843; and practiced law until 1850, when he became editor of the "Burlington Sentinel." In 1851, he was elected State's attorney. "Progress, a Satire, and Other Poems," his first volume, was published in 1849, and several other volumes of great merit attest his originality. For genial humor and good-natured satire, Saxe's writings rank among the best of their kind, and are very popular.

1. It was six men of Indostan,
To learning much inclined,
Who went to see the elephant,
(Though all of them were blind,)
That each by observation
Might satisfy his mind.

2. The first approached the elephant,
   And, happening to fall
Against his broad and sturdy side,
   At once began to bawl:
"God bless me! but the elephant
   Is very like a wall!"

3. The second, feeling of the tusk,
   Cried: "Ho! what have we here,
So very round, and smooth, and sharp?
   To me 't is very clear,
This wonder of an elephant
   Is very like a spear!"

4. The third approached the animal,
   And, happening to take
The squirming trunk within his hands,
   Thus boldly up he spake:
"I see," quoth he, "the elephant
   Is very like a snake!"

5. The fourth reached out his eager hand,
   And fell about the knee:
"What most this wondrous beast is like,
   Is very plain," quoth he;
"'T is clear enough the elephant
   Is very like a tree!"

6. The fifth, who chanced to touch the ear,
   Said: "E'en the blindest man
Can tell what this resembles most:
   Deny the fact who can,
This marvel of an elephant
   Is very like a fan!"

7. The sixth no sooner had begun
About the beast to grope,
Than, seizing on the swinging tail
That fell within his scope,
"I see," quoth he, "the elephant
Is very like a rope!"

8. And so these men of Indostan
Disputed loud and long,
Each in his own opinion
Exceeding stiff and strong,
Though each was partly in the right,
And all were in the wrong!

XCVII. A HOME SCENE.

Donald Grant Mitchell (*b.* 1822, ——). This popular American writer was born in Norwich, Conn. He graduated at Yale in 1841. In 1844 he went to England, and, after traveling through that country on foot, spent some time on the continent. His first volume, "Fresh Gleanings, or a New Sheaf from the Old Fields of Continental Europe, by Ik Marvel," was published in 1847, soon after his return home. He revisited Europe in 1848. On his return, he published "The Battle Summer." Mr. Mitchell has contributed to the "Knickerbocker Magazine," the "Atlantic Monthly," and several agricultural journals. His most popular works are "The Reveries of a Bachelor," 1850, and "Dream Life," 1851. Besides these, he has written "My Farm of Edgewood," "Wet Days at Edgewood," "Doctor Johns," a novel, "Rural Studies," and other works. He is a charming writer. In 1853 he was appointed United States consul at Venice. In 1855 he settled on a farm near New Haven, Conn., where he now resides. The following selection is from "Dream Life."

1. Little does the boy know, as the tide of years drifts by, floating him out insensibly from the harbor of his home, upon the great sea of life,—what joys, what opportunities, what affections, are slipping from him into the shades of that inexorable Past, where no man can go, save on the wings of his dreams.

2. Little does he think, as he leans upon the lap of his mother, with his eye turned to her, in some earnest pleading for a fancied pleasure of the hour, or in some important story of his griefs, that such sharing of his sorrows, and such sympathy with his wishes, he will find nowhere again.

3. Little does he imagine that the fond sister Nelly, ever thoughtful of his pleasures, ever smiling away his griefs, will soon be beyond the reach of either; and that the waves of the years which come rocking so gently under him will soon toss her far away, upon the great swell of life.

4. But *now*, you are there. The fire light glimmers upon the walls of your cherished home. The big chair of your father is drawn to its wonted corner by the chimney side; his head, just touched with gray, lies back upon its oaken top. Opposite sits your mother: her figure is thin, her look cheerful, yet subdued;—her arm perhaps resting on your shoulder, as she talks to you in tones of tender admonition, of the days that are to come.

5. The cat is purring on the hearth; the clock that ticked so plainly when Charlie died is ticking on the mantel still. The great table in the middle of the room, with its books and work, waits only for the lighting of the evening lamp, to see a return to its stores of embroidery and of story.

6. Upon a little stand under the mirror, which catches now and then a flicker of the fire light, and makes it play, as if in wanton, upon the ceiling, lies that big book, reverenced of your New England parents—the Family Bible. It is a ponderous, square volume, with heavy silver clasps, that you have often pressed open for a look at its quaint, old pictures, for a study of those prettily bordered pages, which lie between the Testaments, and which hold the Family Record.

7. There are the Births;—your father's and your mother's; it seems as if they were born a long time ago; and even your own date of birth appears an almost incredible dis-

tance back. Then, there are the Marriages;—only one as yet; and your mother's name looks oddly to you: it is hard to think of her as anyone else than your doting parent.

8. Last of all come the Deaths;—only one. Poor Charlie! How it looks!—"Died, 12 September, 18—, Charles Henry, aged four years." You know just how it looks. You have turned to it often; there you seem to be joined to him, though only by the turning of a leaf.

9. And over your thoughts, as you look at that page of the Record, there sometimes wanders a vague, shadowy fear, which *will* come,—that your own name may soon be there. You try to drop the notion, as if it were not fairly your own; you affect to slight it, as you would slight a boy who presumed on your acquaintance, but whom you have no desire to know.

10. Yet your mother—how strange it is!—has no fears of such dark fancies. Even now, as you stand beside her, and as the twilight deepens in the room, her low, silvery voice is stealing upon your ear, telling you that she can not be long with you;—that the time is coming, when you must be guided by your own judgment, and struggle with the world unaided by the friends of your boyhood.

11. There is a little pride, and a great deal more of anxiety, in your thoughts now, as you look steadfastly into the home blaze, while those delicate fingers, so tender of your happiness, play with the locks upon your brow. To struggle with the world,—that is a proud thing; to struggle alone,—there lies the doubt! Then crowds in swift upon the calm of boyhood the first anxious thought of youth.

12. The hands of the old clock upon the mantel that ticked off the hours when Charlie sighed and when Charlie died, draw on toward midnight. The shadows that the fireflame makes grow dimmer and dimmer. And thus it is, that Home,—boy home, passes away forever,—like the swaying of a pendulum,—like the fading of a shadow on the floor.

Definitions.—1. In-ĕx′or-a-ble, *not to be changed.* 4. Wȯnt′ed, *accustomed.* Ad-mo-nĭ′tion (*pro.* ad-mo-nĭsh′un), *counseling against fault or error.* 6. Pŏn′der-oŭs, *very heavy.* Quāint (*pro.* kwānt), *odd and antique.* 7. In-crĕd′i-ble, *impossible to be believed.* Dōt′-ing, *loving to excess.* 9. Vāgue (*pro.* vāg), *indefinite.* Pre-sūmed′, *pushed upon or intruded in an impudent manner.*

XCVIII. THE LIGHT OF OTHER DAYS.

Thomas Moore (*b.* 1779, *d.* 1852) was born in Dublin, Ireland, and he was educated at Trinity College in that city. In 1799, he entered the Middle Temple, London, as a student of law. Soon after the publication of his first poetical productions, he was sent to Bermuda in an official capacity. He subsequently visited the United States. Moore's most famous works are: "Lalla Rookh," an Oriental romance, 1817; "The Loves of the Angels," 1823; and "Irish Melodies," 1834; a "Life of Lord Byron," and "The Epicurean, an Eastern Tale." "Moore's excellencies," says Dr. Angus, "consist in the gracefulness of his thoughts, the wit and fancy of his allusions and imagery, and the music and refinement of his versification."

1. Oft in the stilly night
Ere slumber's chain has bound me,
Fond memory brings the light
Of other days around me:
The smiles, the tears
Of boyhood's years,
The words of love then spoken;
The eyes that shone,
Now dimmed and gone,
The cheerful hearts now broken!
Thus in the stilly night
Ere slumber's chain has bound me,
Sad memory brings the light
Of other days around me.

2. When I remember all
The friends so linked together
I've seen around me fall
Like leaves in wintry weather,
I feel like one
Who treads alone
Some banquet hall deserted,
Whose lights are fled
Whose garlands dead,
And all but he departed.
Thus in the stilly night
Ere slumber's chain has bound me,
Sad memory brings the light
Of other days around me.

XCIX. A CHASE IN THE ENGLISH CHANNEL.

James Fenimore Cooper (*b.* 1789, *d.* 1851). This celebrated American novelist was born in Burlington, N.J. His father removed to the state of New York about 1790, and founded Cooperstown, on Otsego Lake. He studied three years at Yale, and then entered the navy as a common sailor. He became a midshipman in 1806, and was afterwards promoted to the rank of lieutenant; but he left the service in 1811. His first novel, "Precaution," was published in 1819; his best work, "The Spy," a tale of the Revolutionary War, in 1821. The success of "The Spy" was almost unprecedented, and its author at once took rank among the most popular writers of the day. "The Pilot" and "The Red Rover" are considered his best sea novels. "The Pioneers," "The Last of the Mohicans," "The Prairie," "The Pathfinder," and "The Deerslayer" are among the best of his tales of frontier life. The best of his novels have been translated into nearly all of the European languages, and into some of those of Asia. "The creations of his genius," says Bryant, "shall survive through centuries to come, and only perish with our language." The following selection is from "The Pilot."

1. The ship which the American frigate had now to oppose, was a vessel of near her own size and equipage; and when Griffith looked at her again, he perceived that

she had made her preparations to assert her equality in manful fight.

2. Her sails had been gradually reduced to the usual quantity, and, by certain movements on her decks, the lieutenant and his constant attendant, the Pilot, well understood that she only wanted to lessen the distance a few hundred yards to begin the action.

"Now spread everything," whispered the stranger.

3. Griffith applied the trumpet to his mouth, and shouted, in a voice that was carried even to his enemy, "Let fall — out with your booms — sheet home — hoist away of everything!"

4. The inspiring cry was answered by a universal bustle. Fifty men flew out on the dizzy heights of the different spars, while broad sheets of canvas rose as suddenly along the masts, as if some mighty bird were spreading its wings. The Englishman instantly perceived his mistake, and he answered the artifice by a roar of artillery. Griffith watched the effects of the broadside with an absorbing interest as the shot whistled above his head; but when he perceived his masts untouched, and the few unimportant ropes, only, that were cut, he replied to the uproar with a burst of pleasure.

5. A few men were, however, seen clinging with wild frenzy to the cordage, dropping from rope to rope, like wounded birds fluttering through a tree, until they fell heavily into the ocean, the sullen ship sweeping by them in a cold indifference. At the next instant, the spars and masts of their enemy exhibited a display of men similar to their own, when Griffith again placed the trumpet to his mouth, and shouted aloud, "Give it to them; drive them from their yards, boys; scatter them with your grape; unreeve their rigging!"

6. The crew of the American wanted but little encouragement to enter on this experiment with hearty good will, and the close of his cheering words was uttered amid

the deafening roar of his own cannon. The Pilot had, however, mistaken the skill and readiness of their foe; for, notwithstanding the disadvantageous circumstances under which the Englishman increased his sail, the duty was steadily and dexterously performed.

7. The two ships were now running rapidly on parallel lines, hurling at each other their instruments of destruction with furious industry, and with severe and certain loss to both, though with no manifest advantage in favor of either. Both Griffith and the Pilot witnessed, with deep concern, this unexpected defeat of their hopes; for they could not conceal from themselves that each moment lessened their velocity through the water, as the shot of the enemy stripped the canvas from the yards, or dashed aside the lighter spars in their terrible progress.

8. "We find our equal here," said Griffith to the stranger. "The ninety is heaving up again like a mountain; and if we continue to shorten sail at this rate, she will soon be down upon us!"

"You say true, sir," returned the Pilot, musing, "the man shows judgment as well as spirit; but—"

9. He was interrupted by Merry, who rushed from the forward part of the vessel, his whole face betokening the eagerness of his spirit and the importance of his intelligence.—

"The breakers!" he cried, when nigh enough to be heard amid the din; "we are running dead on a ripple, and the sea is white not two hundred yards ahead."

10. The Pilot jumped on a gun, and, bending to catch a glimpse through the smoke, he shouted, in those clear, piercing tones, that could be even heard among the roaring of the cannon,—

"Port, port your helm! we are on the Devil's Grip! Pass up the trumpet, sir; port your helm, fellow; give it to them, boys—give it to the proud English dogs!"

11. Griffith unhesitatingly relinquished the symbol of his

rank, fastening his own firm look on the calm but quick eye of the Pilot, and gathering assurance from the high confidence he read in the countenance of the stranger. The seamen were too busy with their cannon and the rigging to regard the new danger; and the frigate entered one of the dangerous passes of the shoals, in the heat of a severely contested battle.

12. The wondering looks of a few of the older sailors glanced at the sheets of foam that flew by them, in doubt whether the wild gambols of the waves were occasioned by the shot of the enemy, when suddenly the noise of cannon was succeeded by the sullen wash of the disturbed element, and presently the vessel glided out of her smoky shroud, and was boldly steering in the center of the narrow passages.

13. For ten breathless minutes longer the Pilot continued to hold an uninterrupted sway, during which the vessel ran swiftly by ripples and breakers, by streaks of foam and darker passages of deep water, when he threw down his trumpet and exclaimed —

"What threatened to be our destruction has proved our salvation. — Keep yonder hill crowned with wood one point open from the church tower at its base, and steer east and by north; you will run through these shoals on that course in an hour, and by so doing you will gain five leagues of your enemy, who will have to double their trail."

14. Every officer in the ship, after the breathless suspense of uncertainty had passed, rushed to those places where a view might be taken of their enemies. The ninety was still steering boldly onward, and had already approached the two-and-thirty, which lay a helpless wreck, rolling on the unruly seas that were rudely tossing her on their wanton billows. The frigate last engaged was running along the edge of the ripple, with her torn sails flying loosely in the air, her ragged spars tottering in the breeze, and everything above her hull exhibiting the confusion of a sudden and unlooked-for check to her progress.

15. The exulting taunts and mirthful congratulations of the seamen, as they gazed at the English ships, were, however, soon forgotten in the attention that was required to their own vessel. The drums beat the retreat, the guns were lashed, the wounded again removed, and every individual able to keep the deck was required to lend his assistance in repairing the damages to the frigate, and securing her masts.

16. The promised hour carried the ship safely through all the dangers, which were much lessened by daylight; and by the time the sun had begun to fall over the land, Griffith, who had not quitted the deck during the day, beheld his vessel once more cleared of the confusion of the chase and battle, and ready to meet another foe.

DEFINITIONS.—1. Frĭg'ate, *a war vessel, usually carrying from twenty-eight to forty-four guns, arranged in two tiers on each side.* Eq'ui-paġe (*pro.* ĕk'wĭ-paj), *furniture, fitting out.* 4. Ar'ti-fîçe, *skillful contrivance, trick.* Broạd'sīde, *a discharge of all the guns on one side of a ship, above and below, at the same time.* 7. Măn'i-fest, *visible to the eye, apparent.* 11. As-sụr'ançe (*pro.* ȧ-shụr'ans), *full confidence, courage.* 13. Swāy, *control, rule.*

NOTES.—2. *The Pilot,* who appears in this story, under disguise, is John Paul Jones, a celebrated American naval officer during the Revolution. He was born in Scotland, in 1747, and was apprenticed when only twelve years old as a sailor. He was familiar with the waters about the British Islands, and during part of the war he hovered about their coasts in a daring way, capturing many vessels, often against heavy odds, and causing great terror to the enemy.

8. *The ninety,* refers to a large ninety-gun ship, part of a fleet which was chasing the American vessel.

10. *The Devil's Grip;* the name of a dangerous reef in the English Channel.

13. *One point open.* Directions for steering, referring to the compass.

14. *The two-and-thirty; i.e.,* another of the enemy's ships, carrying thirty-two guns.

C. BURIAL OF SIR JOHN MOORE.

Charles Wolfe (*b.* 1791, *d.* 1823), an Irish poet and clergyman, was born in Dublin. He was educated in several schools, and graduated at the university of his native city. He was ordained in 1817, and soon became noted for his zeal and energy as a clergyman. His literary productions were collected and published in 1825. "The Burial of Sir John Moore," one of the finest poems of its kind in the English language, was written in 1817, and first appeared in the "Newry Telegraph," a newspaper, with the author's initials, but without his knowledge. Byron said of this ballad that he would rather be the author of it than of any one ever written.

1. Not a drum was heard, not a funeral note,
   As his corse to the rampart we hurried;
Not a soldier discharged his farewell shot
   O'er the grave where our hero we buried.

2. We buried him darkly, at dead of night,
   The sods with our bayonets turning,
By the struggling moonbeam's misty light,
   And the lantern dimly burning.

3. No useless coffin inclosed his breast,
   Not in sheet nor in shroud we wound him;
But he lay like a warrior taking his rest,
   With his martial cloak around him.

4. Few and short were the prayers we said,
   And we spoke not a word of sorrow;
But we steadfastly gazed on the face of the dead
   And we bitterly thought of the morrow.

5. We thought, as we hollowed his narrow bed,
   And smoothed down his lonely pillow,
That the foe and the stranger would tread o'er
      his head,
   And we far away on the billow!

6. Lightly they'll talk of the spirit that's gone
And o'er his cold ashes upbraid him;
But little he'll reck, if they'll let him sleep on
In a grave where a Briton has laid him.

7. But half of our heavy task was done,
When the clock struck the hour for retiring
And we heard the distant random gun
That the foe was sullenly firing.

8. Slowly and sadly we laid him down,
From the field of his fame, fresh and gory;
We carved not a line, we raised not a stone,
But we left him alone with his glory!

DEFINITIONS. — 3. Mär'tial (*pro.* mär'shal), *military.* 6. Up-brāid', *to charge with something wrong or disgraceful, to reproach.* Rĕck, *to take heed, to care.* 7. Răn'dom, *without fixed aim or purpose, left to chance.*

NOTE. — *Sir John Moore* (*b.* 1761, *d.* 1809) was a celebrated British general. He was appointed commander of the British forces in Spain, in the war against Napoleon, and fell at the battle of Corunna, by a cannon shot. Marshal Soult, the opposing French commander, caused a monument to be erected to his memory. The British government has also raised a monument to him in St. Paul's Cathedral, while his native city, Glasgow, honors him with a bronze statue.

CI. LITTLE VICTORIES.

1. "O MOTHER, now that I have lost my limb, I can never be a soldier or a sailor; I can never go round the world!" And Hugh burst into tears, now more really afflicted than he had ever been yet. His mother sat on the bed beside him, and wiped away his tears as they

flowed, while he told her, as well as his sobs would let him, how long and how much he had reckoned on going round the world, and how little he cared for anything else in future; and now this was the very thing he should never be able to do!

2. He had practiced climbing ever since he could remember, and now this was of no use; he had practiced marching, and now he should never march again. When he had finished his complaint, there was a pause, and his mother said,

"Hugh, you have heard of Huber?"

"The man who found out so much about bees?" said Hugh.

"Bees and ants. When Huber had discovered more than had ever been known about these, and when he was sure that he could learn still more, and was more and more anxious to peep into their tiny homes and curious ways, he became blind."

3. Hugh sighed, and his mother went on.

"Did you ever hear of Beethoven? He was one of the greatest musical composers that ever lived. His great, his sole delight was in music. It was the passion of his life. When all his time and all his mind were given to music, he suddenly became deaf, perfectly deaf; so that he never more heard one single note from the loudest orchestra. While crowds were moved and delighted with his compositions, it was all silence to him." Hugh said nothing.

4. "Now do you think," asked his mother — and Hugh saw that a mild and gentle smile beamed from her countenance — "do you think that these people were without a Heavenly Parent?"

"O no! but were they patient?" asked Hugh.

"Yes, in their different ways and degrees. Would you suppose that they were hardly treated? Or would you not rather suppose that their Father gave them something better to do than they had planned for themselves?"

5. "He must know best, of course; but it does seem very hard that that very thing should happen to them. Huber would not have so much minded being deaf, perhaps; or that musical man, being blind.

"No doubt their hearts often swelled within them at their disappointments; but I fully believe that they very soon found God's will to be wiser than their wishes. They found, if they bore their trial well, that there was work for their hearts to do far nobler than any the head could do through the eye or the ear. And they soon felt a new and delicious pleasure which none but the bitterly disappointed can feel."

"What is that?"

6. "The pleasure of rousing the soul to bear pain, and of agreeing with God silently, when nobody knows what is in the breast. There is no pleasure like that of exercising one's soul in bearing pain, and of finding one's heart glow with the hope that one is pleasing God."

"Shall I feel that pleasure?"

"Often and often, I have no doubt; every time you can willingly give up your wish to be a soldier or a sailor, or anything else you have set your mind upon, you will feel that pleasure. But I do not expect it of you yet. I dare say it was long a bitter thing to Beethoven to see hundreds of people in raptures with his music, when he could not hear a note of it."

7. "But did he ever smile again?" asked Hugh.

"If he did, he was happier than all the fine music in the world could have made him," replied his mother.

"I wonder, oh, I wonder, if I shall ever feel so!"

"We will pray to God that you may. Shall we ask him now?" Hugh clasped his hands. His mother kneeled beside the bed, and, in a very few words, prayed that Hugh might be able to bear his misfortune well, and that his friends might give him such help and comfort as God should approve.

8. Hugh found himself subject to very painful feelings sometimes, such as no one quite understood, and such as he feared no one was able to pity as they deserved. On one occasion, when he had been quite merry for a while, and his mother and his sister Agnes were chatting, they thought they heard a sob from the sofa. They spoke to Hugh, and found that he was indeed crying bitterly.

"What is it, my dear?" said his mother. "Agnes, have we said anything that could hurt his feelings?"

"No, no," sobbed Hugh. "I will tell you, presently."

9. And, presently, he told them that he was so busy listening to what they said that he forgot everything else, when he felt as if something had gotten between two of his toes; unconsciously he put down his hand as if his foot were there! Nothing could be plainer than the feeling in his toes; and then, when he put out his hand, and found nothing, it was so terrible, it startled him so! It was a comfort to find that his mother knew about this. She came, and kneeled by his sofa, and told him that many persons who had lost a limb considered this the most painful thing they had to bear for some time; but that, though the feeling would return occasionally through life, it would cease to be painful.

10. Hugh was very much dejected, and when he thought of the months and years to the end of his life, and that he should never run and play, and never be like other people, he almost wished that he were dead.

Agnes thought that he must be miserable indeed if he could venture to say this to his mother. She glanced at her mother's face, but there was no displeasure there. On the contrary, she said this feeling was very natural. She had felt it herself under smaller misfortunes than Hugh's; but she had found, though the prospect appeared all strewn with troubles, that they came singly, and were not so hard to bear, after all.

11. She told Hugh that when she was a little girl she

was very lazy, fond of her bed, and not at all fond of dressing or washing.

"Why, mother! you?" exclaimed Hugh.

"Yes; that was the sort of little girl I was. Well, I was in despair, one day, at the thought that I should have to wash, and clean my teeth, and brush my hair, and put on every article of dress, every morning, as long as I lived."

"Did you tell anybody?" asked Hugh.

12. "No, I was ashamed to do that; but I remember I cried. You see how it turns out. When we have become accustomed to anything, we do it without ever thinking of the trouble, and, as the old fable tells us, the clock that has to tick so many millions of times, has exactly the same number of seconds to do it in. So will you find that you can move about on each separate occasion, as you wish, and practice will enable you to do it without any trouble or thought."

"But this is not all, nor half what I mean," said Hugh.

13. "No, my dear, nor half what you will have to bear. You resolved to bear it all patiently, I remember. But what is it you dread the most?"

"Oh! all manner of things. I can never do like other people."

"Some things," replied his mother. "You can never play cricket, as every Crofton boy would like to do. You can never dance at your sister's Christmas parties."

14. "O mamma!" cried Agnes, with tears in her eyes, and with the thought in her mind that it was cruel to talk so.

"Go on! Go on!" cried Hugh, brightening. "You know what I feel, mother; and you don't keep telling me, as others do, and even sister Agnes, sometimes, that it will not signify much, and that I shall not care, and all that; making out that it is no misfortune, hardly, when I know what it is, and they don't. Now, then, go on, mother! What else?"

15. "There will be little checks and mortifications continually, when you see little boys leaping over this, and climbing that, and playing at the other, while you must stand out, and can only look on And some people will pity you in a way you will not like: and some may even laugh at you."

"O mamma!" exclaimed Agnes.

"Well, and what else?" said Hugh.

16. "Sooner or later you will have to follow some way of life determined by this accident instead of one that you would have liked better."

"Well, what else?"

"I must ask you, now. I can think of nothing more; and I hope there is not much else; for, indeed, I think here is quite enough for a boy, or anyone else, to bear."

"I will bear it though; you will see."

17. "You will find great helps. These misfortunes of themselves strengthen one's mind. They have some advantages too. You will be a better scholar for your lameness, I have no doubt. You will read more books, and have a mind richer in thoughts. You will be more beloved by us all, and you yourself will love God more for having given you something to bear for his sake. God himself will help you to bear your trials. You will conquer your troubles one by one, and by a succession of LITTLE VICTORIES will at last completely triumph over all."

— *Harriet Martineau.*

DEFINITIONS. — 1. Af-flĭct'ed, *overwhelmed, dejected.* Rĕck'oned, *calculated, counted.* 3. Com-pōṣ'er, *an author of a piece of music.* Or'ches-trȧ, *a body of instrumental musicians.* 7. Ap-prọve', *sanction, allow.* 10. De-jĕct'ed, *discouraged, low-spirited.*

NOTES. — 2. *François Huber* (*b.* 1750, *d.* 1831) was a Swiss naturalist. He became blind at the age of fifteen, but pursued his studies by the aid of his wife and an attendant.

2. *Ludwig van Beethoven* (*pro.* bā'tō-ven; *b.* 1770, *d.* 1827) was born at Bonn, Prussia, but passed most of his life at Vienna.

CII. THE CHARACTER OF A HAPPY LIFE.

Sir Henry Wotton (*b.* 1568, *d.* 1639) was born at Bocton Hall, Kent, England. He was educated at Winchester and Oxford. About 1598 he was taken into the service of the Earl of Essex, as one of his secretaries. On the Earl's committal to the Tower for treason, Wotton fled to France; but he returned to England immediately after the death of Elizabeth, and received the honor of knighthood. He was King James's favorite diplomatist, and, in 1623, was appointed provost of Eton College. Wotton wrote a number of prose works; but his literary reputation rests mainly on some short poems, which are distinguished by a dignity of thought and expression rarely excelled.

1. How happy is he born and taught,
   That serveth not another's will;
Whose armor is his honest thought,
   And simple truth his utmost skill!

2. Whose passions not his masters are,
   Whose soul is still prepared for death,
Untied unto the worldly care
   Of public fame, or private breath;

3. Who envies none that chance doth raise,
   Or vice; who never understood
How deepest wounds are given by praise;
   Nor rules of state, but rules of good:

4. Who hath his life from rumors freed,
   Whose conscience is his strong retreat;
Whose state can neither flatterers feed,
   Nor ruin make oppressors great;

5. Who God doth late and early pray,
   More of his grace than gifts to lend;
And entertains the harmless day
   With a religious book or friend

6. This man is freed from servile bands,
Of hope to rise, or fear to fall;
Lord of himself, though not of lands;
And having nothing, yet hath all.

CIII. THE ART OF DISCOURAGEMENT.

Arthur Helps (*b.* 1813, *d.* 1875) graduated at Cambridge, England, in 1835. His best known works are: "Friends in Council, a Series of Readings and Discourses," "Companions of my Solitude," and "Realmah," a tale of the "lake dwellers" in southern Europe. He has also written a "History of the Spanish Conquests in America," two historical dramas, and several other works. Mr. Helps was a true thinker, and his writings are deservedly popular with thoughtful readers. In 1859 he was appointed secretary of the privy council.

1. Regarding, one day, in company with a humorous friend, a noble vessel of a somewhat novel construction sailing slowly out of port, he observed, "What a quantity of cold water somebody must have had down his back." In my innocence, I supposed that he alluded to the wet work of the artisans who had been building the vessel; but when I came to know him better, I found that this was the form of comment he always indulged in when contemplating any new and great work, and that his "somebody" was the designer of the vessel.

2. My friend had carefully studied the art of discouragement, and there was a class of men whom he designated simply as "cold-water pourers." It was most amusing to hear him describe the lengthened sufferings of the man who first designed a wheel; of him who first built a boat; of the adventurous personage who first proposed the daring enterprise of using buttons, instead of fish bones, to fasten the scanty raiment of some savage tribe.

3. Warming with his theme, he would become quite eloquent in describing the long career of discouragement which

these rash men had brought upon themselves, and which he said, to his knowledge, must have shortened their lives. He invented imaginary dialogues between the unfortunate inventor, say of the wheel, and his particular friend, some eminent cold-water pourer. For, as he said, every man has some such friend, who fascinates him by fear, and to whom he confides his enterprises in order to hear the worst that can be said of them.

4. The sayings of the chilling friend, probably, as he observed, ran thus: — "We seem to have gone on very well for thousands of years without this rolling thing. Your father carried burdens on his back. The king is content to be borne on men's shoulders. The high priest is not too proud to do the same. Indeed, I question whether it is not irreligious to attempt to shift from men's shoulders their natural burdens.

5. "Then, as to its succeeding, — for my part, I see no chance of that. How can it go up hill? How often you have failed before in other fanciful things of the same nature! Besides, you are losing your time; and the yams about your hut are only half planted. You will be a beggar; and it is my duty, as a friend, to tell you so plainly.

6. "There was Nang-chung: what became of him? We had found fire for ages, in a proper way, taking a proper time about it, by rubbing two sticks together. He must needs strike out fire at once, with iron and flint; and did he die in his bed? Our sacred lords saw the impiety of that proceeding, and very justly impaled the man who imitated heavenly powers. And, even if you could succeed with this new and absurd rolling thing, the state would be ruined. What would become of those who carry burdens on their backs? Put aside the vain fancies of a childish mind, and finish the planting of your yams."

7. It is really very curious to observe how, even in modern times, the arts of discouragement prevail. There are men whose sole pretense to wisdom consists in administering

discouragement. They are never at a loss. They are equally ready to prophesy, with wonderful ingenuity, all possible varieties of misfortune to any enterprise that may be proposed; and when the thing is produced, and has met with some success, to find a flaw in it.

8. I once saw a work of art produced in the presence of an eminent cold-water pourer. He did not deny that it was beautiful; but he instantly fastened upon a small crack in it that nobody had observed; and upon that crack he would dilate whenever the work was discussed in his presence. Indeed, he did not see the work, but only the crack in it. That flaw, — that little flaw, — was all in all to him.

9. The cold-water pourers are not all of one form of mind. Some are led to indulge in this recreation from genuine timidity. They really do fear that all new attempts will fail. Others are simply envious and ill-natured. Then, again, there is a sense of power and wisdom in prophesying evil. Moreover, it is the safest thing to prophesy, for hardly anything at first succeeds exactly in the way that it was intended to succeed.

10. Again, there is the lack of imagination which gives rise to the utterance of so much discouragement. For an ordinary man, it must have been a great mental strain to grasp the ideas of the first projectors of steam and gas, electric telegraphs, and pain-deadening chloroform. The inventor is always, in the eyes of his fellow-men, somewhat of a madman; and often they do their best to make him so.

11. Again, there is the want of sympathy; and that is, perhaps, the ruling cause in most men's minds who have given themselves up to discourage. They are not tender enough, or sympathetic enough, to appreciate all the pain they are giving, when, in a dull plodding way, they lay out argument after argument to show that the project which the poor inventor has set his heart upon, and upon which, perhaps, he has staked his fortune, will not succeed.

12. But what inventors suffer, is only a small part of

what mankind in general endure from thoughtless and unkind discouragement. Those high-souled men belong to the suffering class, and must suffer; but it is in daily life that the wear and tear of discouragement tells so much. Propose a small party of pleasure to an apt discourager, and see what he will make of it. It soon becomes sicklied over with doubt and despondency; and, at last, the only hope of the proposer is, that his proposal, when realized, will not be an ignominious failure. All hope of pleasure, at least for the proposer, has long been out of the question.

Definitions. — 2. Dĕş'ĭg-nāt-ed, *called by a distinctive title, named.* 5. Yăm, *the root of a climbing plant, found in the tropics, which is used for food.* 6. Im-pāled', *put to death by being fixed on an upright, sharp stake.* 8. Dĭ-lāte', *to speak largely, to dwell in narration.* 10. Rīse (*pro.* rīs, *not* rīz), *source, origin.* Pro-jĕc'tor, *one who forms a scheme or design.*

CIV. THE MARINER'S DREAM.

William Dimond (*b.* 1780, *d.* 1837) was a dramatist and poet, living at Bath, England, where he was born and received his education. He afterwards studied for the bar in London. His literary productions are for the most part dramas, but he has also written a number of poems, among them the following:

1. In slumbers of midnight the sailor boy lay;
   His hammock swung loose at the sport of the wind;
But watch-worn and weary, his cares flew away,
   And visions of happiness danced o'er his mind.

2. He dreamed of his home, of his dear native bowers,
   And pleasures that waited on life's merry morn;
While Memory each scene gayly covered with flowers,
   And restored every rose, but secreted the thorn.

3. Then Fancy her magical pinions spread wide,
And bade the young dreamer in ecstasy rise;
Now, far, far behind him the green waters glide,
And the cot of his forefathers blesses his eyes.

4. The jessamine clambers in flowers o'er the thatch,
And the swallow chirps sweet from her nest in the wall;
All trembling with transport, he raises the latch,
And the voices of loved ones reply to his call.

5. A father bends o'er him with looks of delight;
His cheek is impearled with a mother's warm tear;
And the lips of the boy in a love kiss unite
With the lips of the maid whom his bosom holds dear.

6. The heart of the sleeper beats high in his breast;
Joy quickens his pulses, — all his hardships seem o'er;
And a murmur of happiness steals through his rest, —
"O God! thou hast blest me, — I ask for no more."

7. Ah! whence is that flame which now bursts on his eye?
Ah! what is that sound that now 'larums his ear?
'T is the lightning's red glare painting hell on the sky!
'T is the crashing of thunders, the groan of the sphere!

8. He springs from his hammock, — he flies to the deck;
Amazement confronts him with images dire;
Wild winds and mad waves drive the vessel a wreck;
The masts fly in splinters; the shrouds are on fire.

9. Like mountains the billows tremendously swell;
In vain the lost wretch calls on Mercy to save;
Unseen hands of spirits are ringing his knell,
And the death angel flaps his broad wings o'er the wave!

10. O sailor boy, woe to thy dream of delight!
In darkness dissolves the gay frostwork of bliss!
Where now is the picture that Fancy touched bright,—
Thy parents' fond pressure, and love's honeyed kiss?

11. O sailor boy! sailor boy! never again
Shall home, love, or kindred, thy wishes repay;
Unblessed and unhonored, down deep in the main,
Full many a fathom, thy frame shall decay.

12. No tomb shall e'er plead to remembrance for thee,
Or redeem form or fame from the merciless surge;
But the white foam of waves shall thy winding sheet be,
And winds in the midnight of winter thy dirge.

13. On a bed of green sea flowers thy limbs shall be laid,—
Around thy white bones the red coral shall grow;
Of thy fair yellow locks threads of amber be made,
And every part suit to thy mansion below.

14. Days, months, years, and ages shall circle away,
And still the vast waters above thee shall roll;
Earth loses thy pattern forever and aye;
O sailor boy! sailor boy! peace to thy soul!

Definitions.—1. Hăm'mock, *a hanging or swinging bed, usually made of netting or hempen cloth.* 4. Trăns'pōrt, *ecstasy, rapture.* 5. Im-pēarled' (*pro.* im-pẽrled'), *decorated with pearls, or with things resembling pearls.* 7. 'Lăr'ums (*an abbreviation of* alarums, *for* alarms), *affrights, terrifies.* 12. Dĩrge, *funeral music.*

Notes.—13. *Coral* is the solid part of a minute sea animal, corresponding to the bones in other animals. It grows in many fantastic shapes, and is of various colors.

Amber is a yellow resin, and is the fossilized gum of buried trees. It is mined in several localities in Europe and America; it is also found along the seacoast, washed up by the waves.

CV. THE PASSENGER PIGEON.

John James Audubon (*b.* 1780, *d.* 1851). This celebrated American ornithologist was born in Louisiana. When quite young he was passionately fond of birds, and took delight in studying their habits. In 1797 his father, an admiral in the French navy, sent him to Paris to be educated. On his return to America, he settled on a farm in eastern Pennsylvania, but afterwards removed to Henderson, Ky., where he resided several years, supporting his family by trade, but devoting most of his time to the pursuit of his favorite study. In 1826 he went to England, and commenced the publication of the "Birds of America," which consists of ten volumes — five of engravings of birds, natural size, and five of letterpress. Cuvier declares this work to be "the most magnificent monument that art has ever erected to ornithology." In 1830 Audubon returned to America, and soon afterwards made excursions into nearly every section of the United States and Canada. A popular edition of his great work was published, in seven volumes, in 1844, and "The Quadrupeds of America," in six volumes, — three of plates and three of letterpress, in 1846–50. He removed to the vicinity of New York about 1840, and resided there until his death.

1. THE multitudes of wild pigeons in our woods are astonishing. Indeed, after having viewed them so often, and under so many circumstances, I even now feel inclined to pause and assure myself that what I am going to relate is a fact. Yet I have seen it all, and that, too, in the company of persons who, like myself, were struck with amazement.

2. In the autumn of 1813 I left my house at Henderson, on the banks of the Ohio, on my way to Louisville. In passing over the Barrens, a few miles beyond Hardinsburgh, I observed the pigeons flying, from northeast to southwest, in greater numbers than I thought I had ever seen them before, and feeling an inclination to count the flocks that might pass within the reach of my eye in one hour, I dismounted, seated myself on an eminence, and began to mark with my pencil, making a dot for every flock that passed.

3. In a short time, finding the task which I had undertaken impracticable, as the birds poured in in countless multitudes, I rose, and, counting the dots then put down,

found that one hundred and sixty-three had been made in twenty-one minutes. I traveled on, and still met more the farther I proceeded. The air was literally filled with pigeons; the light of noonday was obscured as by an eclipse; and the continued buzz of wings had a tendency to lull my senses to repose.

4. Whilst waiting for dinner at Young's inn, at the confluence of Salt River with the Ohio, I saw, at my leisure, immense legions still going by, with a front reaching far beyond the Ohio on the west, and the beech wood forests directly on the east of me. Not a single bird alighted, for not a nut or acorn was that year to be seen in the neighborhood. They consequently flew so high that different trials to reach them with a capital rifle proved ineffectual; nor did the reports disturb them in the least.

5. I can not describe to you the extreme beauty of their aërial evolutions when a hawk chanced to press upon the rear of a flock. At once, like a torrent, and with a noise like thunder, they rushed into a compact mass, pressing upon each other towards the center. In these almost solid masses, they darted forward in undulating and angular lines, descended and swept close over the earth with inconceivable velocity, mounted perpendicularly so as to resemble a vast column, and, when high, were seen wheeling and twisting within their continued lines, which then resembled the coils of a gigantic serpent.

6. As soon as the pigeons discover a sufficiency of food to entice them to alight, they fly round in circles, reviewing the country below. During their evolutions, on such occasions, the dense mass which they form exhibits a beautiful appearance, as it changes its direction, now displaying a glistening sheet of azure, when the backs of the birds come simultaneously into view, and anon suddenly presenting a mass of rich, deep purple.

7. They then pass lower, over the woods, and for a moment are lost among the foliage, but again emerge, and are

seen gliding aloft. They now alight; but the next moment, as if suddenly alarmed, they take to wing, producing by the flappings of their wings a noise like the roar of distant thunder, and sweep through the forests to see if danger is near. Hunger, however, soon brings them to the ground.

8. When alighted, they are seen industriously throwing up the withered leaves in quest of the fallen mast. The rear ranks are continually rising, passing over the main body, and alighting in front, in such rapid succession, that the whole flock seems still on wing. The quantity of ground thus swept is astonishing; and so completely has it been cleared that the gleaner who might follow in their rear would find his labor completely lost.

9. On such occasions, when the woods are filled with these pigeons, they are killed in immense numbers, although no apparent diminution ensues. About the middle of the day, after their repast is finished, they settle on the trees to enjoy rest and digest their food. As the sun begins to sink beneath the horizon, they depart *en masse* for the roosting place, which not unfrequently is hundreds of miles distant, as has been ascertained by persons who have kept an account of their arrivals and departures.

10. Let us now inspect their place of nightly rendezvous. One of these curious roosting places, on the banks of the Green River, in Kentucky, I repeatedly visited. It was, as is always the case, in a portion of the forest where the trees were of great magnitude, and where there was little underwood. I rode through it upwards of forty miles, and, crossing it in different parts, found its average breadth to be rather more than three miles. My first view of it was about a fortnight subsequent to the period when they had made choice of it, and I arrived there nearly two hours before sunset.

11. Many trees, two feet in diameter, I observed, were broken off at no great distance from the ground; and the

branches of many of the largest and tallest had given way, as if the forest had been swept by a tornado. Everything proved to me that the number of birds resorting to this part of the forest must be immense beyond conception.

12. As the period of their arrival approached, their foes anxiously prepared to receive them. Some were furnished with iron pots containing sulphur, others with torches of pine knots, many with poles, and the rest with guns. The sun was lost to our view, yet not a pigeon had arrived. Everything was ready, and all eyes were gazing on the clear sky, which appeared in glimpses amidst the tall trees. Suddenly there burst forth the general cry of, "Here they come!"

13. The noise which they made, though yet distant, reminded me of a hard gale at sea passing through the rigging of a close-reefed vessel. As the birds arrived and passed over me, I felt a current of air that surprised me. Thousands were soon knocked down by the pole men. The birds continued to pour in. The fires were lighted, and a magnificent as well as wonderful and almost terrifying sight presented itself.

14. The pigeons, arriving by thousands, alighted everywhere, one above another, until solid masses, as large as hogsheads, were formed on the branches all round. Here and there the perches gave way under the weight with a crash, and falling to the ground destroyed hundreds of the birds beneath, forcing down the dense groups with which every stick was loaded. It was a scene of uproar and confusion. I found it quite useless to speak or even to shout to those persons who were nearest to me. Even the reports of the guns were seldom heard, and I was made aware of the firing only by seeing the shooters reloading.

15. The uproar continued the whole night; and as I was anxious to know to what distance the sound reached, I sent off a man, accustomed to perambulate the forest, who, returning two hours afterwards, informed me he had

heard it distinctly when three miles distant from the spot. Towards the approach of day, the noise in some measure subsided; long before objects were distinguishable, the pigeons began to move off in a direction quite different from that in which they had arrived the evening before, and at sunrise all that were able to fly had disappeared.

DEFINITIONS. — 5. A-ē'ri-al, *belonging or pertaining to the air.* 6. A-nŏn', *in a short time, soon.* 8. Màst, *the fruit of oak and beech or other forest trees.* 10. Rĕn'dez-vous (*pro.* rĕn'de-vōō), *an appointed or customary place of meeting.* Sŭb'se-quent, *following in time.* 15. Per-ăm'bu-lāte, *to walk through.*

NOTES. — The wild pigeon, in common with almost every variety of game, is becoming more scarce throughout the country each year; and Audubon's account, but for the position he holds, would in time, no doubt, be considered ridiculous.

9. *En masse* (*pro.* àN mäs), a French phrase meaning in a body.

CVI. THE COUNTRY LIFE.

Richard Henry Stoddard (*b.* 1825, ——) was born at Hingham, Mass., but removed to New York City while quite young. His first volume of poems, "Foot-prints," appeared in 1849, and has been followed by many others. Of these may be mentioned "Songs of Summer," "Town and Country," "The King's Bell," "Abraham Lincoln" (an ode), and the "Book of the East," from which the last of which the following selection is abridged. Mr. Stoddard's verses are full of genuine feeling, and some of them show great poetic power.

1. NOT what we would, but what we must,
   Makes up the sum of living:
Heaven is both more and less than just,
   In taking and in giving
Swords cleave to hands that sought the plow,
And laurels miss the soldier's brow.

2. Me, whom the city holds, whose feet
   Have worn its stony highways,
Familiar with its loneliest street, —
   Its ways were never my ways.
My cradle was beside the sea,
And there, I hope, my grave will be.

3. Old homestead! in that old gray town
   Thy vane is seaward blowing;
Thy slip of garden stretches down
   To where the tide is flowing;
Below they lie, their sails all furled,
The ships that go about the world.

4. Dearer that little country house,
   Inland with pines beside it;
Some peach trees, with unfruitful boughs,
   A well, with weeds to hide it:
No flowers, or only such as rise
Self-sown — poor things! — which all despise.

5. Dear country home! can I forget
   The least of thy sweet trifles?
The window vines that clamber yet,
   Whose blooms the bee still rifles?
The roadside blackberries, growing ripe,
And in the woods the Indian pipe?

6. Happy the man who tills his field,
   Content with rustic labor;
Earth does to him her fullness yield,
   Hap what may to his neighbor.
Well days, sound nights — oh, can there be
A life more rational and free?

NOTE. — 5. *The Indian pipe* is a little, white plant, bearing a white, bell-shaped flower.

CVII. THE VIRGINIANS.

William Makepeace Thackeray (*b.* 1811, *d.* 1863). This popular English humorist, essayist, and novelist was born in Calcutta. He was educated at the Charterhouse school in London, and at Cambridge, but he did not complete a collegiate course of study. He began his literary career as a contributor to "Fraser's Magazine," under the assumed name of Michael Angelo Titmarsh, and afterwards contributed to the columns of "Punch." The first novel published under Thackeray's own name was "Vanity Fair," which is regarded by many as his greatest work. He afterwards wrote a large number of novels, tales, and poems, most of which were illustrated by sketches drawn by himself. His course of "Lectures on the English Humorists" was delivered in London in 1851, and the following year in several cities in the United States. He revisited the United States in 1856, and delivered a course of lectures on "The Four Georges," which he repeated in Great Britain soon after his return home. In 1860 he became the editor of "The Cornhill Magazine," the most successful serial ever published in England.

1. Mr. Esmond called his American house Castlewood, from the patrimonial home in the old country. The whole usages of Virginia, indeed, were fondly modeled after the English customs. It was a loyal colony. The Virginians boasted that King Charles the Second had been king in Virginia before he had been king in England. English king and English church were alike faithfully honored there.

2. The resident gentry were allied to good English families. They held their heads above the Dutch traders of New York, and the money-getting Roundheads of Pennsylvania and New England. Never were people less republican than those of the great province which was soon to be foremost in the memorable revolt against the British Crown.

3. The gentry of Virginia dwelt on their great lands after a fashion almost patriarchal. For its rough cultivation, each estate had a multitude of hands — of purchased and assigned servants — who were subject to the command of the master. The land yielded their food, live stock, and game.

4. The great rivers swarmed with fish for the taking. From their banks the passage home was clear. Their ships took the tobacco off their private wharves on the banks of the Potomac or the James River, and carried it to London or Bristol,—bringing back English goods and articles of home manufacture in return for the only produce which the Virginian gentry chose to cultivate.

5. Their hospitality was boundless. No stranger was ever sent away from their gates. The gentry received one another, and traveled to each other's houses, in a state almost feudal. The question of slavery was not born at the time of which we write. To be the proprietor of black servants shocked the feelings of no Virginia gentleman; nor, in truth, was the despotism exercised over the negro race generally a savage one. The food was plenty: the poor black people lazy and not unhappy. You might have preached negro emancipation to Madam Esmond of Castlewood as you might have told her to let the horses run loose out of her stables; she had no doubt but that the whip and the corn bag were good for both.

6. Her father may have thought otherwise, being of a skeptical turn on very many points, but his doubts did not break forth in active denial, and he was rather disaffected than rebellious. At one period, this gentleman had taken a part in active life at home, and possibly might have been eager to share its rewards; but in latter days he did not seem to care for them. A something had occurred in his life, which had cast a tinge of melancholy over all his existence.

7. He was not unhappy,—to those about him most kind,—most affectionate, obsequious even to the women of his family, whom he scarce ever contradicted; but there had been some bankruptcy of his heart, which his spirit never recovered. He submitted to life, rather than enjoyed it, and never was in better spirits than in his last hours when he was going to lay it down.

8. When the boys' grandfather died, their mother, in great state, proclaimed her eldest son George her successor and heir of the estate; and Harry, George's younger brother by half an hour, was always enjoined to respect his senior. All the household was equally instructed to pay him honor; the negroes, of whom there was a large and happy family, and the assigned servants from Europe, whose lot was made as bearable as it might be under the government of the lady of Castlewood.

9. In the whole family there scarcely was a rebel save Mrs. Esmond's faithful friend and companion, Madam Mountain, and Harry's foster mother, a faithful negro woman, who never could be made to understand why her child should not be first, who was handsomer, and stronger, and cleverer than his brother, as she vowed; though, in truth, there was scarcely any difference in the beauty, strength, or stature of the twins.

10. In disposition, they were in many points exceedingly unlike; but in feature they resembled each other so closely, that, but for the color of their hair, it had been difficult to distinguish them. In their beds, and when their heads were covered with those vast, ribboned nightcaps, which our great and little ancestors wore, it was scarcely possible for any but a nurse or a mother to tell the one from the other child.

11. Howbeit, alike in form, we have said that they differed in temper. The elder was peaceful, studious, and silent; the younger was warlike and noisy. He was quick at learning when he began, but very slow at beginning. No threats of the ferule would provoke Harry to learn in an idle fit, or would prevent George from helping his brother in his lesson. Harry was of a strong military turn, drilled the little negroes on the estate, and caned them like a corporal, having many good boxing matches with them, and never bearing malice if he was worsted; — whereas George was sparing of blows, and gentle with all about him.

12. As the custom in all families was, each of the boys had a special little servant assigned him: and it was a known fact that George, finding his little wretch of a blackamoor asleep on his master's bed, sat down beside it, and brushed the flies off the child with a feather fan, to the horror of old Gumbo, the child's father, who found his young master so engaged, and to the indignation of Madam Esmond, who ordered the young negro off to the proper officer for a whipping. In vain George implored and entreated — burst into passionate tears, and besought a remission of the sentence. His mother was inflexible regarding the young rebel's punishment, and the little negro went off beseeching his young master not to cry.

13. On account of a certain apish drollery and humor which exhibited itself in the lad, and a liking for some of the old man's pursuits, the first of the twins was the grandfather's favorite and companion, and would laugh and talk out all his infantine heart to the old gentleman, to whom the younger had seldom a word to say.

14. George was a demure, studious boy, and his senses seemed to brighten up in the library, where his brother was so gloomy. He knew the books before he could well-nigh carry them, and read in them long before he could understand them. Harry, on the other hand, was all alive in the stables or in the wood, eager for all parties of hunting and fishing, and promised to be a good sportsman from a very early age.

15. At length the time came when Mr. Esmond was to have done with the affairs of this life, and he laid them down as if glad to be rid of their burden. All who read and heard that discourse, wondered where Parson Broadbent of James Town found the eloquence and the Latin which adorned it. Perhaps Mr. Dempster knew, the boys' Scotch tutor, who corrected the proofs of the oration, which was printed, by the desire of his Excellency and many persons of honor, at Mr. Franklin's press in Philadelphia.

16. No such sumptuous funeral had ever been seen in the country as that which Madam Esmond Warrington ordained for her father, who would have been the first to smile at that pompous grief.

17. The little lads of Castlewood, almost smothered in black trains and hatbands, headed the procession and were followed by my Lord Fairfax, from Greenway Court, by his Excellency the Governor of Virginia (with his coach), by the Randolphs, the Careys, the Harrisons, the Washingtons, and many others; for the whole country esteemed the departed gentleman, whose goodness, whose high talents, whose benevolence and unobtrusive urbanity, had earned for him the just respect of his neighbors.

18. When informed of the event, the family of Colonel Esmond's stepson, the Lord Castlewood of Hampshire in England, asked to be at the charges of the marble slab which recorded the names and virtues of his lordship's mother and her husband; and after due time of preparation, the monument was set up, exhibiting the arms and coronet of the Esmonds, supported by a little, chubby group of weeping cherubs, and reciting an epitaph which for once did not tell any falsehoods.

Definitions. — 1. Păt-ri-mō'ni-al, *inherited from ancestors.* 6. Dĭs-af-fĕct'ed, *discontented.* 7. Ob-sē'qui-oŭs, *compliant to excess.* 12. Blăck'a-mōōr, *a negro.* 17. Ur-băn'i-ty, *civility or courtesy of manners, refinement.* 18. Ep'i-taph (*pro.* ĕp'i-taf), *an inscription on a monument, in honor or in memory of the dead.*

Notes. — 2. *Roundhead* was the epithet applied to the Puritans by the Cavaliers in the time of Charles I. It arose from the practice among the Puritans of cropping their hair peculiarly.

3. *Patriarchal.* 5. *Feudal.* The Jewish patriarch, in olden times, and the head of a noble family in Europe, during the Middle Ages, when the "Feudal System," as it is called, existed, both held almost despotic sway, the one over his great number of descendants and relations, and the other over a vast body of sub-

jects or retainers. Both patriarch and feudal lord were less restricted than the modern king, and the feudal lord, especially, lived in a state of great magnificence.

15. *Proofs.* When matter is to be printed, a rough impression of it is taken as soon as the type is set up, and sent to the editor or some other authority for correction. These first sheets are called proofs.

His Excellency was the title applied to the governor.

CVIII. MINOT'S LEDGE.

Fitz-James O'Brien (*b.* 1828, *d.* 1862) was of Irish birth, and came to America in 1852. He has contributed a number of tales and poems to various periodicals, but his writings have never been collected in book form. Mr. O'Brien belonged to the New York Seventh Regiment, and died at Baltimore of a wound received in a cavalry skirmish.

1. Like spectral hounds across the sky,
   The white clouds scud before the storm;
And naked in the howling night
   The red-eyed lighthouse lifts its form.
The waves with slippery fingers clutch
   The massive tower, and climb and fall,
And, muttering, growl with baffled rage
   Their curses on the sturdy wall.

2. Up in the lonely tower he sits,
   The keeper of the crimson light:
Silent and awe-struck does he hear
   The imprecations of the night.
The white spray beats against the panes
   Like some wet ghost that down the air
Is hunted by a troop of fiends,
   And seeks a shelter anywhere.

3. He prays aloud, the lonely man,
 For every soul that night at sea,
But more than all for that brave boy
 Who used to gayly climb his knee, —
Young Charlie, with his chestnut hair,
 And hazel eyes, and laughing lip.
"May Heaven look down," the old man cries,
 "Upon my son, and on his ship!"

4. While thus with pious heart he prays,
 Far in the distance sounds a boom:
He pauses; and again there rings
 That sullen thunder through the room.
A ship upon the shoals to-night!
 She cannot hold for one half hour;
But clear the ropes and grappling hooks,
 And trust in the Almighty Power!

5. On the drenched gallery he stands,
 Striving to pierce the solid night:
Across the sea the red eye throws
 A steady crimson wake of light;
And, where it falls upon the waves,
 He sees a human head float by,
With long drenched curls of chestnut hair,
 And wild but fearless hazel eye.

6 Out with the hooks! One mighty fling!
 Adown the wind the long rope curls.
Oh! will it catch? Ah, dread suspense!
 While the wild ocean wilder whirls.
A steady pull; it tightens now:
 Oh! his old heart will burst with joy,
As on the slippery rocks he pulls
 The breathing body of his boy.

7. Still sweep the specters through the sky;
Still scud the clouds before the storm;
Still naked in the howling night
The red-eyed lighthouse lifts its form.
Without, the world is wild with rage;
Unkenneled demons are abroad;
But with the father and the son
Within, there is the peace of God.

NOTE.—*Minot's Ledge* (also called the "Cohasset Rocks") is a dangerous reef in Boston Harbor, eight miles southeast of Boston Light. It has a fixed light of its own, sixty-six feet high.

CIX. HAMLET.

William Shakespeare (*b.* 1564, *d.* 1616), by many regarded as the greatest poet the world has ever produced, was born at Stratford-upon-Avon, England. He was married, when very young, to a woman eight years his senior, went to London, was joint proprietor of Blackfriar's Theater in 1589, wrote poems and plays, was an actor, accumulated some property, and retired to Stratford three or four years before his death. He was buried in Stratford church, where a monument has been erected to his memory. This is all that is known of him with any degree of certainty.

Shakespeare's works consist chiefly of plays and sonnets. They show a wonderful knowledge of human nature, expressed in language remarkable for its point and beauty.

(ACT I, SCENE II. HAMLET *alone in a room of the castle. Enter* HORATIO, MARCELLUS, *and* BERNARDO.)

Hor. HAIL to your lordship!
Ham. I am glad to see you well:
Horatio,—or I do forget myself.
Hor. The same, my lord, and your poor servant ever.
Ham. Sir, my good friend; I'll change that name with you:
And what make you from Wittenberg, Horatio?—
Marcellus?

Mar. My good lord —

Ham. I am very glad to see you. [*To* BER.] Good even, sir.
But what, in faith, make you from Wittenberg?

Hor. A truant disposition, good my lord.

Ham. I would not hear your enemy say so,
Nor shall you do mine ear that violence,
To make it truster of your own report
Against yourself: I know you are no truant.
But what is your affair in Elsinore?
We'll teach you to drink deep ere you depart.

Hor. My lord, I came to see your father's funeral.

Ham. I pray thee, do not mock me, fellow-student;
I think it was to see my mother's wedding.

Hor. Indeed, my lord, it follow'd hard upon.

Ham. Thrift, thrift, Horatio! the funeral baked meats
Did coldly furnish forth the marriage tables.
Would I had met my dearest foe in heaven
Or ever I had seen that day, Horatio!
My father! — methinks I see my father.

Hor. Where, my lord?

Ham. In my mind's eye, Horatio.

Hor. I saw him once; he was a goodly king.

Ham. He was a man, take him for all in all,
I shall not look upon his like again.

Hor. My lord, I think I saw him yesternight.

Ham. Saw? who?

Hor. My lord, the king your father.

Ham. The king my father!

Hor. Season your admiration for a while
With an attent ear, till I may deliver,
Upon the witness of these gentlemen,
This marvel to you.

Ham. For God's love, let me hear.

Hor. Two nights together had these gentlemen,
Marcellus and Bernardo, on their watch,
In the dead vast and middle of the night,

Been thus encounter'd. A figure like your father,
Armed at point exactly, *cap-a-pie*,
Appears before them, and with solemn march
Goes slow and stately by them: thrice he walk'd

By their oppress'd and fear-surprised eyes,
Within his truncheon's length; whilst they, distill'd
Almost to jelly with the act of fear,
Stand dumb and speak not to him. This to me
In dreadful secrecy impart they did;
And I with them the third night kept the watch:
Where, as they had deliver'd, both in time,
Form of the thing, each word made true and good,
The apparition comes: I knew your father;
These hands are not more like.

Ham. But where was this?
Mar. My lord, upon the platform where we watch'd.
Ham. Did you speak to it?
Hor. My lord, I did;
But answer made it none: yet once methought
It lifted up its head and did address
Itself to motion, like as it would speak;
But even then the morning cock crew loud,
And at the sound it shrunk in haste away,
And vanish'd from our sight.
Ham. 'T is very strange.
Hor. As I do live, my honor'd lord, 't is true;
And we did think it writ down in our duty
To let you know of it.
Ham. Indeed, indeed, sirs, but this troubles me.
Hold you the watch to-night?
Mar. } *Ber.* } We do, my lord.
Ham. Arm'd, say you?
Mar. } *Ber.* } Arm'd, my lord.
Ham. From top to toe?
Mar. } *Ber.* } My lord, from head to foot.
Ham. Then saw you not his face?
Hor. Oh, yes, my lord; he wore his beaver up.

Ham. What, look'd he frowningly?
Hor. A countenance more in sorrow than in anger.
Ham. Pale or red?
Hor. Nay, very pale.
Ham. And fix'd his eyes upon you?
Hor. Most constantly.
Ham. I would I had been there.
Hor. It would have much amazed you.
Ham. Very like, very like. Stay'd it long?
Hor. While one with moderate haste might tell a hundred.
Mar. } Longer, longer.
Ber. }
Hor. Not when I saw 't.
Ham. His beard was grizzled,—no?
Hor. It was, as I have seen it in his life,
A sable silver'd.
Ham. I will watch to-night;
Perchance 't will walk again.
Hor. I warrant it will.
Ham. If it assume my noble father's person,
I'll speak to it, though hell itself should gape
And bid me hold my peace. I pray you all,
If you have hitherto conceal'd this sight,
Let it be tenable in your silence still;
And whatsoever else shall hap to-night,
Give it an understanding, but no tongue:
I will requite your loves. So, fare you well:
Upon the platform, 'twixt eleven and twelve,
I'll visit you.

Definitions. — Trụ̈'ant, *wandering from business, loitering.* Trŭst'er, *a believer.* At-tĕnt', *attentive, heedful.* De-lĭv'er, *to communicate, to utter.* Căp-a-pie' (*from the French, pro.* kăp-ä-pee'), *from head to foot.* Trŭn'çheon (*pro.* trŭn'shun), *a short staff, a baton.* Bēa'ver, *a part of the helmet covering the face, so constructed that the wearer could raise or lower it.* Tĕn'a-ble, *capable of being held.*

Notes. — *What make you from Wittenberg?* i.e., what are you doing away from Wittenberg?

Wittenberg is a university town in Saxony, where Hamlet and Horatio had been schoolfellows.

Elsinore is a fortified town on one of the Danish islands, and was formerly the seat of one of the royal castles. It is the scene of Shakespeare's "Hamlet."

Hard upon; i.e., soon after.

Funeral baked meats. This has reference to the ancient custom of funeral feasts.

My dearest foe; i.e., my greatest foe. A common use of the word "dearest" in Shakespeare's time.

Or ever; i.e., before.

Season your admiration; i.e., restrain your wonder.

The dead vast; i.e., the dead void.

Armed at point; i.e., armed at all points.

Did address itself to motion; i.e., made a motion.

Give it an understanding, etc.; i.e., understand, but do not speak of it.

I will requite your loves, or, as we should say, I will repay your friendship.

CX. DISSERTATION ON ROAST PIG.

Charles Lamb (*b.* 1775, *d.* 1834) was born in London. He was educated at Christ's Hospital, where he was a schoolfellow and intimate friend of Coleridge. In 1792 he became a clerk in the India House, London, and in 1825 he retired from his clerkship on a pension of £441. Lamb never married, but devoted his life to the care of his sister Mary, who was at times insane. He wrote "Tales founded on the Plays of Shakespeare," and several other works of rare merit; but his literary fame rests principally on the inimitable "Essays of Elia" (published originally in the "London Magazine"), from one of which the following selection is adapted.

1. Mankind, says a Chinese manuscript, which my friend M. was obliging enough to read and explain to me, for the first seventy thousand ages ate their meat raw, clawing or biting it from the living animal, just as they do in Abyssinia to this day.

2. This period is not obscurely hinted at by their great Confucius in the second chapter of his "Mundane Mutations," where he designates a kind of golden age by the term *Cho-fang*, literally the Cooks' Holiday. The manuscript goes on to say that the art of roasting, or rather broiling (which I take to be the elder brother), was accidentally discovered in the manner following:

3. The swineherd, Ho-ti, having gone out into the woods one morning, as his manner was, to collect mast for his hogs, left his cottage in the care of his eldest son, Bo-bo, a great lubberly boy, who, being fond of playing with fire, as younkers of his age commonly are, let some sparks escape into a bundle of straw, which, kindling quickly, spread the conflagration over every part of their poor mansion till it was reduced to ashes.

4. Together with the cottage,—a sorry, antediluvian makeshift of a building, you may think it,—what was of much more importance, a fine litter of newborn pigs, no less than nine in number, perished. China pigs have been esteemed a luxury all over the East from the remotest periods we read of.

5. Bo-bo was in the utmost consternation, as you may think, not so much for the sake of the tenement, which his father and he could easily build up again with a few dry branches, and the labor of an hour or two, at any time, as for the loss of the pigs. While he was thinking what he should say to his father, and wringing his hands over the smoking remnants of one of those untimely sufferers, an odor assailed his nostrils unlike any scent which he had before experienced.

6. What could it proceed from? Not from the burnt cottage,—he had smelt that smell before,—indeed, this was by no means the first accident of the kind which had occurred through the negligence of this unlucky young firebrand. Much less did it resemble that of any known herb, weed, or flower. A premonitory moistening at the same

time overflowed his nether lip. He knew not what to think.

7. He next stooped down to feel the pig, if there were any signs of life in it. He burnt his fingers, and to cool them he applied them in his booby fashion to his mouth. Some of the crumbs of the scorched skin had come away with his fingers, and for the first time in his life (in the world's life, indeed, for before him no man had known it) he tasted — *crackling!* Again he felt and fumbled at the pig. It did not burn him so much now; still he licked his fingers from a sort of habit.

8. The truth at length broke into his slow understanding that it was the pig that smelt so, and the pig that tasted so delicious; and surrendering himself up to the newborn pleasure, he fell to tearing up whole handfuls of the scorched skin with the flesh next it, and was cramming it down his throat in his beastly fashion, when his sire entered amid the smoking rafters, armed with a retributory cudgel, and, finding how affairs stood, began to rain blows upon the young rogue's shoulders as thick as hailstones, which Bo-bo heeded not any more than if they had been flies.

9. His father might lay on, but he could not beat him from his pig till he had fairly made an end of it, when, becoming a little more sensible of his situation, something like the following dialogue ensued:

"You graceless whelp, what have you got there devouring? Is it not enough that you have burnt me down three houses with your dog's tricks, and be hanged to you! but you must be eating fire, and I know not what? What have you got there, I say?"

"O father, the pig, the pig! do come and taste how nice the burnt pig eats!"

10. The ears of Ho-ti tingled with horror. He cursed his son, and he cursed himself that he should ever have a son that should eat burnt pig.

Bo-bo, whose scent was wonderfully sharpened since

morning, soon raked out another pig, and, fairly rending it asunder, thrust the lesser half by main force into the fists of Ho-ti, still shouting out, "Eat, eat, eat the burnt pig, father! only taste! Oh!" with such like barbarous ejaculations, cramming all the while as if he would choke.

11. Ho-ti trembled in every joint while he grasped the abominable thing, wavering whether he should not put his son to death for an unnatural young monster, when the crackling scorching his fingers, as it had done his son's, and applying the same remedy to them, he in his turn tasted some of its flavor, which, make what sour mouths he would for a pretense, proved not altogether displeasing to him. In conclusion (for the manuscript here is a little tedious), both father and son fairly sat down to the mess, and never left off till they had dispatched all that remained of the litter.

12. Bo-bo was strictly enjoined not to let the secret escape, for the neighbors would certainly have stoned them for a couple of abominable wretches, who could think of improving upon the good meat which God had sent them. Nevertheless strange stories got about. It was observed that Ho-ti's cottage was burnt down now more frequently than ever. Nothing but fires from this time forward. Some would break out in broad day, others in the nighttime; and Ho-ti himself, which was the more remarkable, instead of chastising his son, seemed to grow more indulgent to him than ever.

13. At length they were watched, the terrible mystery discovered, and father and son summoned to take their trial at Pekin, then an inconsiderable assize town. Evidence was given, the obnoxious food itself produced in court, and verdict about to be pronounced, when the foreman of the jury begged that some of the burnt pig, of which the culprits stood accused, might be handed into the box.

14. He handled it, and they all handled it; and burning

their fingers, as Bo-bo and his father had done before them, and nature prompting to each of them the same remedy, against the face of all the facts, and the clearest charge which the judge had ever given, — to the surprise of the whole court, townsfolk, strangers, reporters, and all present, — without leaving the box, or any manner of consultation whatever, they brought in a simultaneous verdict of "Not Guilty."

15. The judge, who was a shrewd fellow, winked at the manifest iniquity of the decision; and when the court was dismissed, went privily, and bought up all the pigs that could be had for love or money. In a few days his lordship's townhouse was observed to be on fire.

16. The thing took wing, and now there was nothing to be seen but fire in every direction. Fuel and pigs grew enormously dear all over the district. The insurance offices one and all shut up shop. People built slighter and slighter every day, until it was feared that the very science of architecture would in no long time be lost to the world.

17. Thus this custom of firing houses continued till in process of time, says my manuscript, a sage arose, like our Locke, who made a discovery that the flesh of swine, or indeed of any other animal, might be cooked (*burnt*, as they called it) without the necessity of consuming a whole house to dress it.

18. Then first began the rude form of a gridiron. Roasting by the string or spit came in a century or two later; I forget in whose dynasty. By such slow degrees, concludes the manuscript, do the most useful, and seemingly the most obvious, arts make their way among mankind.

19. Without placing too implicit faith in the account above given, it must be agreed that if a worthy pretext for so dangerous an experiment as setting houses on fire (especially in these days) could be assigned in favor of any culinary object that pretext and excuse might be found in Roast Pig.

Definitions. — 3. Youn'kers, *young persons.* 4. An-te-dĭ-lū'-vi-an (literally, *existing before the flood*), *very ancient.* Māke'shĭft, *that which answers a need with the best means at hand.* 6. Pre-mŏn'i-to-ry, *giving previous warning.* 8. Re-trĭb'u-to-ry, *rewarding, retaliating.* 12. En-joined', *ordered, commanded.* 13. Ob-nŏx'-ioŭs (*pro.* ob-nŏk'shus), *liable to censure, offensive.* 18. Dȳ'nas-ty, *sovereignty, reign.* 19. Im-plĭç'it, *trusting without doubt.* Cū'li-na-ry, *relating to the kitchen.*

Notes. — 1. *Abyssinia* is a country of eastern Africa.

2. *Confucius* (*pro.* Con-fū'she-ŭs; *the Chinese name is* Kong-fu-tse', *pro.* Kong-fōōt-sā') was a celebrated Chinese philosopher (*b.* 551 B.C.) who did much for the moral improvement of his country.

The *Golden Age* was supposed to be that period in the various stages of human civilization when the greatest simplicity existed; the fruits of the earth sprang up without cultivation, and spring was the only season.

13. *Pekin* is the capital of China.

An *assize town* is a town where the assizes, or periodical sittings of a court, are held.

17. *Locke* (*b.* 1632, *d.* 1704) was one of the most illustrious of English philosophers.

CXI. A PEN PICTURE.

William Black (*b.* 1841, - —) is one of the leading modern novelists of England. The scenes of his stories are for the most part laid in Scotland, and he excels in the delineation of Scotch character. But his most remarkable power is seen in those vivid, poetical descriptions of scenery, of which the following selection, adapted from "The Princess of Thule," is a good example. Mr. Black's most noted works, in addition to the one named, are: "A Daughter of Heth," "The Strange Adventures of a Phaëton," "Kilmeny," and "McLeod of Dare."

1. Lavender had already transformed Sheila into a heroine during the half hour of their stroll from the beach

and around the house; and as they sat at dinner on this still, brilliant evening in summer, he clothed her in the garments of romance.

2. Her father, with his great, gray beard and heavy brow, became the King of Thule, living in this solitary house overlooking the sea, and having memories of a dead sweetheart. His daughter, the Princess, had the glamour of a thousand legends dwelling in her beautiful eyes; and when she walked by the shores of the Atlantic, that were now getting yellow under the sunset, what strange and unutterable thoughts must appear in the wonder of her face!

3. After dinner they went outside and sat down on a bench in the garden. It was a cool and pleasant evening. The sun had gone down in red fire behind the Atlantic, and there was still left a rich glow of crimson in the west, while overhead, in the pale yellow of the sky, some filmy clouds of rose color lay motionless. How calm was the sea out there, and the whiter stretch of water coming into Loch Roag! The cool air of the twilight was scented with sweetbrier. The wash of the ripples along the coast could be heard in the stillness.

4. The girl put her hand on her father's head, and reminded him that she had had her big greyhound, Bras, imprisoned all the afternoon, and that she had to go down to Borvabost with a message for some people who were leaving by the boat in the morning.

"But you can not go away down to Borvabost by yourself, Sheila," said Ingram. "It will be dark before you return."

"It will not be darker than this all the night through," said the girl.

5. "But I hope you will let us go with you," said Lavender, rather anxiously; and she assented with a gracious smile, and went to fetch the great deerhound that was her constant companion. And lo! he found himself

walking with a Princess in this wonderland, through the magic twilight that prevails in northern latitudes. Mackenzie and Ingram had gone to the front. The large deerhound, after regarding him attentively, had gone to its mistress's side, and remained closely there.

6. Even Sheila, when they had reached the loftiest part of their route, and could see beneath them the island and the water surrounding it, was struck by the exceeding beauty of the twilight; and as for her companion, he remembered it many a time thereafter, as if it were a dream of the sea.

7. Before them lay the Atlantic—a pale line of blue, still, silent, and remote. Overhead the sky was of a clear, thin gold, with heavy masses of violet cloud stretched across from north to south, and thickening as they got near the horizon. Down at their feet, near the shore, a dusky line of huts and houses was scarcely visible; and over these lay a pale blue film of peat smoke that did not move in the still air.

8. Then they saw the bay into which the White Water runs, and they could trace the yellow glimmer of the river stretching into the island through a level valley of bog and morass. Far away towards the east lay the bulk of the island,—dark green undulations of moorland and pasture; and there, in the darkness, the gable of one white house had caught the clear light of the sky, and was gleaming westward like a star.

9. But all this was as nothing to the glory that began to shine in the southeast, where the sky was of a pale violet over the peaks of Mealasabhal and Suainabhal. There, into the beautiful dome, rose the golden crescent of the moon, warm in color, as though it still retained the last rays of the sunset. A line of quivering gold fell across Loch Roag, and touched the black hull and spars of the boat in which Sheila had been sailing in the morning.

10. That bay down there, with its white sands and mass-

ive rocks, its still expanse of water, and its background of mountain peaks palely covered by the yellow moonlight, seemed really a home for a magic princess who was shut off from all the world. But here, in front of them, was another sort of sea, and another sort of life, — a small fishing village hidden under a cloud of pale peat smoke, and fronting the great waters of the Atlantic itself, which lay under a gloom of violet clouds.

11. On the way home it was again Lavender's good fortune to walk with Sheila across the moorland path they had traversed some little time before. And now the moon was still higher in the heavens, and the yellow lane of light that crossed the violet waters of Loch Roag quivered in a deeper gold. The night air was scented with the Dutch clover growing down by the shore. They could hear the curlew whistling and the plover calling amid that monotonous plash of the waves that murmured all around the coast.

12. When they returned to the house, the darker waters of the Atlantic and the purple clouds of the west were shut out from sight; and before them there was only the liquid plain of Loch Roag, with its pathway of yellow fire, and far away on the other side the shoulders and peaks of the southern mountains, that had grown gray and clear and sharp in the beautiful twilight. And this was Sheila's home.

Definitions. — 2. Glā'mo̤ur (*pro.* g̅lā'mo͞or), *witchery, or a charm on the eyes, making them see things differently from what they really are.* 3. Lŏch (*pro.* lŏk), *a lake, a bay or arm of the sea.* 7. Pēat, *a kind of turf used for fuel.* 11. Cûr'lew (*pro.* kûr'lū), *an aquatic bird which takes its name from its cry.* Plŏv'er (*pro.* plŭv'er), *a game bird frequenting river banks and the seashore.*

Notes. — Of the characters mentioned in this selection, *Sheila* is a young Scotch girl living on the small island of Borva, which her father owns: it lies just west of Lewis, one of the

Hebrides. *Ingram* is an old friend and frequent visitor, while *Lavender*, a friend of Ingram's, is on his first visit to the island.

2. *Thule* (*pro.* Thū'le) is the name given by an ancient Greek navigator, Pytheas, to the northernmost region of Europe. The exact locality of Thule is a disputed point.

3. *Loch Roag* (*pro.* Rōg) is an inlet of the sea, west of Lewis, in which Borva is situated.

4. *Borvabost*, a little town of Borva. *Bost* means *an inhabited place*.

9. *Mealasabhal* and *Suainabhal* are mountains on the island of Lewis. *Bhal* is Gaelic for *mountain*.

CXII. THE GREAT VOICES.

Charles T. Brooks (*b.* 1813, *d.* 1833) was born at Salem, Mass., and was the valedictorian of his class at Harvard College, where he graduated in 1832. He shortly afterwards entered the ministry, and had charge of a congregation at Newport, R.I. He was a great student of German literature, and began his own literary career by a translation of Schiller's "William Tell." This was followed by numerous translations from the German, mainly poetry, which have been published from time to time, in several volumes. Of these translations, Goethe's "Faust," Richter's "Titan" and "Hesperus," and a humorous poem by Dr. Karl Arnold Kortum, "The Life, Opinions, Actions, and Fate of Hieronimus Jobs, the Candidate," deserve especial mention. Mr. Brooks also published a number of original poems, addresses, etc.

1. A VOICE from the sea to the mountains,
 From the mountains again to the sea;
A call from the deep to the fountains,—
 "O spirit! be glad and be free."

2. A cry from the floods to the fountains;
 And the torrents repeat the glad song
As they leap from the breast of the mountains,—
 "O spirit! be free and be strong."

3. The pine forests thrill with emotion
 Of praise, as the spirit sweeps by:
With a voice like the murmur of ocean
 To the soul of the listener they cry.

4. Oh! sing, human heart, like the fountains,
 With joy reverential and free,
Contented and calm as the mountains,
 And deep as the woods and the sea.

CXIII. A PICTURE OF HUMAN LIFE.

Samuel Johnson (*b.* 1709, *d.* 1784). This remarkable man was born in Lichfield, Staffordshire, England. He was the son of a bookseller and stationer. He entered Pembroke College, Oxford, in 1728; but his poverty compelled him to leave at the end of three years. Soon after his marriage, in 1736, he opened a private school, but obtained only three pupils, one of whom was David Garrick, afterwards a celebrated actor. In 1737, he removed to London, where he resided most of the rest of his life. The most noted of his numerous literary works are his "Dictionary," the first one of the English language worthy of mention, "The Vanity of Human Wishes," a poem, "The Rambler," "Rasselas," "The Lives of the English Poets," and his edition of Shakespeare. An annual pension of £300 was granted him in 1762.

In person, Johnson was heavy and awkward; in manner, boorish and overbearing; but his learning and his great powers caused his company to be sought by many eminent men.

1. Obidah, the son of Abnesina, left the caravansary early in the morning, and pursued his journey through the plains of Hindostan. He was fresh and vigorous with rest; he was animated with hope; he was incited by desire; he walked swiftly forward over the valleys, and saw the hills gradually rising before him.

2. As he passed along, his ears were delighted with the morning song of the bird of paradise; he was fanned by the last flutters of the sinking breeze, and sprinkled with dew by groves of spices; he sometimes contemplated the

towering height of the oak, monarch of the hills; and sometimes caught the gentle fragrance of the primrose, eldest daughter of the spring; all his senses were gratified, and all care was banished from his heart.

3. Thus he went on, till the sun approached his meridian, and the increasing heat preyed upon his strength; he then looked round about him for some more commodious path. He saw, on his right hand, a grove that seemed to wave its shades as a sign of invitation; he entered it, and found the coolness and verdure irresistibly pleasant. He did not, however, forget whither he was traveling, but found a narrow way, bordered with flowers, which appeared to have the same direction with the main road, and was pleased, that, by this happy experiment, he had found means to unite pleasure with business, and to gain the rewards of diligence without suffering its fatigues.

4. He, therefore, still continued to walk for a time, without the least remission of his ardor, except that he was sometimes tempted to stop by the music of the birds, which the heat had assembled in the shade, and sometimes amused himself with picking the flowers that covered the banks on each side, or the fruits that hung upon the branches. At last, the green path began to decline from its first tendency, and to wind among the hills and thickets, cooled with fountains, and murmuring with waterfalls.

5. Here Obidah paused for a time, and began to consider whether it was longer safe to forsake the known and common track; but, remembering that the heat was now in its greatest violence, and that the plain was dusty and uneven, he resolved to pursue the new path, which he supposed only to make a few meanders, in compliance with the varieties of the ground, and to end at last in the common road.

6. Having thus calmed his solicitude, he renewed his pace, though he suspected he was not gaining ground.

This uneasiness of his mind inclined him to lay hold on every new object, and give way to every sensation that might soothe or divert him. He listened to every echo, he mounted every hill for a fresh prospect, he turned aside to every cascade, and pleased himself with tracing the course of a gentle river that rolled among the trees, and watered a large region, with innumerable circumvolutions.

7. In these amusements, the hours passed away uncounted; his deviations had perplexed his memory, and he knew not toward what point to travel. He stood pensive and confused, afraid to go forward lest he should go wrong, yet conscious that the time of loitering was now past. While he was thus tortured with uncertainty, the sky was overspread with clouds, the day vanished from before him, and a sudden tempest gathered round his head.

8. He was now roused by his danger to a quick and painful remembrance of his folly; he now saw how happiness is lost when ease is consulted; he lamented the unmanly impatience that prompted him to seek shelter in the grove, and despised the petty curiosity that led him on from trifle to trifle. While he was thus reflecting, the air grew blacker and a clap of thunder broke his meditation.

9. He now resolved to do what remained yet in his power; to tread back the ground which he had passed, and try to find some issue where the wood might open into the plain. He prostrated himself upon the ground, and commended his life to the Lord of nature. He rose with confidence and tranquillity, and pressed on with his saber in his hand; for the beasts of the desert were in motion, and on every hand were heard the mingled howls of rage, and fear, and ravage, and expiration; all the horrors of darkness and solitude surrounded him; the winds roared in the woods, and the torrents tumbled from the hills.

10. Thus, forlorn and distressed, he wandered through the wild without knowing whither he was going or whether

he was every moment drawing nearer to safety or to destruction. At length, not fear but labor began to overcome him; his breath grew short, and his knees trembled, and he was on the point of lying down, in resignation to his fate, when he beheld, through the brambles, the glimmer of a taper. He advanced toward the light, and finding that it proceeded from the cottage of a hermit, he called humbly at the door, and obtained admission. The old man set before him such provisions as he had collected for himself, on which Obidah fed with eagerness and gratitude.

11. When the repast was over, "Tell me," said the hermit, "by what chance thou hast been brought hither; I have been now twenty years an inhabitant of this wilderness, in which I never saw a man before." Obidah then related the occurrences of his journey, without any concealment or palliation.

12. "Son," said the hermit, "let the errors and follies, the dangers and escapes, of this day, sink deep into your heart. Remember, my son, that human life is the journey of a day. We rise in the morning of youth, full of vigor, and full of expectation; we set forward with spirit and hope, with gayety and with diligence, and travel on awhile in the straight road of piety toward the mansions of rest. In a short time we remit our fervor, and endeavor to find some mitigation of our duty, and some more easy means of obtaining the same end.

13. "We then relax our vigor, and resolve no longer to be terrified with crimes at a distance, but rely upon our own constancy, and venture to approach what we resolve never to touch. We thus enter the bowers of ease, and repose in the shades of security. Here the heart softens, and vigilance subsides; we are then willing to inquire whether another advance can not be made, and whether we may not at least turn our eyes upon the gardens of pleasure. We approach them with scruple and hesitation; we

enter them, but enter timorous and trembling, and always hope to pass through them without losing the road of virtue, which we for a while keep in our sight, and to which we propose to return.

14. "But temptation succeeds temptation, and one compliance prepares us for another; we, in time, lose the happiness of innocence, and solace our disquiet with sensual gratifications. By degrees we let fall the remembrance of our original intention, and quit the only adequate object of rational desire. We entangle ourselves in business, immerge ourselves in luxury, and rove through the labyrinths of inconstancy till the darkness of old age begins to invade us, and disease and anxiety obstruct our way. We then look back upon our lives with horror, with sorrow, and with repentance; and wish, but too often vainly wish, that we had not forsaken the paths of virtue.

15. "Happy are they, my son, who shall learn, from thy example, not to despair, but shall remember that though the day is past, and their strength is wasted, there yet remains one effort to be made; that reformation is never hopeless, nor sincere endeavors ever unassisted; that the wanderer may at length return after all his errors; and that he who implores strength and courage from above, shall find danger and difficulty give way before him. Go now, my son, to thy repose: commit thyself to the care of Omnipotence; and when the morning calls again to toil, begin anew thy journey and thy life."

DEFINITIONS. — 1. Căr-a-văn'sa-ry, *a kind of inn in the East, where caravans (or large companies of traders) rest at night.* 5. Me-ăn'derș, *windings, turnings.* 6. Cĭr-eum-vo-lū'tionș, *windings or flowings around.* 7. Dē-vi-ā'tionș, *wanderings from one's course.* 9. Ex-pi-rā'tion, *death.* 11. Păl-li-ā'tion, *concealment of the most blamable circumstances of an offense.* 12. Mĭt-i-gā'tion, *abatement, the act of rendering less severe.* 14. Ad'e-quāte, *fully sufficient.* Lăb'y-rĭnth, *a place full of winding passages.*

CXIV. A SUMMER LONGING.

George Arnold (*b.* 1834, *d.* 1865) was born in New York, but removed with his parents to Illinois while yet an infant. There he passed his boyhood, being educated at home by his parents. In 1849 the family again removed to Strawberry Farms, Monmouth County, N.J. When eighteen years old he began to study painting, but soon gave up the art and devoted himself to literature. He became a journalist of New York City, and his productions include almost every variety of writings found in the literary magazines. After his death, two volumes of his poems, "Drift: a Seashore Idyl," and "Poems, Grave and Gay," were edited by Mr. William Winter.

1. I MUST away to the wooded hills and vales,
   Where broad, slow streams flow cool and silently
And idle barges flap their listless sails.
For me the summer sunset glows and pales,
   And green fields wait for me.

2. I long for shadowy founts, where the birds
   Twitter and chirp at noon from every tree;
I long for blossomed leaves and lowing herds;
And Nature's voices say in mystic words,
   "The green fields wait for thee."

3. I dream of uplands, where the primrose shines
   And waves her yellow lamps above the lea;
Of tangled copses, swung with trailing vines;
Of open vistas, skirted with tall pines,
   Where green fields wait for me.

4. I think of long, sweet afternoons, when I
   May lie and listen to the distant sea,
Or hear the breezes in the reeds that sigh,
Or insect voices chirping shrill and dry,
   In fields that wait for me.

5. These dreams of summer come to bid me find
The forest's shade, the wild bird's melody,
While summer's rosy wreaths for me are twined,
While summer's fragrance lingers on the wind,
And green fields wait for me.

CXV. FATE.

Francis Bret Harte (*b.* 1839, ——) was born in Albany, N.Y. When seventeen years old he went to California, where he engaged in various employments. He was a teacher, was employed in government offices, worked in the gold mines, and learned to be a compositor in a printing office. In 1868 he started the "Overland Monthly," and his original and characteristic poems and sketches soon made it a popular magazine. Mr. Harte has been a contributor to some of the leading periodicals of the country, but principally to the "Atlantic Monthly."

1. "The sky is clouded, the rocks are bare;
The spray of the tempest is white in air;
The winds are out with the waves at play,
And I shall not tempt the sea to-day.

2. "The trail is narrow, the wood is dim,
The panther clings to the arching limb;
And the lion's whelps are abroad at play,
And I shall not join in the chase to-day."

3. But the ship sailed safely over the sea,
And the hunters came′from the chase in glee;
And the town that was builded upon a rock
Was swallowed up in the earthquake shock.

CXVI. THE BIBLE THE BEST OF CLASSICS.

Thomas S. Grimké (*b.* 1786, *d.* 1834). This eminent lawyer and scholar was born in Charleston, S.C. He graduated at Yale College in 1807. He gained considerable reputation as a politician, but is best known as an advocate of peace, Sunday schools, and the Bible. He was a man of deep feeling, earnest purpose, and pure life.

1. THERE is a classic, the best the world has ever seen, the noblest that has ever honored and dignified the language of mortals. If we look into its antiquity, we discover a title to our veneration unrivaled in the history of literature. If we have respect to its evidences, they are found in the testimony of miracle and prophecy; in the ministry of man, of nature, and of angels, yea, even of "God, manifest in the flesh," of "God blessed forever."

2. If we consider its authenticity, no other pages have survived the lapse of time that can be compared with it. If we examine its authority, for it speaks as never man spake, we discover that it came from heaven in vision and prophecy under the sanction of Him who is Creator of all things, and the Giver of every good and perfect gift.

3. If we reflect on its truths, they are lovely and spotless, sublime and holy as God himself, unchangeable as his nature, durable as his righteous dominion, and versatile as the moral condition of mankind. If we regard the value of its treasures, we must estimate them, not like the relics of classic antiquity, by the perishable glory and beauty, virtue and happiness, of this world, but by the enduring perfection and supreme felicity of an eternal kingdom.

4. If we inquire who are the men that have recorded its truths, vindicated its rights, and illustrated the excellence of its scheme, from the depth of ages and from the living world, from the populous continent and the isles of the sea, comes forth the answer: "The patriarch and the prophet, the evangelist and the martyr."

5. If we look abroad through the world of men, the victims of folly or vice, the prey of cruelty, of injustice,